In the name of God, the Con

Sayyid Quṭb

IN THE SHADE OF THE QUR'ĀN

Fī Ẓilāl al-Qur'ān

VOLUME VII

SŪRAH 8

Al-Anfāl

Translated and Edited by
Adil Salahi

THE ISLAMIC FOUNDATION
AND
ISLAMONLINE.NET

Published by

THE ISLAMIC FOUNDATION,

Markfield Conference Centre,
Ratby Lane, Markfield, Leicestershire LE67 9SY, United Kingdom
Tel: (01530) 244944, Fax: (01530) 244946
E-mail: i.foundation@islamic-foundation.org.uk
Website: www.islamic-foundation.org.uk

Quran House, PO Box 30611, Nairobi, Kenya

PMB 3193, Kano, Nigeria

ISLAMONLINE.NET,
PO Box 22212, Doha, Qatar
E-mail: webmaster@islam-online.net
Website: www.islamonline.net

British Library Cataloguing-in-Publication Data
Qutb, Sayyid, 1903–1966
In the shade of the Qur'an: Fi zilal al-Qur'an,
Vol. 7: Surah 8: Al-Anfal
1. Koran – Commentaries
I. Title II. Salahi, Adil III. Islamic Foundation
IV. Fi zilal al-Qur'an
297.1'227

ISBN 0 86037 318 5
ISBN 0 86037 323 1 pbk

Typeset by: N.A.Qaddoura
Cover design by: Imtiaze A. Manjra

Printed and bound in Great Britain by
Antony Rowe Ltd., Chippenham, Wiltshire

بسم الله الرحمن الرحيم

Contents

Transliteration Table

Consonants. Arabic

initial: unexpressed medial and final:

ء	ʾ	د	d	ض	ḍ	ك	k
ب	b	ذ	dh	ط	ṭ	ل	l
ت	t	ر	r	ظ	ẓ	م	m
ث	th	ز	z	ع	ʿ	ن	n
ج	j	س	s	غ	gh	هـ	h
ح	ḥ	ش	sh	ف	f	و	w
خ	kh	ص	ṣ	ق	q	ي	y

Vowels, diphthongs, etc.

Short:	ـَ	a	ـِ	i	ـُ	u
long:	ـَا	ā	ـُو	ū	ـِي	ī
diphthongs:			ـَوْ	aw		
			ـَىْ	ay		

Jihād and Freedom

Introduction by Adil Salahi

Over the past fourteen centuries of the history of Islam scores of commentaries on the Qur'ān have been written, many of which run into thousands of pages. In addition hundreds, if not thousands, of volumes have been written on different aspects of the Qur'ān: its style, language, special word usage, rhythm, imagery and other distinctive qualities. Although we have today the benefit of many of these, many others have been lost without trace, due to the different calamities that befell many cities and learning centres in the Muslim world. Yet there is always room for more. For one thing, the Qur'ān is the word of God, documented as He revealed it to His last Messenger to mankind, Muḥammad (peace be upon him). It is common practice that a meritorious literary work becomes the subject of numerous essays and different aspects of research. Yet a poem or a play merely expresses the thoughts, feelings and ideas of its writer: a human being who interacts with life in a more pronounced way than most of us.

The Qur'ān is God's constitution for human life for as long as people continue to live on earth. Its importance is thus far greater than what may be attached to any literary work, legal document, or constitution. Only God can give us a legal code and a constitution that combine both the consistency and flexibility to ensure its easy applicability to all generations. Hence, it is only natural that as life develops, scholars need to look at the Qur'ān afresh, in order to learn how it applies to their generation and how they and their children should approach God's book.

During the twentieth century, several studies of the Qur'ān were produced in Arabic, Urdu, Persian and other languages of the Muslim world. While every writer is greatly influenced by his or her own social and scholarly environment, works of exceptional merit soon find themselves translated into other languages. This has been the case with *In the Shade of the Qur'ān*. Translations in different 'Islamic' languages began to appear in the late 1950s, but the translation work gathered far greater momentum in the 1960s, after the author's third unjust imprisonment, military trial and execution. Parts of it were published in periodicals in some European languages, and now this English translation will, God willing, present the whole work to a wider audience of Muslims and non-Muslims alike.

It may be significant to relate here a story I heard from Mr Wahbah Ḥasan Wahbah, Sayyid Quṭb's publisher who, as a member of the Muslim Brotherhood, shared with him the last two periods of imprisonment. One day in prison, Sayyid Quṭb related to his fellow prisoners a dream in which he saw himself sitting at his desk in his home in Helwan, a picturesque town to the south of Cairo. He was writing and some of his books were on the desk. There was also a jar of honey. As he tried to reach a book or a document, he knocked the jar and spilled the honey. It was not a mere drop or two, but rather a large quantity of honey which poured out of the jar, and moved through the room towards the door of the apartment. It soon reached the door of the building and moved into the street. It went further into Cairo, and then out of the city, until it reached the airport, where he could no longer see it.

Sayyid Quṭb asked his fellow Muslim Brotherhood prisoners if they could interpret his dream. Some of them came up with some ideas, but he said that he felt that it was an indication that his books would be more widely circulated in other countries than in Egypt. How true! At the time of his last imprisonment, his books were banned in Egypt, but extracts from them were broadcast on a daily basis from various Arab radio stations. Later the Egyptian ban was relaxed and his books, including *In the Shade of the Qur'ān*, were on the shelves of most Egyptian bookshops.

It is in the nature of things that any attempt to bring about an Islamic revival should meet with strong opposition. Islam aims to reform people's lives, so that everyone should enjoy freedom of thought, belief and expression; equality becomes a reality; and justice is maintained in the fullest sense of the word. Advocating such values is bound to be met with opposition from different quarters. Not only will the people who benefit by the absence of these values put up determined resistance, trying to defend their privileges, but they will also be helped by many others. In a social set-up that gives many privileges to those in power, there will be a number of social groups that have their own privileges to protect. A commercial company is able to ensure much better success in its enterprises if its staff members realize that they benefit from such success. By contrast, a company that gives poor wages to its workers, allowing its owners to monopolize all benefits will not gain that most essential quality for success, namely full commitment by its employees. Similarly, governments realize that they have to put in place machinery committed to the survival of the system. The people serving in such positions feel that their own survival depends on the continuity of the system. These will be opposed to any serious reform, particularly one that ensures equality of all people.

Such secondary layers of beneficiaries exist in all systems, even those that uphold democratic values and principles. We always find that even the most democratic regimes are prepared to sidestep their own values and principles when they feel their existence threatened. They feel that they lack the strength to sustain them against all opposition. But in fact, even the longest functioning democracies are prepared to raise the spectre of defending 'national security' in order to justify shedding even their own basic values and the most essential of human rights. The first couple of years of the twenty-first century provide a wide range of examples.

It comes as no surprise that any genuine call for Islamic revival meets with stiff opposition. People simply try to defend their privileges and political regimes try to ensure their survival. Hence resistance to Islamic revival will come in different forms. Over the last decade or more of the twentieth century, we witnessed a sustained media effort linking Islam with terrorism, to the extent that the two became almost synonymous in the minds of many people even in Western democratic countries. Perhaps nowhere was this effort more determined than in the United States. Numerous have been the attempts to distort the image of Islam in the minds of ordinary people, in order to ensure popular acceptance of depriving its advocates of their basic human rights.

But Islam is the faith God has laid down for humanity and for all times. Hence, the motive to preserve the rights God has established for mankind is built in its very structure. This is the very essence of Islamic *jihād*, which means an endeavour to establish right and justice in human life. This endeavour may take any type or form, as long as it is suitable for resisting aggression against man and his rights granted by his Creator.

In this volume, the author takes up the issue of *jihād* and explains it fully. Needless to say, the author discusses major Islamic issues only within the context of the Qur'ānic statements he is commenting on. The only reason why he takes up this subject in this volume is that the *sūrah* under discussion comments on the Battle of Badr, the first major military encounter during the life of the Prophet, and the events leading to it.

However, the publication of this volume now, with its strong emphasis on *jihād*, is particularly useful. To start with, it provides a full explanation of the motives and logical arguments for *jihād*, explaining it in its true colour. *Jihād* is an active movement which aims to defend man throughout the world, and to ensure that human rights are maintained. Foremost among these is the right to freedom, which is given a higher priority than the right to life, as clearly indicated in the two Qur'ānic statements: "Oppression is even worse than killing." (2: 191) "Religious persecution is worse than killing." (2: 217) And when Islam refers to freedom, it gives it its fullest sense, and ensures that it applies to all people, particularly those who are liable to persecution, or who fall victim to injustice. This is summed up by Abū Bakr, the first ruler of the Islamic state after the Prophet, who said in his first address after being elected as Caliph: "I have been given this position of leadership when I am not the best among you. A weak person will be treated as powerful until I ensure that he gets his full rights; and a person who has power will be treated as weak until I take from him whatever he has no right to have." This is the main policy that every Muslim ruler should adopt. Everyone should have what is rightfully his or hers, without encroaching on the rights of others. The state should make sure that none is deprived of their rights and none takes more than what is rightfully theirs.

It is for the defence of human rights, particularly freedom, that Islam enshrines the principle of *jihād* as central to its policy. However, this principle has been maligned, particularly in recent years, by two types of people. The first are the enemies of Islam who try to distort its image, painting Islam as an extreme and aggressive movement. The second are the fringe groups of Muslims who adopt an exceedingly narrow view of Islam and *jihād*, and in their rigid approach tend to confirm what the hostile camp alleges. Needless to say, these fringe groups tend to provide further ammunition to those who level every accusation at the door of Islam and its advocates.

The defence of freedom, and of human rights generally, requires an active movement which Islam establishes through its concept of *jihād*. When we look at it in this light, *jihād* appears to be a proactive principle that seeks to elevate human life through freedom and justice. As such, it needs no apology to answer criticism from those who mistake its purpose and motives. What it needs is that it should be understood for what it really is: a means to defend man against all injustice, and to elevate human life to its optimum standard.

However, under the dual attack of the enemies of Islam and the fringe, narrow-minded Muslim factions, *jihād* itself needs to be defended. Its defence need not be anything other than an accurate exposition of the principle of *jihād* and its motives, as clearly stated in the Qur'ān. This is what the author attempts in this volume, particularly in the Prologue. He aptly describes Islam as a universal declaration of the liberation of man throughout the world from every form of oppression. His defence of *jihād* is both lucid and powerful. Hence, it is not surprising that it was exploited by forces hostile to Islam, who twist words and ideas, making use of his refutation of the narrow 'defensive' view of *jihād*, to gain currency to their accusation of Islam as being aggressive. Nor is it surprising that the author's ideas have been wrongly understood by the other groups who try to see in it a justification for their rigid views. Both have been grossly unjust to the author.

It must be said that it is not difficult to twist and distort writers' ideas, particularly when they take a clear stand in support of what they believe in. An English proverb says: "The devil can quote from the Scriptures." The pagan Arabs laid too many false accusations at the door of Islam. It is not surprising that in our present world, when the media shape and influence public opinion, that the same tactics are used with far more sophistication. Hence Sayyid Quṭb's views on *jihād* can be grossly misrepresented to play into the hands of both groups.

The fact is that Sayyid Quṭb was committed to the principle of freedom for all. To him, people must be free to choose their beliefs. No pressure must be brought to bear on them in order to toe any line or maintain any status quo. God's message to mankind must be placed before them, clear, lucid and accurate, so that they may choose to accept it if they wish, without fearing any social or political repercussions.

It is only natural that a person like Sayyid Quṭb should value freedom very highly. In the late 1940s, when he was writing three articles a week in support of social justice and political freedom, the authorities tried to get rid of him, sending him to the US to obtain a Master's degree in Statistics, a subject far removed from his literary specialization. Later, under the Nasser dictatorship, he was unfairly imprisoned three times, for a total of over 11 years, culminating in his summary trial by a military court and subsequent execution in 1966. A writer, who was exceedingly sensitive to the pulse of his community, suffering such sustained persecution under different regimes, and believing in the ideals and values of Islam, should know the value of freedom of thought, feeling and belief for all people. In Islam he finds that the right to freedom is given the top position among human rights. Hence, his powerful exposition of the concept of *jihād* as the means to ensure freedom for all people.

It may be said, perhaps with some justification, that Sayyid Quṭb was a bit too strong in his argument, providing a platform for extremism to stand on. Here we find ourselves trying to answer the question: to what extent may a writer be blamed for being misunderstood by his readers? In the case of Sayyid Quṭb, the overwhelming majority of his readers maintain that he reflects the middle path Islam adopts. In history, there were numerous examples of groups who used the Qur'ān as the basis for their extremist ideas, violent tactics, or both. Should the blame be put on God for revealing the Qur'ān? Or on the Prophet for showing us how it is implemented in human life?

What is needed is an objective, unbiased reading of Sayyid Quṭb's ideas. Such reading is bound to support the conclusion that powerful as his exposition of the concept of *jihād* is, it never advocates extremism. It only defends the right of Islam to act in defence of mankind generally, of each person's right to have free access to God's message, and their freedom to choose their beliefs without pressure or coercion.

London **Adil Salahi**
Shawwāl 1423
December 2002

SŪRAH 8

Al-Anfāl

(The Spoils of War)

Prologue

Like *Sūrah*s 2–5, discussed in Volumes I–IV, this *sūrah* was revealed in the Madinah period of the Prophet's mission, while *Sūrahs* 6 and 7, discussed in Volumes V and VI, were revealed earlier when the Prophet was still in Makkah. As is already clear, our approach in this commentary is to follow the order adopted in the Qur'ān, in preference to the chronological order of revelation. For one thing, it is not possible to be absolutely certain about the time of revelation of each *sūrah*, except in general terms indicating that one *sūrah* is a Makkan revelation and another belongs to the Madinah period, but even then there are some differences of views. To try to determine the exact order of when each verse, passage or *sūrah* was revealed is practically impossible, despite the fact that in the case of a small number of verses we have confirmed reports concerning the exact time of revelation.

Valuable as the endeavour to trace the chronological order of revelation may be in trying to establish the pattern of progress of the Islamic movement at the time of the Prophet, the lack of clear and firm evidence makes this endeavour both hard and problematic. The conclusions that we may arrive at will always remain uncertain, and could lead to serious or erroneous results. Therefore, I have chosen to present the Qur'ān in the traditional order given in the original copy finalized at the time of 'Uthmān, the third Caliph. However, I try to look at the historical events associated with the revelation of each *sūrah*, knowing that this can only be done in general and tentative terms. In so doing, I am only trying to give a general and tentative idea of the circumstances leading to the revelation of each *sūrah*.

This *sūrah*, al-Anfāl, or The Spoils of War, was revealed after *Sūrah* 2, The Cow, shortly after the Battle of Badr which took place in Ramaḍān, in the second year of the Islamic calendar, approximately 19 months after the Prophet's migration to Madinah. However, when we say that it was revealed after *Sūrah* 2, our statement does not give a complete picture, because *Sūrah* 2 was not revealed in full on one occasion. Some of its passages were revealed early in the Madinan period, and some towards its end, stretching over a period of nearly nine years. The present *sūrah*, al-Anfāl, was revealed sometime between these two dates, while *Sūrah* 2 was still in the process leading to its completion. This meant that a passage would be revealed and placed in its appropriate position, according to divine instruction given through the Prophet. Normally, however, when we say that a particular *sūrah* was revealed on such and such date, we are simply referring to the beginning of its revelation.

Some reports suggest that verses 30–36 were revealed in Makkah, since they refer to events that took place there before the Prophet's migration to Madinah. This, however, is not a sufficient reason to draw such a conclusion. Many are the verses revealed in Madinah that refer to past events from the Makkan period. In this *sūrah*, verse 26 provides such a case. Moreover, verse 36, the last one in the passage claimed to have been revealed in Makkah, speaks of how the idolaters allocated funds to prepare for the Battle of Uḥud, which took place after their defeat at Badr.

The reports that claim that these verses were a Makkan revelation also mention a conversation that is highly improbable. They mention that "Abū Ṭālib, the Prophet's uncle who provided him with protection, asked the Prophet: 'What are your people plotting against you?' He answered: 'They want to cast a magic spell on me, or to banish or kill me.' He said: 'Who told you this?' The Prophet replied: 'My Lord.' Abū Ṭālib then said: 'Your Lord is a good one. Take care of him.' The Prophet said: 'I take care of Him! No, it is He who takes good care of me.' By way of comment on this, verse 26 was revealed, saying: '*Remember when you were few and helpless in the land, fearful lest people do away with you: how He sheltered you, strengthened you with His support and provided you with many good things so that you might be grateful.*'" (Verse 26)

Ibn Kathīr mentions this report and discounts it, saying: "This is highly improbable, because this verse was revealed in Madinah. Besides, the entire event, when the Quraysh convened a meeting of its notables to discuss how they could get rid of the Prophet and the suggestions they made of imprisoning, banishing or killing him, took place on the eve of the Prophet's migration, about three years after Abū Ṭālib's death. When Abū Ṭālib died, the Prophet lost his uncle who had given him full support and protection. The Quraysh were thus able to abuse him and concoct a plot to kill him."

Muḥammad ibn Isḥāq, a very early biographer of the Prophet, transmits a couple of long reports on the authority of Ibn 'Abbās, the Prophet's cousin who was an eminent scholar, concerning these plots by the Quraysh. He concludes by saying: "God then gave him permission to depart. After he settled in Madinah, He revealed to him the *sūrah* entitled *al-Anfāl*, reminding him of His grace: '*Remember how the unbelievers were scheming against you, seeking to keep you in chains or have you slain or banished. Thus they plot and plan, but God also plans. God is above all schemers.*'" (Verse 30)

This report by Ibn 'Abbās fits well with the general text of the complete *sūrah*, and its reminders to the Prophet and his companions of His grace. When they remember these aspects of God's grace, they are motivated to fulfil their duty, fight the enemies of their faith and stand firm. Hence, to say that the whole *sūrah* was revealed after the Muslims' migration to Madinah is more accurate.

Characteristics of the Islamic Approach

This *sūrah* takes up the Battle of Badr as its subject matter. This battle, its circumstances, results and effects on human history constitute a major landmark in the progress of the Islamic movement. God describes this battle as '*the day when the true was distinguished from the false, the day when the two hosts met in battle.*' (Verse 41) He also makes it the parting point not merely in this life or in human history, but also in the life to come. He says in the Qur'ān: "*These two adversaries have become engrossed in contention about their Lord. For the unbelievers garments of fire shall be cut out; and scalding water will be poured over their heads, melting all that is in their bellies and their skin. In addition, there will be grips of iron for them. Whenever, in their anguish, they try to get out, they are returned there, and will be told: 'Taste the torment of fire.' God will certainly admit those who believe and do righteous deeds into gardens through which running waters flow, wherein they will be adorned with bracelets of gold and pearls, and where silk will be their raiment. For they were guided to the best of words; and so they were guided to the way that leads to the One to whom all praise is due.*" (22: 19–24) Some reports suggest that these verses speak of the two hosts that met in battle at Badr. This confirms that this battle provides the criterion by which people shall be distinguished in the life to come. This statement by God Almighty is sufficient to give us a clear idea of the importance of that day of battle. We will try to give an idea of its great value as we discuss the battle, the events leading to it and its outcome.

Exceptionally important as that battle is, its true value cannot be clearly seen unless we understand its nature and realize that it was merely one episode of *jihād*. To appreciate it fully we also need to understand the motives and objectives of *jihād*; and we certainly cannot understand those unless we fully understand the nature of Islam itself.

In his priceless book *Zād al-Ma'ād*, Imām Ibn al-Qayyim includes a chapter with the title, The Progress of the Prophet's Guidance on Dealing with the Unbelievers and the Hypocrites from the Start of His Mission to the End of His Life. This is given below in a highly summarized form:

> The first revelation given to the Prophet by his Lord – limitless is He in His glory – was his order to him, "*Read in the name of your Lord who created man out of a germ-cell.*" (96: 1–2) This was the start of his prophethood. The instruction to him was to read within himself. At that point, He did not order him to convey anything to anyone. He subsequently revealed to him: "*You who are enfolded, arise and warn!*" (74: 1–2) This means that God made him a prophet by telling him to read, and He gave him his mission by saying, "*You who are enfolded, arise and warn!*" (74: 1–2) God then ordered him to warn his immediate clan. Subsequently, he gave the same warning to his own people, then to the surrounding Arabian tribes, then all Arabs, then mankind generally.
>
> For more than a decade after the start of his prophethood, Muḥammad [peace be upon him] continued to advocate the faith without resorting to fighting or the imposition of any loyalty tax, i.e. *jizyah*. Throughout this period he was ordered to stay his hand, forbear patiently and overlook all opposition. Later, God

gave him permission to migrate [from Makkah to Madinah] and permitted him to fight. He then instructed him to fight those who wage war against him and to maintain peace with those who refrain from fighting him. At a later stage, God ordered him to fight the idolaters until all submission is made to God alone.

After the order was given to the Prophet to strive and fight for God's cause [i.e. *jihād*], unbelievers were in three categories with regard to their relations with him: those with whom he was in peace and truce, combatants fighting him, and those under his protection [i.e. *ahl al-dhimmah*]. God ordered him to honour his treaties with those whom he had a peace treaty, as long as they honoured their commitments. If he feared treachery on their part, he was to revoke the treaty but would not fight them until he had informed them of the termination of their peace treaty. On the other hand, he was to fight those who violated their treaties with him.

When *Sūrah* 9, *al-Tawbah*, was revealed, it outlined the policy towards all these three categories. The Prophet is ordered there to fight his enemies from among the people of earlier faiths until they submit to his authority, paying the loyalty tax, *jizyah*, or embrace Islam. He is also ordered in the same *sūrah* to strive hard against the unbelievers and the idolaters. He strove against the unbelievers with arms, and against the hypocrites with argument and proof.

A further order to the Prophet in *Sūrah* 9 was to terminate all treaties with unbelievers, classifying such people into three groups. The first group he was ordered to fight, because these were the ones who violated their treaties with him and who were untrue to their commitments. He fought them and was victorious. The second group consisted of those with whom he had a peace treaty which they had honoured fully, and the treaty was to run for a specific term. They had given no support to any person or group who opposed the Prophet. With these he was to honour the peace treaty until it had run its course. The third group included those with whom the Prophet had no treaty and no previous fighting engagements, as well as those who had an open-ended agreement. The Prophet was instructed to give these groups four months' notice, after which he was to fight them. The Prophet acted on these instructions, fought those who violated their treaties, and gave four months, notice to those who had no treaty or had one without a specific term. Those who honoured their treaty were to have it honoured by the Prophet until the end of its term. All these embraced Islam before the end of their term. As for those who pledged loyalty to him, they were to pay the loyalty tax, *jizyah*.

Thus, after the revelation of *Sūrah* 9, the unbelievers were in three different categories with regard to the Prophet's relations with them: combatants, or bound by a specified-term treaty, or loyal. The second category embraced Islam shortly thereafter, leaving the other two groups: combatants who feared him, and those who were loyal. Thus, all mankind were divided into three classes: Muslims who believed in the Prophet's message; those at peace with him who enjoyed security; and those who were hostile and feared him.

As for the hypocrites, he was instructed to accept from them what they professed, leaving the final verdict on them to God. He was to strive against them with informed argument. He was further instructed to turn away from them and to be hard so that he would deliver his message to them in a way that they could not refute. He was forbidden to pray for them when they died, or to visit their graves. He was informed that if he were to pray for them to be forgiven, God would not forgive them.

Such was the Prophet's policy towards his opponents, both unbelievers and hypocrites.[1]

This excellent summary of the different stages of the development of *jihād*, or striving for God's cause, reveals a number of profound features of the Islamic approach which merit discussion; but we can only present them here very briefly.

The first of these features is the serious realism of the Islamic approach. Islam is a movement confronting a human situation with appropriate means. What it confronts is a state of ignorance, or *jāhiliyyah*, which prevails over ideas and beliefs, giving rise to practical systems that are supported by political and material authority. Thus,

1. Ibn al-Qayyim, *Zād al-Ma'ād,* Mu'assasat Al-Risālah, Beirut, 1994, Vol. 3, pp.158–161.

the Islamic approach is to confront all this with vigorous means and suitable resources. It presents its arguments and proofs to correct concepts and beliefs; and it strives with power to remove the systems and authorities that prevent people from adopting the right beliefs, forcing them to follow their errant ways and worship deities other than God Almighty. The Islamic approach does not resort to the use of verbal argument when confronting material power. Nor does it ever resort to compulsion and coercion in order to force its beliefs on people. Both are equally alien to the Islamic approach as it seeks to liberate people from subjugation so that they may serve God alone.

Secondly, Islam is a practical movement that progresses from one stage to the next, utilizing for each stage practically effective and competent means, while at the same time preparing the ground for the next stage. It does not confront practical realities with abstract theories, nor does it use the same old means to face changing realities. Some people ignore this essential feature of the Islamic approach and overlook the nature of the different stages of development of this approach. They cite Qur'ānic statements stating that they represent the Islamic approach, without relating these statements to the stages they addressed. When they do so, they betray their utter confusion and give the Islamic approach a deceptive appearance. They assign to Qur'ānic verses insupportable rules and principles, treating each verse or statement as outlining final Islamic rules. Themselves a product of the sorry and desperate state of contemporary generations who have nothing of Islam other than its label, and defeated both rationally and spiritually, they claim that Islamic *jihād* is always defensive. They imagine that they are doing Islam a service when they cast away its objective of removing all tyrannical powers from the face of the earth, so that people are freed from serving anyone other than God. Islam does not force people to accept its beliefs; rather, it aims to provide an environment where people enjoy full freedom of belief. It abolishes oppressive political systems depriving people of this freedom, or forces them into submission so that they allow their peoples complete freedom to choose to believe in Islam if they so wish.

Thirdly, such continuous movement and progressive ways and means do not divert Islam from its definitive principles and well-defined objectives. Right from the very first day, when it made its initial address to the Prophet's immediate clan, then to the Quraysh, and then to the Arabs and finally putting its message to all mankind, its basic theme remained the same, making the same requirement. It wants people to achieve the same objective of worshipping God alone, submitting themselves to none other than Him. There can be no compromise over this essential rule. It then moves towards this single goal according to a well-thought-out plan, with progressive stages, and fitting means.

Finally, we have a clear legal framework governing relations between the Muslim community and other societies, as is evident in the excellent summary quoted from *Zād al-Ma'ād*. This legal framework is based on the main principle that submission to God alone is a universal message which all mankind must either accept or be at peace with. It must not place any impediment to this message, in the form of a political system or material power. Every individual must remain free to make his or her absolutely free choice to accept or reject it, feeling no pressure or opposition. Anyone who puts such impediments in the face of the message of complete submission to God, must be resisted and fought by Islam.

The Liberation of Mankind

Writers with a defeatist and apologetic mentality who try to defend Islamic *jihād* often confuse two clearly different principles. The first is that Islam comes out clearly against forcing people to accept any particular belief, while the second is its approach that seeks to remove political and material forces that try to prevent it from addressing people, so that they may not submit themselves to God. These are clearly distinct principles that should never be confused. Yet it is because of their defeatism that such writers try to limit *jihād* to what is called today 'a defensive war'. But Islamic *jihād* is a totally different matter that has nothing to do with the wars people fight today, or their motives and presentation. The motives of Islamic *jihād* can be found within the nature of Islam, its role in human life, the objectives God has set for it and for the achievement of which He has sent His final Messenger with His perfect message.

We may describe the Islamic faith as a declaration of the liberation of mankind from servitude to creatures, including man's own desires. It also declares that all Godhead and Lordship throughout the universe belong to God alone. This represents a challenge to all systems that assign sovereignty to human beings in any shape or form. It is, in effect, a revolt against any human situation where sovereignty, or indeed

Godhead, is given to human beings. A situation that gives ultimate authority to human beings actually elevates those humans to the status of deities, usurping God's own authority. As a declaration of human liberation, Islam means returning God's authority to Him, rejecting the usurpers who rule over human communities according to man-made laws. In this way, no human being is placed in a position of Lordship over other people. To proclaim God's authority and sovereignty means the elimination of all human kingship and to establish the rule of God, the Lord of the universe. In the words of the Qur'ān: "*He alone is God in the heavens and God on earth.*" (43: 84) "*All judgement rests with God alone. He has ordered that you should worship none but Him. That is the true faith, but most people do not know it.*" (12: 40) "*Say: 'People of earlier revelations! Let us come to an agreement which is equitable between you and us: that we shall worship none but God, that we shall associate no partners with Him, and that we shall not take one another for lords beside God.' And if they turn away, then say: 'Bear witness that we have surrendered ourselves to God.'*" (3: 64)

Establishing the rule of God on earth does not mean that sovereignty is assigned to a particular group of people, as was the case when the Church wielded power in Christian Europe, or that certain men become spokesmen for the gods, as was the case under theocratic rule. God's rule is established when His law is enforced and all matters are judged according to His revealed law.

Nothing of all this is achieved through verbal advocacy of Islam. The problem is that the people in power who have usurped God's authority on earth will not relinquish their power at the mere explanation and advocacy of the true faith. Otherwise, it would have been very simple for God's messengers to establish the divine faith. History, however, tells us that the reverse was true throughout human life.

This universal declaration of the liberation of man on earth from every authority other than that of God, and the declaration that all sovereignty belongs to God alone as does Lordship over the universe, are not a theoretical, philosophical and passive proclamation. It is a positive, practical and dynamic message which seeks to bring about the implementation of God's law in human life, freeing people from servitude to anyone other than God alone. This cannot be achieved unless advocacy is complemented with a movement that confronts the existing human situation with adequate and competent means.

In actual life, Islam is always confronted with a host of obstacles placed in its way: some belong to the realm of beliefs and concepts, others are physical, in addition to political, social, economic, racial obstacles. Deviant beliefs and superstitions add further obstacles trying to impede Islam. All these interact to form a very complex mixture working against Islam and the liberation of man.

Verbal argument and advocacy face up to beliefs and ideas, while the movement confronts material obstacles, particularly political authority that rests on complex yet interrelated ideological, racial, class, social and economic systems. Thus, employing both verbal advocacy and its practical movement, Islam confronts the existing human situation in its totality with adequately effective methods. Both are necessary for the achievement of the liberation of all mankind throughout the world. This is a very important point that merits strong emphasis.

This religion of Islam is not a declaration for the liberation of the Arabs, nor is its message addressed to the Arabs in particular. It addresses itself to all humanity, considering the entire earth its field of work. God is not the Lord of the Arabs alone, nor is His Lordship limited to Muslims only. God is the Lord of all worlds. Hence, Islam wants to bring all mankind back to their true Lord, liberating them from servitude to anyone else. From the Islamic point of view, true servitude or worship, takes the form of people's submission to laws enacted by other human beings. It is such submission, or servitude, that is due to God alone, as Islam emphasizes. Anyone that serves anyone other than God in this sense takes himself out of Islam, no matter how strongly he declares himself to be a Muslim. The Prophet clearly states that adherence to laws and authorities was the type of worship which classified the Jews and Christians as unbelievers, disobeying God's orders to worship Him alone.

Al-Tirmidhī relates on the authority of 'Adiy ibn Ḥātim that when the Prophet's message reached him, he fled to Syria. [He had earlier accepted Christianity.] However, his sister and a number of people from his tribe were taken prisoner by the Muslims. The Prophet [peace be upon him] treated his sister kindly and gave her gifts. She went back to her brother and encouraged him to adopt Islam, and to visit the Prophet. People were speaking about his expected arrival. When he came into the Prophet's presence, he was wearing a silver cross. As he entered, the Prophet was reciting the verse which says: "*They [i.e. the people of earlier revelations] have taken their rabbis and their monks, as well as the Christ, son of Mary, for their lords beside God.*" (9: 31) 'Adiy reports: "I said, 'They did not worship their priests.' God's Messenger replied, 'Yes they did. Their priests and rabbis forbade them what is lawful, and declared permissible what is unlawful, and they accepted that. This is how they worshipped them.'"

The explanation given by the Prophet is a clear statement that obedience to man-made laws and judgements constitutes worship that takes people out of Islam. It is indeed how some people take others for their lords. This is the very situation Islam aims to eradicate in order to ensure man's liberation.

When the realities of human life run contrary to the declaration of general human liberation, it becomes incumbent on Islam to take appropriate action, on both the advocacy and the movement fronts. It strikes hard against political regimes that rule over people according to laws other than that of God, or in other words, force people to serve beings other than God, and prevent them from listening to the message of Islam and accepting it freely if they so desire. Islam will also remove existing powers whether they take a purely political or racial form or operate class distinction within the same race. It then moves to establish a social, economic and political system that allows the liberation of man and man's unhindered movement.

It is never the intention of Islam to force its beliefs on people, but Islam is not merely a set of beliefs. Islam aims to make mankind free from servitude to other people. Hence, it strives to abolish all systems and regimes that are based on the servitude of one person to another. When Islam has thus freed people from all political pressure and enlightened their minds with its message, it gives them complete freedom to choose the faith they wish. However, this freedom does not mean that they can make their desires their gods, or that they choose to remain in servitude to people like them, or that some of them are elevated to the status of lordship over the rest. The system to be established in the world should be based on complete servitude to God alone, deriving all its laws from Him only. Within this system, every person is free to adopt whatever beliefs he or she wants. This is the practical meaning of the principle that 'all religion must be to God alone.' Religion means submission, obedience, servitude and worship, and all these must be to God. According to Islam, the term 'religion' is much wider in scope than belief. Religion is actually a way of life, and in Islam this is based on belief. But in an Islamic system, it is possible that different groups live under it even though they may choose not to adopt Islamic beliefs. They will, however, abide by its laws based on the central principle of submission to God alone.

How Defensive Is *Jihād*?

When we understand the nature of Islam, as it has already been explained, we realize the inevitability of *jihād*, or striving for God's cause, taking a military form in addition to its advocacy form. We will further recognize that *jihād* was never defensive, in the narrow sense that the term 'defensive war' generally denotes today. It is this narrow sense that is emphasized by the defeatists who succumb to the pressure of the present circumstances and to the Orientalists' wily attacks. Indeed the concept of striving, or *jihād*, for God's cause represents a positive movement that aims to liberate man throughout the world, employing appropriate means to face every situation at every stage.

If we must describe Islamic *jihād* as defensive, then we need to amend the meaning of the term 'defence' so that it means the defending of mankind against all factors that hinder their liberation and restrict their freedom. These may take the form of concepts and beliefs, as well as political regimes that create economic, class and racial distinctions. When Islam first came into existence, this world was full of such hindrances, some forms of which persist in present-day *jāhiliyyah*.

When we give the term 'defence' such a broader meaning we can appreciate the motives for Islamic *jihād* all over the world, and we can understand the nature of Islam. Otherwise, any attempt to find defensive justification for *jihād*, within the contemporary narrow sense of defence, betrays a lack of understanding of the nature of Islam and its role in this world. Such attempts try to find any evidence to prove that early Muslims went on *jihād* to repel aggression by their neighbours against the Muslim land, which to some people is confined to the Arabian Peninsula. All this betrays stark defeatism.

Had Abū Bakr, 'Umar and 'Uthmān, the first three Caliphs, felt secure against any attack on Arabia by the Byzantine or the Persian Empires, would they have refrained from carrying the message of Islam to the rest of the world? How could they present Islam to the world when they had all types of material obstacles to contend with: political regimes, social, racial and class systems, as well as economic systems based on such social discrimination; and all these are guaranteed protection by the state?

Jihād is essential for the Islamic message, if it is to be taken seriously as a declaration of the liberation of man, because it cannot confine itself to theoretical and philosophical arguments. It must confront existing situations with effective means, whether the land of Islam is secure or under threat from neighbouring powers. As Islam works for peace, it is not satisfied with a cheap peace that applies only to the area where people of the Muslim faith happen to live. Islam aims to achieve the sort of peace which ensures that all submission is made to God alone. This means that all people submit themselves to God, and none of them takes others for their lords. We must form our view on the basis of the ultimate stage of the *jihād* movement, not on the early or middle stages of the Prophet's mission. All these stages led to the situation described by Imām Ibn al-Qayyim as follows:

> Thus, after the revelation of *Sūrah* 9, the unbelievers were in three different categories with regard to the Prophet's relations with them: combatants, or bound by a specified-term treaty, or loyal. The second category embraced Islam shortly thereafter, leaving the other two groups: combatants who feared him, and those who were loyal. Thus, all mankind were divided into three classes: Muslims who believed in the Prophet's message; those at peace with him who enjoyed security; and those who were hostile and feared him.[2]

Such is the attitude that is consistent with the nature of Islam and its objectives.

When Islam was still confined to Makkah, and in the early period of the Prophet's settlement in Madinah, God restrained the Muslims from fighting. They were told: "*Hold back your hands [from fighting], and attend regularly to prayer, and pay your* zakāt." (4: 77) They were later permitted to fight, when they were told: "*Permission to fight is given to those against whom war is being wrongfully waged. Most certainly, God has the power to grant them victory. These are the ones who have been driven from their homelands against all right for no other reason than their saying, 'Our Lord is God!' Were it not that God repels some*

2. Ibn al-Qayyim, Ibid, p. 161.

people by means of others, monasteries, churches, synagogues and mosques – in all of which God's name is abundantly extolled – would surely have been destroyed. God will most certainly succour him who succours God's cause. God is certainly most Powerful, Almighty. They are those who, if We firmly establish them on earth, attend regularly to their prayers, give in charity, enjoin the doing of what is right and forbid the doing of what is wrong. With God rests the final outcome of all events." (22: 39–41) They were then required to fight those who fight them, but not other people: "*Fight for the cause of God those who wage war against you, but do not commit aggression.*" (2: 190) But then they were ordered to fight against all idolaters: "*fight against the idolaters all together as they fight against you all together.*" (9: 36) They were also told: "*Fight against those among the people of the scriptures who do not believe in God or the Last Day, and do not forbid what God and His Messenger have forbidden, and do not follow the religion of truth until they pay the submission tax with a willing hand and are utterly subdued.*" (9: 29) This means, as Ibn al-Qayyim puts it, that "fighting was first forbidden, then permitted, then ordered against those who fight Muslims, and finally against all unbelievers who associate partners with God."

The seriousness that is characteristic of the Qur'ānic texts and the Prophet's traditions on *jihād*, and the positive approach that is very clear in all events of *jihād* in the early Islamic periods and over many centuries make it impossible to accept the explanation concocted by defeatist writers. They have come up with such an explanation under pressure from the present weakness of the Muslim community and the unsavoury attacks on the concept of *jihād* by Orientalists.

When we listen to God's words and the Prophet's traditions on *jihād*, and follow the events of early Islamic *jihād*, we cannot imagine how anyone can consider it a temporary measure, subject to circumstances that may or may not come into play, or having the limited objective of securing national borders.

In the very first Qur'ānic verse that gives Muslims permission to fight for His cause, God makes it clear to believers that the normal situation in this present life is that one group of people is checked by another so as to prevent the spread of corruption on earth: "*Permission to fight is given to those against whom war is being wrongfully waged. Most certainly, God has the power to grant them victory. These are the ones who have been driven from their homelands against all right for no other reason than their saying, 'Our Lord is God!' Were it not that God repels some people by means of others, monasteries, churches, synagogues and mosques – in all of which God's name is abundantly extolled – would surely have been destroyed.*" (22: 39–40) We thus see that it is the permanent state of affairs for truth to be unable to co-exist with falsehood on earth. Hence, when Islam makes its declaration for the liberation of mankind on earth, so that they may only serve God alone, those who usurp God's authority try to silence it. They will never tolerate it or leave it in peace. Islam will not sit idle, either. It will move to deprive them of their power so that people can be freed of their shackles. This is the permanent state of affairs which necessitates the continuity of *jihād* until all submission is made to God alone.

A Stage of No Fighting

Holding back from fighting in Makkah, by divine order, was only a stage in a long-term strategy. The same was the case in the early days after the Prophet's migration to Madinah. However, what made the Muslim community in Madinah take its stance was not merely the need to defend Madinah and make it secure against attack. This was certainly a primary objective, but it was by no means the ultimate one. Achieving this objective provided the means and the secure base from which to remove the obstacles that fettered man and deprived him of his freedom.

Besides, it is perfectly understandable that Muslims should refrain from taking up arms in Makkah. Advocacy of Islam was reasonably free. Assured of protection by his own clan, the Hāshimites, the Prophet was able to declare his message, addressing it to individuals and groups and putting to them its clear principles and beliefs. There was no organized political power to stop him from doing so, or to stop individuals from listening to him. Hence, there was no need at this stage to resort to force. There were other reasons which we outlined in Volume III, pp. 234–236, when commenting on the verse that says: "*Are you not aware of those who have been told, 'Hold back your hands [from fighting], and attend regularly to prayer, and pay your* zakāt*...?'*" It may be useful to quote here a part of what we stated there:

1. One reason could be that the Makkan period was one of training, educating and preparing a particular group of people under certain conditions. One of the aims of such a programme

is to discipline the Arab mind to persevere and endure personal and collective hardship as a means to transcend personal egos. One's own self and immediate community should no longer be the focus and prime movers in one's life. People needed to be taught restraint and self-control and how not to react with immediate rage and anger, as was their nature. They needed to learn to behave as members of an organized society with a central leadership to be consulted and obeyed in all matters, regardless of how different that was from their customs and traditions. This was the cornerstone in remodelling the Arab character to establish a civilized, orderly, non-tribal Muslim society that recognizes a governing leadership.

2. Another possible reason is that peaceful action was more effective in that particular Arab society of the Quraysh, which attached much importance to self-image and honour. The use of force in such a situation could only harden attitudes and result in fresh bloody grudges, reminiscent of the famous inter-Arab feuds of Dāḥis and al-Ghabrā', and of al-Basūs which raged for many years, wiping out complete tribes. Such a new conflict would always be associated in the Arab memory with Islam as the cause of vengeance and bloodshed rather than Islam as a universal Divine mission. The basic essence of Islam would, in that case, be forever obscured and obliterated.

3. There was also the need to avoid a bloodbath within every Arab household in Makkah since there was no organized authority perpetrating the persecution of Muslim converts. The harassment was unsystematic, following no specific order. Every household dealt with their converts as they saw fit. Prescription of armed confrontation in such circumstances would mean battles and massacres in every home for which Islam would be blamed. In fact, the Quraysh propaganda, spread during the pilgrimage and trading seasons, was already blaming Islam for family splits, feuds and divisions among the Arabs even before the use of force was eventually permitted.

4. Another reason for the delay in prescribing *jihād* by force of arms could be God's prior knowledge that many of the tormentors and perpetrators of maltreatment against the

Muslims would, one day soon, themselves be converts and ardent defenders, indeed leaders, of Islam. Was not 'Umar ibn al-Khaṭṭāb one such person?

5. Another reason could be that Arab tribal chivalry was known to provoke sympathy with the weak and the oppressed when they persevere in the face of adversity, especially if some of these hailed from the noble sections of society. This is borne out in several incidents including that whereby Ibn al-Dughunnah tried to persuade Abū Bakr, a noble man, not to leave Makkah and offered him protection, seeing it as a shame on all the Arabs that he should have to emigrate. Another incident was the repeal of the boycott on Hāshim, Muḥammad's clan, and the ending of their siege in the Hāshimite quarters in Makkah, after an extended period of starvation and hardship. In other ancient civilizations, persecution might have led to the adulation of the oppressor and further humiliation for the oppressed, but not in Arab society.

6. It could have been due to the small number of Muslims at the time and their confinement in Makkah when Islam had not spread widely in Arabia, and the neutral stand that other Arab tribes would take in an internal conflict within Makkah. Confrontation could very well lead to the annihilation of the small band of Muslim converts, even if they were to kill twice as many as their own number, and the infidels would thus prevail. In this case, the religion of Islam, which was meant to be a universal way of life and a practical and realistic system, would no longer exist.

As for the early period in Madinah, the treaty the Prophet agreed with the Jews and the Arab unbelievers in the city and the neighbouring areas was a suitable arrangement at this stage. Besides, there was an open opportunity for delivering God's message, with no political authority standing in opposition to it. All groups recognized the new Muslim state and the Prophet as its leader who conducted its political affairs. The treaty stipulated that no party or group could wage war against, or make peace or establish any relations with, any outside group without the express permission of the Prophet. Moreover, it was clear that real power in Madinah was wielded by the Muslim leadership. Hence, God's message could be freely addressed to people and they could choose to accept it if they so wanted.

Moreover, the Prophet wanted to concentrate his efforts at this stage on the struggle against the Quraysh, whose relentless opposition to Islam constituted a hard obstacle preventing its spread to other tribes. Most Arabian tribes adopted a wait-and-see attitude to the struggle which they viewed as an internal conflict between the Quraysh and a group of its own members. Hence the Prophet started to send out expeditions, beginning in Ramaḍān, only seven months after his migration to Madinah when his uncle Ḥamzah ibn 'Abd al-Muṭṭalib was the first commander.

Other expeditions followed, with the second taking place nine months after the Prophet's migration, and another after 13 months, and a fourth three months later on. Shortly after that the Prophet sent a small company commanded by 'Abdullāh ibn Jaḥsh, 17 months after his migration. It was on this particular expedition that fighting took place for the first time and one man was killed. This was in one of the four sacred months. In a comment on this incident the Qur'ān says: "*They ask you about fighting in the sacred month. Say, 'Fighting in it is a grave offence, but to turn people away from God's path, to disbelieve in Him and in the Sacred Mosque, and to expel its people from it – [all this] is far more grave in God's sight.' Religious persecution is worse than killing. They shall not cease to fight you until they force you to renounce your faith, if they can.*" (2: 217)[3]

In Ramaḍān of the same year, the Battle of Badr took place, on which the present *sūrah* provides detailed commentary.

What Justification for *Jihād*?

When we review the situation with all its relevant circumstances, we realize that the argument that *jihād* is nothing more than a defensive war, in the narrow sense of the term, cannot hold. Those who try to find pure defensive reasons to justify the expansion of Islam find themselves cornered by Orientalists' attacks at a time when Muslims are powerless. Indeed Muslims today are far removed from Islam, except

3. For details of this expedition with our commentary on this verse please refer to Vol.I, Chapter 13.

for a small minority who are determined to implement the Islamic declaration of man's liberation from all authority except that of God.

The spread of Islam does not need to find any justification other than those stated in the Qur'ān: "*Let them fight in God's cause – all who are willing to barter the life of this world for the life to come. To him who fights in God's cause, whether he be slain or be victorious, We shall grant a rich reward. And why should you not fight in the cause of God and the utterly helpless men, women and children who are crying, 'Our Lord! Deliver us from this land whose people are oppressors, and send forth to us, out of Your grace, a protector, and send us one that will help us.' Those who believe fight in the cause of God, and those who reject the faith fight in the cause of evil. Fight, then, against the friends of Satan. Feeble indeed is the cunning of Satan.*" (4: 74–76)

"*Say to the unbelievers that if they desist, all that is past shall be forgiven them; but if they persist [in their erring ways], let them remember what happened to the like of them in former times. Fight them until there is no more oppression, and all submission is made to God alone. If they desist, God is certainly aware of all they do. But if they turn away, know that God is your Lord Supreme. How splendid is this Lord Supreme, and how splendid is this giver of support.*" (8: 38–40)

"*Fight against those among the people of earlier revelations who do not believe in God or the Last Day, and do not forbid what God and His Messenger have forbidden, and do not follow the religion of truth until they pay the submission tax with a willing hand and are utterly subdued. The Jews say: 'Ezra is the son of God', while the Christians say: 'The Christ is the son of God.' Such are the assertions they utter with their mouths, echoing assertions made by the unbelievers of old. May God destroy them! How perverse they are! They make of their rabbis and their monks, and of the Christ, son of Mary, lords besides God. Yet they have been ordered to worship none but the One God, other than whom there is no deity. Exalted be He above those to whom they ascribe divinity. They seek to extinguish God's light with their mouths, but God will not allow anything to interfere with His will to bring His light to perfection, however hateful this may be to the unbelievers.*" (9: 29–32)

The justification carried in these verses is that of the need to establish the truth of Godhead on earth, and implement the way of life God has decreed in human life. Moreover, satanic forces and methods must be chased out and abolished; and the lordship of one man over others must be ended. Human beings are God's creatures and they serve Him alone. No one may be allowed to hold authority over them so as to make them his servants or enact arbitrary laws for them. This is sufficient justification, not forgetting at the same time the main principle that "*there shall be no compulsion in religion.*" (2: 256) No one will ever be compelled or pressurized to adopt the Islamic faith after the liberation of all people and the acknowledgement that all submission must be to God alone, and that all authority belongs to Him.

It is sufficient to remember that Islam aims to free all mankind from servitude to creatures so that they may serve God alone to justify Islamic *jihād*. This was clearly in the minds of the early Muslims when they went out to fight the Byzantine and the Persian Empires. None of them justified their action by saying, 'We want to defend our country against external threats,' or, 'We want to repel Byzantine or Persian aggression,' or, 'We want to annex land and add to our wealth.' Their representatives, Rib'iy ibn 'Āmir, Ḥudhayfah ibn Muḥṣin and al-Mughīrah ibn Shu'bah, each met Rustam, the Persian army commander in the Battle of al-Qādisiyyah, alone on three successive days. In response to Rustam's question about their objectives, they all said the same thing: "It is God who has commanded us so that we may liberate anyone who wishes from servitude to human beings into the service of God alone, from the narrowness of this world into the expanse of this world and the hereafter, and from the injustices of different religions to the justice of Islam. God has sent His Messenger to deliver His message to His creatures. Whoever accepts it from us, we let him be, turn back and give him his land. We fight only those who rebel until we achieve martyrdom or victory."

The justification for *jihād* is inherent in the nature of this faith, its declaration of man's liberation, and its confrontation with existing human situations using adequate and effective means, suitably adapted and renewed for every stage. This justification exists in the first place, even though there may be no threat to the Muslim land or the Muslim community. It is of the essence of the Islamic approach and the nature of the practical obstacles that stand in its way in different communities. Islamic *jihād* cannot be linked merely to some limited and temporary defensive needs.

It is sufficient that a Muslim goes out on *jihād* laying down his life and sacrificing all his money, for God's cause, not for any considerations of any personal gain. Before going out on *jihād* a Muslim would have won the greater battle within himself, against his own desires, ambitions, personal and national interests and against any motive other than serving God and establishing His authority on earth after winning it back from rebellious usurpers.

People who try to justify Islamic *jihād* on the grounds of protecting or defending the Islamic homeland underrate the Islamic way of life, placing its importance below that of the homeland. Theirs is a new consideration that is alien to the Islamic outlook. The faith, the way of life based on it and the community that implements it are the considerations valued by Islam. The land in itself has no significance. It acquires its value when the Islamic way of life is implemented in it, so as to become the cradle of the faith, the practical model, the homeland of Islam, and the starting point for the liberation of mankind.

It is true that defending the homeland of Islam means protecting the faith, the way of life and the Muslim community, all at the same time; but this is not the ultimate objective of Islamic *jihād*. Defending the homeland of Islam is the means to establish God's authority within it, and to use it as the base from which to address all mankind. Islam is a message to all humanity, and the whole earth is its sphere of action.

As already stated, any effort that tries to spread the Islamic way of life is bound to meet obstacles created by the power of the state, the social system and the general environment. Islam aims to remove all these obstacles so that it can address people freely, appealing to their minds and consciences, after breaking their fetters so that they have genuine freedom of choice.

We must not be intimidated by the Orientalists' attacks on the concept of Islamic *jihād*, or allow the pressures of world political powers to weigh heavily on us, so as to seek justifications for *jihād* that do not fit with the nature of Islam.

When we look at historical events, we must not lose sight of the inherent factors in the nature of Islam, its universal declaration and practical way of life. We must not confuse these with temporary defensive needs. It was inevitable that Islam would defend itself against aggression, because its very existence, general objective, the movement it forms under a new leadership, and the birth of a new community which recognizes only God's sovereignty – all this is bound to provoke other societies, based on *jāhiliyyah*, into trying to smash it in order to defend their own interests. It is inevitable that the new Muslim community will also have to defend itself. This is an inescapable situation that arises with the advent of Islam in any society. There is no question that Islam wants to fight such a battle; it is imposed on it, and the struggle that follows is a natural one, between two systems that cannot co-exist for long. All this is undeniable. Hence, Islam has no choice but to defend itself against aggression.

A much more important fact, however, is that, by nature, Islam will take the initiative and move to save humanity and free people throughout the world from servitude to anyone other than God. It is not possible that Islam will confine itself to geographical boundaries, or racial limits, abandoning the rest of mankind and leaving them to suffer from evil, corruption and servitude to lords other than God Almighty.

A time may come when enemies of Islam may find it expedient not to try to suppress Islam if it is willing to leave them alone, practising within their national boundaries their own systems that allow some people to be lords over others. They may offer such a state of co-existence if Islam is willing not to extend its declaration of universal freedom to their people. But Islam will not accept such a truce, unless they are willing to acknowledge its authority in the form of paying the loyalty or submission tax, *jizyah*, to guarantee that the message of Islam may address their people freely, without putting any material obstacle in its way.

Such is the nature of Islam and its role of liberating all mankind from servitude to anyone other than God. The gulf is wide indeed between this understanding and confining Islam to a local status within national borders or racial limits, acting only to defend itself against outside aggression. To think of Islam in this light is to deprive it of its reasons for action.

The underlying reasons for *jihād* are clearly identified when we remember that Islam is the way of life God has given to man. It is not a system devised by an individual or a group of people, nor is it the ideology of a certain race. It is only when we begin to lose sight of this fundamental truth of God's absolute sovereignty and people's servitude to Him that we try to find external reasons to justify *jihād*. No one who is fully cognizant of this basic Islamic principle will need to look for any other justification for *jihād*.

The gulf may not seem too great between thinking that Islam had to fight a war imposed on it by the very fact of its existence alongside *jāhiliyyah* societies, which were bound to attack it, and the recognition that Islam would have taken the initiative and embarked on its struggle. In both situations, Islam would have had to fight. But at the end the gulf between the two views is very wide indeed. It gives Islamic ideas and concepts a totally different colour. This is very serious indeed.

A Gulf Too Wide!

Islam is a system given by God and it aims to establish the fundamental principle of God's sovereignty and people's servitude to Him alone. It gives practical implementation of this principle in the form of a human society where people are totally free from servitude to anyone other than God. Thus, people are governed only by God's law, demonstrating His authority, or, in other words, His Godhead. As such, Islam has the right to remove all obstacles in its way and address people freely, without any impediments such as a political system or social customs and traditions. Viewing Islam in this way is far removed from viewing it as a local system of a particular country or nationality, having the right to defend itself within its national borders.

The two views are worlds apart, even though in both cases Islam would have had to fight. However, the reasons, motives, objectives and results of *jihād* under the two concepts are widely different. Our understanding of these is part of our beliefs, strategies and aims.

It is the right of Islam to take the initiative. It is not the creed of a particular people or the system of a particular country. It is a system given by God for the entire world. As such, it has the right to take action to remove all obstacles that fetter man's freedom of choice. It is a faith that does not force itself on any individual; it only attacks situations and regimes in order to free individuals from deviant influences that corrupt human nature and restrict man's freedom.

It is right that Islam should liberate people from servitude to other individuals in order that they serve God alone. It thus puts into practice its universal declaration of God's Lordship over the entire universe and the liberation of all mankind. Servitude to God alone cannot be realized, from the Islamic point of view and in practice, except under the Islamic system. It is only under this system that God's law applies equally and in the same way to all people, rulers and ruled, white and black, rich and poor. Under all other systems, people serve other people who enact laws for them. Legislation is a most fundamental attribute of Godhead. Any human being who claims the right to decree laws of his own for a community of people actually and practically claims Godhead, even though he may not put such a claim in words. Anyone who recognizes such an authority as belonging to a human being admits that Godhead belongs to that human being, whether he calls it as such or not.

Islam is not a mere ideology to be explained to people by normal ways of communication. It is a way of life represented in a social set-up that takes the necessary action to liberate mankind. Other communities try to prevent it from addressing their individuals to convince them of adopting its way of life. Therefore, it becomes imperative that Islam should try to remove those regimes that impede the freedom of mankind. As stated earlier, this is the meaning of ensuring that all submission is made to God alone, so that no submission or obedience is given to any human being on account of his own position or status, as is the case with all other systems.

Defeated by the combined pressures of the present situation and Orientalists' attacks, some contemporary Muslim writers feel too embarrassed to state these facts. Orientalists have tried to paint a false picture of Islam, showing it to have been spread by the sword. These Orientalists know very well that this is absolutely false, but they deliberately try to distort the underlying reasons for Islamic *jihād*. In reply, some of our people try to disprove this charge by seeking defensive justifications for *jihād*, overlooking the nature of Islam, its role in human life and its right to take the initiative to liberate mankind. Such defeatist writers are heavily influenced by the Western outlook and how it views religion as a mere set of beliefs that have nothing to do with day-to-day life. Hence, to fight for a religious cause means fighting to compel people to adopt a particular faith.

But this is not the case with Islam, which is a way of life given by God for all mankind, ascribing Lordship and sovereignty to God alone, and providing a system for the conduct of all life affairs. To fight for Islam is to fight for the implementation of this way of life and its systems. Faith, on the other hand, is a matter for free personal conviction, after the removal of all pressures and obstacles. The whole issue thus appears in a totally different light.

Thus, whenever an Islamic community comes into existence and begins to implement the Islamic way of life, God gives it the right to move, take power and establish that system, guaranteeing total freedom of belief. The fact that God held back the early Muslim community from fighting at a particular stage is only a question of strategy, not a matter of principle.

When we have this fundamental principle clear in our minds, we can easily understand the different Qur'ānic texts, applicable to different historical stages, without being confused as to their overall significance in relation to the constant Islamic approach.

A Further Point of View

Further explanation of the nature of *jihād* and the nature of Islam itself is given in a paper written by the great Muslim scholar, Abu'l Aʿlā Mawdūdī, which we will quote here at length.[4] This is very important for anyone who wishes to formulate a clear understanding of this issue which is central to the way of thinking of the Islamic movement.

> In common parlance the word '*jihād*' equates with holy war in English. For a considerable time now unfriendly interpreters have been adding spin to it as if it were nothing but pure zealotry – giving an image of a horde of religious fanatics surging forward, swords in hands, beards tucked under their lips, and chanting *Allāhu Akbar* (God is great). To intensify this imagery, their eyes are shown as filled with blood. Wherever they see an infidel (non-Muslim) they lay their hand on him and force him to declare that there is no deity except God or face execution. The spin masters have thus painted us masterly with their tag: "This nation's history smells of blood."
>
> Ironically, our picture makers are our old well wishers who have themselves been involved in an unholy war for the past many centuries against the poor and the wretched of the earth. History reveals a very ungainly picture of Westerners: equipped with all kinds of deadly weapons, they have thrown themselves on the

4. This translation of Mawdūdī's quote relies on the Urdu version of his paper, which was originally a speech given in Lahore in 1939. Sayyid Quṭb quoted from an Arabic translation which appears to have been expanded in some places and abridged in others. It also appears that the Arabic translation utilizes an expansive style, using many synonymous phrases and expressions. Hence, a reader who compares this text with the Arabic quote is bound to notice differences in many paragraphs. However, the ideas expressed are the same, and the lines the two versions follow are identical. – Editor's note.

peoples of the world establishing markets for their goods, searching for raw material resources, looking for lands to colonize, and minerals to exploit so that they can fuel their never-ending lust for other people's wealth. Their war is not for God but for greed to satisfy the demands of their baser selves. For them, it is enough of a reason for their bloodletting pursuits if others have resources to enrich them. Worse, they have annexed other people's lands where they have settled their surplus manpower. Some people even qualified themselves for such punitive action if their geographical areas provided access to a territory that they wanted to overpower.

What we, Muslims, have done is now history while the West's accomplishments are part of the contemporary scene witnessed by humanity every day. Asia, Africa, Europe, America – which part of the world is left unsoiled with the blood of the innocents owing to the West's unholy war? Horrible as it is, it redounds to their painting skills that they have brushed us in such exaggerated colours. Ghastly as it may be, they have succeeded in concealing their own ugly face behind ours. And so great is our naïvety that when we see our portrait thus made we are so terrified that we forget to see the faces of the painters behind it. Worse, we become apologetic, pleading: "Your Excellencies, we do not have anything to do with war; we are as peaceful a missionary as the Buddhists and the priests are. All we do is to refute a few beliefs and replace them with some others. Weapons are not our business. We do, however, admit that occasionally when someone comes to beat us we counter him against our will. But now we have discarded even our right to self-defence. To please your Excellencies we have officially proscribed weapon-wielding *jihād*. Now *jihād* is an effort waged with our mouths and pens. To fight with weapons is your prerogative."

Misgivings about jihād

Rhetoric aside, when we try to analyze the causes that have made *jihād* for God's sake an ungainly proposition for the non-Muslims as well as Muslims, we find two primary misconceptions behind it. The first lies in the fact that Islam has been misconceived as just another religion. The second centres around the fact that the Muslims are being viewed as a nation in the sense that this noun is generally perceived. Thus, two misconceptions have distorted not only the concept of *jihād* but have also damaged the whole complexion of Islam, giving Muslims a very bad image.

In common parlance, religion is nothing but a combination of a few articles of faith, and a few worship rituals. In this sense religion is doubtless a matter of private concern. One has the right to choose any faith one likes. One can also follow one's conscience in worshipping any deity one wants. And if one feels comfortable with it, one can even become part of the effort to spread it across the globe engaging others in polemics. This kind of faith does not need a sword for support. The proponents of traditional religion may rightly ask: "Do you want to beat people into embracing your faith?" This is a valid question that will inevitably be asked if one reduces Islam to a religion, in the common nuance of the word. In fact, once Islam is reduced to just another faith, then *jihād* invalidates itself in the overall scheme of Islam.

Likewise, what is a nation other than a homogeneous group of people which assumes distinction from other groups on account of its shared belief in some foundational values. In this sense a group having become a nation may rise in arms only for two reasons: when others attempt to deprive it of its legitimate rights or when it invades others to divest them of their rights. In the first situation, it has the moral ground to fight back; but even then some pacifists may disapprove. The second situation lacks moral content to justify armed invasion. None, other than a ruthless dictator, tries to justify such aggression. Indeed, intellectuals and statesmen of modern-day empires like France and Britain would not try to justify it.

The essence of jihād

Thus, if Islam is a religion and the Muslims are a nation, then *jihād* loses its most significant qualities that make it an important part of Islamic worship. Strictly speaking, Islam is neither a mere religion in the common sense, nor is the denomination "Muslim" the name of a nation.

So what is Islam? Islam is a revolutionary concept and a way of life, which seeks to change the prevalent social order and remould it according to its own vision. Based on this definition, the word 'Muslim' becomes the name of an international revolutionary party that Islam seeks to form in order to put its revolutionary programme into effect. *Jihād* signifies that revolutionary struggle involving the utmost use of resources that the Islamic party mobilizes in the service of its cause.

Like other revolutionary concepts, Islam avoids common words already in currency and opts for a more precise terminology so that its radical aspects stand distinct. As part of this special terminology, *jihād* serves a clear purpose. Islam deliberately discards words denoting war. Instead, it uses the word *jihād*, which is the equivalent of the English word "struggle". The Arabic word, however, is far more expressive and carries broader connotations, as it stands for exerting one's utmost endeavour to promote a cause.

One may ask why the old words were discarded and new expressions coined? The answer lies in the fact that the word 'war' has always been used for armed conflict between nations and empires aiming to achieve personal or national interests, devoid of any ideology or higher principles. Since Islam is not concerned with such mundane considerations, it dropped the old vocabulary altogether. Nor does Islam feel itself bound by a national concern. It has no interest in who occupies a particular piece of land. The only thing that matters for Islam is the well-being of humanity, for which it has its own particular perspective and action plan. Wherever there are governments opposed to its perspective, Islam aims to change them, regardless of where they function and the people they govern. Its ultimate objective is to establish its way of life and to put in place governments that implement its programme. Islam wants space – not a piece of the earth but the whole planet. It has no wish to monopolize resources for the benefit of a particular community; on the contrary, it wants to give all humanity spiritual and moral elevation through the implementation of its unique programme. To make it happen, it marshals every bit of manpower and material resource.

Islam gives the name *jihād* to such cumulative efforts. This includes efforts to change people through verbal advocacy. It also includes the possible armed struggle to end an oppressive system and establish justice. Spending money for the cause and physical exertion are also *jihād*.

For God's cause

Islamic *jihād* is not the mere exertion of effort; it has to be for God alone. Thus, it is imperative that *jihād* be undertaken only for God's cause, or to use the Arabic phrase, '*fī sabīl-illāh*'. This is a special phrase that belongs to the particular repertoire of terminology that I have mentioned. Literally translated, it means 'in the way of God.' True as this translation is, some narrow-minded people imagine that coercing others to accept Islam falls under this heading. Such understanding only betrays their rigidly narrow concepts. The fact remains that in the Islamic lexicon it has much wider connotations and implications.

For example, any work that involves collective well-being with no worldly considerations is for God. That is why a charity dispensed by a person for a moral or material return is not altruistic. If, however, the intention is to please God by helping the poor, it will fall within the purview of *fī sabīlillāh*. Thus, this term is specific to those works that are unsoiled by selfish considerations, solely motivated by the desire to help improve the human situation. And that in doing so will please God the Exalted, who is the end-all of all human endeavours. This is the sole reason for adding the condition of *fī sabīlillāh*. Meaning thereby that when a person aims at replacing a system of life with Islam he should have no self-centred considerations. In other words, he should not seek to replace Caesar with another Caesar. Nor should his struggle for the mission bear even a shade of seeking wealth, fame, or honour for himself. Instead, his whole effort and sacrifice should be directed toward establishing a just system for humanity, and to please no one but God.

Says the Qur'ān: "Those who believe fight in the cause of God, and those who reject the faith fight in the cause of evil. Fight, then, against the friends of Satan. Feeble indeed is the cunning of Satan." (4: 76)

The word *ṭaghūt* has its root in *ṭughyān,* which means crossing the limits. When a river swells outgrowing its banks, we say it is flooded. Likewise, when a person goes beyond his limits and uses power to become god over humanity or garners for himself monetary and other benefits then he follows the way of *ṭaghūt*. Opposed to this is fighting in the way of God to establish His laws of justice, and which calls for a sense of altruism not found elsewhere.

Thus says the Qur'ān: "*As for that happy life in the hereafter, We grant it only to those who do not seek to exalt themselves on earth, nor yet to spread corruption. The future belongs to the God-fearing.*" (28: 83)

A *ḥadīth* says that a person asked the Prophet "what does fighting in the way of God mean? One person fights for booty, another fights to prove his bravery; and a third fights for enmity toward someone or because he has a bias for his nation. Among them whose fight is in God's way?" The Prophet's reply was as follows: "Nobody's. The fight *fī sabīlillāh* is only of a person who has no other considerations but that the word of God prevails."

Another *ḥadīth* says "if a person fought and had the intention to secure for himself even a camel's halter, he would lose his reward." God accepts only that deed which is performed solely for Him without any personal or group considerations. Thus, the conditionality of *fī sabīlillāh* is crucial from the Islamic viewpoint. For every living being (animal or human) is engaged in the *jihād* of survival with the full vigour of its existence.

Among the radical concepts of the revolutionary party named "Muslim" the most foundational is to engage every rebellious force that comes in Islam's way: fight them, muster everything possible to replace them. But make sure that you do not become rebellious instead. Your mandate is contingent on your cleansing the world of rebellion and wickedness and subjecting it to God's laws of justice and fair play.

After spelling out *jihād's* meaning and its link with *fī sabīlillāh*, I will now deal with Islam's revolutionary message so that you may understand the reason for waging *jihād* as a tool for the spread of Islam.

Islam's revolutionary message

One can summarize the Islamic message as follows: "*Mankind, worship your Lord who has created you and those who lived before you, so that you may become God-fearing.*" (2: 21) Islam does not address itself to the farm holders and the moneyed class of industrialists, or to the peasants and industrial workers, but rather to the whole of mankind. Its audiences are human beings (not classes): for if you are subservient to someone other than God, then you should give this up. If you crave to be a deity over humanity, then push this out of your mind for none has the right to exalt himself over others. You must all enter into God's servitude as equals. Thus, the Islamic call is universal, inviting a total change. It is to God alone that the right to rule belongs, and none else. Expressed differently, nobody has the authority to become the master of others, dictating to them what he thinks is right and wrong. To acknowledge anyone as such is to attribute Godhead to him, which undoubtedly complicates the human situation.

What causes distortion in the true human self and derails humans from the God-given straight path is that they lose sight of Him in their lives and thus forget their true nature. The result it formulates is equally disastrous. On the one hand, some people, class or group rise with claims to divinity and by virtue of their power reduce others into their servitude. On the other hand, because of this tendency to oust God from our lives and the consequent distortion of our true nature, a large number of people surrender themselves to the divinity of the powerful, accepting their right to decide for them. This, as I said, is the source of oppression in the world: Islam makes its first strike at this apparatus of divinity. It says loudly and clearly: "*Pay no heed to the counsel of those who are given to excesses – those who spread corruption on earth instead of setting things to rights.*" (26: 151–152) "*Contain yourself in patience with those who call on their Lord morning and evening, seeking His countenance. Let not your eyes pass beyond them in quest of the beauties of the life of this world. Pay no heed to any whose heart We have left to be negligent of all remembrance of Us because he had always followed his own desires, and whose case has gone beyond all bounds.*" (18: 28) "*Those [are the ones] who debar others from the path of God and would have it crooked, and who deny the life to come.*" (11: 18)

Islam asks people: do you want to continue with a servitude forced upon you by these small and petty multitude of deities or do you want one God who is all-powerful? If you refuse to return to the worship of one God, you will never liberate yourselves from the slavery of these hordes of self-made gods. They will overpower you one way or the other and cause disruption throughout human life. "*She said: 'Whenever kings enter a country, they corrupt it, and turn the noblest of its people into the most abject. This is the way they always behave.*'" (27: 34) "*Yet, no sooner does he turn his back than he strives to spread corruption in the world, destroying crops and progeny. God does not love corruption.*" (2: 205)

Without elaborating upon it further, I will be brief in presenting to you the fact that Islam's advocacy of God's oneness was not toward a religion, which invites people to certain articles of belief constituting a faith.

In fact, it was a social revolution that gave a direct blow to the stratified classes, which had institutionalized themselves into a priesthood, a kingship, moneylenders, feudal lords and cartel owners reducing people to bondage.

In some places they had even become gods unto themselves asking people in the name of their birth or class right to surrender themselves to their worship. In other places, while making use of the masses' ignorance, the ruling regime had carved for them artificial gods and built temples inducing them to accept their claims to divinity, under the patronage of those gods.

Thus, when Islam, opposed to idol worship and polytheism, invited humanity to worship one true God, the people in power and those who supported them and shared the privileges arising from power felt threatened. Hence why whenever a prophet raised the call of "My people, worship God alone, for you have no God other than Him," it triggered opposition towards him. The power elite along with the exploitative classes combined to crush the message, for they knew it was not merely a metaphysical proposition but a call for social change. In its very first reverberation they smelled rebellion of a political nature.

Characteristics of the call for an Islamic change

There is not a shadow of doubt that all the prophets were revolutionary leaders. And the most revolutionary among them was Muḥammad (peace be upon him). However, what separated the prophets from the rest of the revolutionaries is their balanced approach towards life, their untainted sense of justice and equality.

The non-prophet revolutionaries, despite their being well intentioned, had a tilted sense of justice and equality. [The problem being their relative backgrounds.]

Either such revolutionaries came from the oppressed classes or they rose with their support. Small wonder then that they viewed everything from a class perspective. Their vantage was coloured by their class bias and not by humanity considerations or impartiality. They swung between hatred for a particular class and their bias for the class that supported them. Hence why their solution for oppression was reactive, leading them to fall into the same trap and making them a new class of oppressors. For them to formulate a balanced collective system was an impossible proposition. Contrary to this, no matter how much the prophets and their companions were persecuted, their revolutionary movement remained free from resentment and bitterness. This was possible for they worked under the direct supervision of God, the Exalted, who does not suffer from any human weakness nor does He have a particular relation with any class of people or a grudge against anyone. This is why the prophets viewed things with justice. Their sole desire was to make sure that humanity's interests were served by bringing about a system in which people could exercise their due rights while living within legitimate means, and by creating a perfect balance between individual and societal interests. This perhaps explains why the prophet-led movements never turned into class warfare. Their reconstruction programme was not designed to impose one class over another. Rather, they followed the course of justice in a manner that people had equal space for their material and spiritual growth.

The need for jihād and its objective

In this short presentation it is difficult for me to spell out the entire socio-political order of Islam. Keeping within the constraints of my subject, I wish to emphasize the point that Islam is not merely the amalgamation of certain dogmas and rituals but rather a comprehensive code of life that seeks to blot out all oppressive modes of life and introduce its own programme for human welfare.

To meet this end, Islam seeks a wider audience by embracing humanity and not just a particular group. In fact, it even goes to the extent of inviting oppressors, including kings and the super rich, to come and live within the legitimate bounds fixed by their Creator. If they accept the truth, it says, they will have peace and security. Here, there is no enmity toward human beings. If there is hostility, it is towards oppression, social disorder, and immorality. In other words, it is towards those who by taking what is not theirs, transgress their natural limits.

Besides, whoever embraces this message no matter to what class, race, nation, and state he or she belongs, will have equal rights and status in the Islamic society, creating thus that universal revolutionary party which the Qur'ān describes as "*Ḥizb Allāh*" or what is also known as the "Islamic party" or "the Muslim ummah".

The moment this party comes into being, it takes up *jihād* to pursue the objectives of its creation. This should not be surprising for it is logical to the demand of its existence – that it will strive to replace paganism in human life with a balanced code of social reconstruction that the Qur'ān alludes to as *kalimatullāh*, or God's word.

Thus, sluggishness on its part to any change in the current administrative set-up aiming at substituting it with Islamic governance will deny it its justification to continue, for that is the sole purpose of its inception. Explaining the reason for its birth, the Qur'ān says: "*You are the best community that has ever been raised for mankind; you enjoin the doing of what is right and forbid what is wrong, and you believe in God.*" (3: 110)

It is not a party of preachers and missionaries but rather of divine enforcers. Its mission is to blot out, by force if necessary, oppression, moral anarchy, social disorder and exploitation so as to finish the so-called divine role of self-styled gods and replace evil with good. "*Fight them,*" the Qur'ān says, "*until there is no more oppression, and all submission is made to God alone.*" (Verse 39) "*Unless you do likewise, there will be oppression on earth and much corruption.*" (Verse 73) "*He it is who has sent forth His Messenger with guidance and the religion of truth, to the end that He may cause it to prevail over all religions, however hateful this may be to those who associate partners with God.*" (9: 33)

Thus, this Muslim party has no choice but to go for and control the power centres, for the simple reason that an oppressive immoral civilization derives its sustenance from an immoral governmental set-up. Likewise, a righteous state apparatus cannot be implemented unless the reins of government pass from the mischief-makers to the peacemakers.

That being the case, not to talk of reforming the world, this party will not be able to live up to its convictions if the ruling system is tied to some other mode of thought. For example, a person of a socialist bent will not be able to live by the norms of his preferred system if he resides under the capitalist systems of Britain and the United States. Likewise, if a Muslim seeks to live in a non-Islamic ambience, his desire to live a Muslim life will be hard to realize. This is due to the fact that the laws he considers defective, the taxes he considers wrong, the matters he considers illegitimate, the culture he considers ridden with immorality, the education system he considers horrible will be imposed upon him and his family, and he will not find a way out. Thus a person or a group who believes in a value system is forced by the logic of its truth to seek its establishment in place of the opposing value system. If he does not become part of the effort to change the situation, he will prove himself to be false in his faith. "*May God forgive you (Prophet)! Why did you grant them permission to stay behind before you had come to know who were speaking the truth and who were the liars? Those who believe in God and the Last Day will not ask you to exempt them from striving with their wealth and with their persons. God has full knowledge as to who are the God-fearing. Only those who do not truly believe in God and the Last Day ask for exemption. Their hearts are filled with doubt, and so do they waver.*" (9: 43–45)

In the preceding words the Qur'ān gives a clear verdict that an Islamic party must strive to make its value system reign supreme for that is the only touchstone to validate its sincerity. Should it accept the supremacy of the opposite value system, the falsity of its claim starts to unravel itself. That such a group will eventually lose even its alleged faith in Islam is only natural, though this happens in phases. It starts with the tacit acceptance of the reigning value system as a compulsive situation which is hard to change followed by an imperceptible shift of feeling from discomfort to ease with a non-Islamic situation. So much so that you will become part of the auxiliary forces supporting the system. You will give your wealth and your life in the cause of sustaining the reigning value system and opposing the call of Islam. At this point, there will hardly remain any difference between you and the unbelievers other than some hypocritical claims to belief in Islam. In a *ḥadīth*, the Prophet clearly describes the consequence of such a state: "By Him who holds my soul in His hand, you will either call for goodness [to the people] and restrain them from evil and hold the hand of the evildoer and turn him toward the truth by force or God's natural law will move to its inexorable result: the evildoers will affect your hearts as well and like them you will become the accursed ones."

The universal revolution

The discussion so far should clarify the point that Islamic *jihād* seeks to replace the dominance of non-Islamic systems. This revolution is not territorial but international, though as a starter the members of the Muslim party, wherever they live, should focus on that place. Their eventual goal should, however, be a world revolution for the simple reason that any revolutionary ideology, which is humanity specific and seeking universal welfare, cannot reduce itself to a particular state or nation. It is innate in its nature to embrace the whole world, for the truth refuses to be confined to geography. For it, truth is indivisible: if it is truth on one side of a river, it is the same truth on the other side as well. No segment of humanity should be barred of its compassion. Wherever humans are oppressed, it must come to their rescue. Such is the dictate of its message. The Qur'ān says the same: "*And why should you not fight in the cause of God and the utterly helpless men, women and children who are crying, 'Our Lord! Deliver us from this land whose people are oppressors, and send forth to us, out of Your grace, a protector, and send us one that will help us.'*" (4: 75)

Besides, split as the peoples are into national confines, human relations are universal by their nature. In fact, no state can live up to its ideological moorings if neighbouring states do not share its vision of humanity. For the spread of the Muslim party's mission of improving the human situation, it is thus inevitable that the Islamic system should rise above the parochial outlook and embrace the universal. On the one hand, it should seek a global reach for its message inviting everyone to its fold for a better life. On the other hand, depending on its power resource, it should force non-Islamic governments to clean their stables or face the cleansing sweep of Islamic governance.

This was the policy that the Prophet [peace be upon him] and his successors followed. Arabia, the birthplace of the Muslim party, was Islamized first, and this was followed by extending the Islamic call to neighbouring states. It was only when they refused to accept the call and set on a direct course of opposing it that military action was taken against them. The Tabūk Expedition was the beginning of this policy. After the Prophet, his successor Abū Bakr engaged the non-Islamic empires of Rome and Persia. 'Umar concluded the conquest. At first, the Egyptians and Syrians took the new event in history as an extension of Arabian imperialism. Looking for its parallel in the past, they thought that like previous nations which annexed other lands to enslave their populations, it wanted to tread the same path. For this very reason the Egyptians and Syrians came out to fight the Muslims under the banners of Caesar and Kisra. But when they came to know the revolutionary message of the Muslim party they could not believe it: the Muslims were not the bearers of an aggressive nationalism; they were above national interests and had come to deliver them from the inhuman yoke of their tyrant rulers. Those who were exploited thus felt themselves inclined toward the Muslim party and thus began a process of disenchantment in Caesar's and Kisra's camps. Where they were forced to fight the Muslims, they fought without any real zest, paving the way for those spectacular strings of victories in the early period of Muslim history. This is also because once the Islamic system was introduced and people saw it functioning they willingly joined the cadres of this international Muslim party and embraced its cause to facilitate its spread elsewhere.

The Battle of Badr

In the light of this exposition of the nature of Islam, the role of *jihād* and its importance, as well as the way of life Islam seeks to implement and its strategy of jihad and what it involves of progressive stages we can now consider the Battle of Badr and its importance. This was a battle which God describes as the Day of Distinction. We can also look at this *sūrah*, *al-Anfāl*, which comments on this battle.

As stated earlier, the Battle of Badr was not the first action of Islamic *jihād*. Prior to it, a number of expeditions were sent out, but fighting took place during only one of these, involving the small company led by 'Abdullāh ibn Jaḥsh, 17 months after the Prophet's migration to Madinah. All of these were in line with the fundamental principle underlying the concept of Islamic *jihād*, which I have fully discussed in this Prologue. They were all, it is true, directed against the Quraysh which drove the Prophet and his noble companions away from their homes, violating the sanctity of the Inviolable House of worship that was rightly observed under Islam and prior to its advent. But this was not the basis upon which the concept of Islamic *jihād* is founded. The basis is that Islam wants to liberate all mankind from servitude to any creature, so that they may serve only the Creator. It wants to establish Godhead as belonging to God alone, and remove all tyrannical authority that enslaves human beings. The Quraysh was the immediate tyrannical power which prevented people in Arabia from turning to the worship of God alone and acknowledging only His sovereignty. Hence, in line with its overall strategy, Islam had no option but to fight this tyrannical power. This had the added advantage of removing the injustice suffered by the noble companions of the Prophet in Makkah, and ensuring the security of the Muslim homeland in Madinah against any possible aggression. However, when we state these immediate or local causes, we must not lose sight of the nature of Islam and its strategy that allows no power to usurp God's sovereignty, bringing people into servitude to anyone other than God.

We need to give a brief outline of the events of the Battle of Badr[5] before discussing this *sūrah* which comments on it. This will enable us to appreciate the general atmosphere prevailing at the time of its revelation, understand the meaning of its text, its practicality both in dealing with events and in explaining them. Qur'ānic statements cannot be properly understood on the basis of their linguistic import alone. Their proper understanding requires, first and foremost, that we try

5. For a full discussion of the Battle of Badr, its events and consequences, see Adil Salahi, *Muhammad: Man and Prophet,* The Islamic Foundation, Leicester, 2002, pp. 253–295. – Editor's note.

to live in their historical atmosphere, appreciate their practical and positive approach to events and circumstances. Although their significance stretches well beyond the historical reality they deal with, Qur'ānic statements do not reveal the full extent of their significance except in the light of such historical reality. Thus, they will continue to have their permanent significance and inspiration for those who work for the implementation of Islam, facing situations and circumstances that are not unlike those faced by the early Muslims. The Qur'ān will never reveal its secrets to those who passively deal with its statements on the basis of their linguistic import alone.

Muḥammad ibn Isḥāq[6] reports:

> Intelligence was brought to the Prophet (peace be upon him) that a large trade caravan, in which almost every household in the Quraysh had a share, was returning from Syria, led by Abū Sufyān ibn Ḥarb, and travelling with 30 or 40 men from the Quraysh. He suggested to his Companions: "Here is a caravan of the Quraysh, with much of their wealth. If you intercept it, God may reward you with it." People began to get ready, while others did not. No one thought that the Prophet would have to fight a battle.

In *Zād al-Ma'ād* and in *Imtā' al-Asmā'* it is mentioned that the Prophet only ordered those whose mounts were ready to move immediately to march, without giving too much importance to numbers. Ibn al-Qayyim states:

> The total number of Muslims to take part in Badr was 317 men, 86 of them were from the Muhājirīn, 61 from the Aws and 170 from the Khazraj. The number of the Aws people was much less than the Khazraj, despite the fact that the Aws were the stronger fighters and more steadfast, because their quarters were further away from the city, and the call to get ready came as a surprise.

6. Muḥammad ibn Isḥāq was one of the earliest biographers of the Prophet. His report of the Battle of Badr is the basis of its account in *al-Bidāyah wa'l-Nihāyah* by Ibn Kathīr. In his book, *Imtā' al-Asmā'*, al-Maqrīzī provides more or less the same account. Similarly, Imām Ibn al-Qayyim gives a summarized version of it in *Zād al-Ma'ād*, as does Imām 'Alī ibn Ḥazm in *Jawāmi' al-Sīrah*. We have incorporated parts of all these accounts into our summary of the events of this battle.

> The Prophet said that he wanted only those who were ready to move, and had their mounts available. Some people who lived in the outskirts requested him to wait until they got their mounts, but he refused. Indeed, there was no intention to fight a battle, and no preparations were taken for such an eventuality, but God caused them to meet their enemy when they were totally unprepared.[7]

As Abū Sufyān drew near the Hijaz, he tried to obtain intelligence, seeking information from any traveller he met on his way. He was worried for the safety of people's property he carried with him. Some travellers told him that Muḥammad had mobilized his followers to intercept his caravan. Abū Sufyān hired Ḍamḍam ibn ʿAmr al-Ghifārī, sending him to Makkah to alert its people to the need to defend their property and to tell them that Muḥammad and his Companions were about to intercept the caravan. Ḍamḍam moved very fast towards Makkah. Al-Maqrīzī reports:

> The people of Makkah were alarmed to hear Ḍamḍam shouting: "People of the Quraysh! Descendants of Lu'ayy ibn Ghālib! A tragedy! A disaster! Your property with Abū Sufyān is being intercepted by Muḥammad and his Companions. I doubt whether you can save the caravan. Help! Help!" To indicate the gravity of his message Ḍamḍam cut his camel's ears, and tore his own shirt. The Quraysh immediately started to mobilize all their resources, getting ready in three days, and in only two days according to some reports. The strong among them helped those who were weak. Suhayl ibn ʿAmr, Zamʿah ibn al-Aswad, Ṭuʿaymah ibn ʿAdiy, Ḥanẓalah ibn Abī Sufyān and ʿAmr ibn Abī Sufyān were all urging people to join the Quraysh army. Suhayl said to his people: "Are you going to allow Muḥammad and the apostates from Yathrib to confiscate your property and caravan? Whoever needs money or power, he may have these." Umayyah ibn Abī al-Ṣalt praised him in a short poem.
>
> Nawfal ibn Muʿāwiyah al-Dīlī spoke to a number of rich people urging them to make financial contributions so as to provide

7. Ibn al-Qayyim, Ibid, p. 188.

mounts for people to join the army, who did not have their own. ʿAbdullāh ibn Abī Rabīʿah gave him 500 Dinar [a gold currency] to spend in the way he wished in strengthening the army. He also received 200 Dinars from Ḥuwayṭib ibn ʿAbd al-ʿUzzā, and a further 300 Dinars to buy arms and mounts. Ṭuʿaymah ibn ʿAdiy provided 20 camels and undertook to look after the fighters' families. Anyone who did not wish to join the army in person sent someone in his place. They spoke to Abū Lahab, but he refused to join or send anyone in his place, but it is also reported that he sent in his place al-ʿĀṣī ibn Hishām ibn al-Mughīrah, who owed money to him, saying to him that he would write off his debt if he went in his place, which he did.

ʿAddās,[8] a Christian slave, tried hard to dissuade his masters, ʿUtbah and Shaybah, sons of Rabīʿah, as well as al-ʿĀṣ ibn Munabbih from joining. Umayyah ibn Khalaf, on the other hand, decided not to join the army, but ʿUqbah ibn Abī Muʿayṭ and Abū Jahl rebuked him severely. He said to them: "Buy me the best camel in this valley." They bought him a camel for 300 Dirhams [a silver currency], but it was part of the spoils of war taken by the Muslims.

None was less enthusiastic to go than al-Ḥārith ibn ʿĀmir. Ḍamḍam ibn ʿAmr had seen the valley of Makkah with blood running from both of its two ends. ʿĀtikah bint ʿAbd al-Muṭṭalib, the Prophet's aunt, had seen in her dream, warning of death and blood in every home. Hence, people known for sound judgement were disinclined to march for war. They began to exchange views. Among those unwilling to go were al-Ḥārith ibn ʿĀmir, Umayyah ibn Khalaf, ʿUtbah ibn Rabīʿah, Shaybah ibn Rabīʿah, Ḥakīm ibn Ḥizām, Abū al-Bakhtarī ibn Hishām, ʿAlī ibn Umayyah ibn Khalaf, and al-ʿĀṣ ibn Munabbih, but Abū Jahl rebuked them all, aided in this task by ʿUqbah ibn Abī Muʿayṭ and al-Naḍr ibn

---

8. When the Prophet went to Ṭā'if some four years earlier to address its people with the message of Islam, they treated him very badly, and set on him their slaves and children to stone him, and his two feet bled as a result. He sought refuge in an orchard belonging to ʿUtbah and Shaybah, and when they saw him, they sent ʿAddās to him carrying a bunch of grapes. When ʿAddās spoke to the Prophet he recognized his position and kissed his hands and feet.

al-Ḥārith ibn Kildah. Thus the Quraysh settled for marching to meet the Muslims.

The Quraysh army left in a festive mood, with singers and music playing, and feeding themselves well. Their army was 950 men strong, with 100 horses mounted by 100 heavily armoured soldiers, and a large number of body armour for those who were walking. They had 700 camels. They were most aptly described in the Qur'ān: "*Do not be like those who left their homes full of self-conceit, seeking to be seen and praised by others. They debar others from the path of God; but God has knowledge of all that they do.*" (Verse 47)

As they marched, they were nursing great hatred against the Prophet and his Companions because of their intention to intercept their trade caravan. The Muslims had earlier killed 'Amr ibn al-Haḍramī and took the small caravan he was leading.[9] Abū Sufyān was leading the caravan accompanied by 70 men,[10] among whom were Makhramah ibn Nawfal and 'Amr ibn al-'Āṣ. The caravan had no less than 1000 camels, loaded with merchandise. When they were near to Madinah, they were extremely alarmed, particularly because they felt that Ḍamḍam ibn 'Amr and the help from the Quraysh were slow in coming. As Abū Sufyān arrived in Badr at the head of the caravan, he was worried lest he should be detected. Therefore, he changed route and took his caravan closer to the sea, leaving Badr to his left and marching with speed.

Meanwhile, the Quraysh army was marching at leisure, feeding anyone who caught up with them and slaughtering many camels for food. Then Qays ibn Imri' al-Qays came to them with a message from Abū Sufyān advising them to go back "so that you do not leave yourselves liable to be killed by the people of Yathrib [i.e. the old name of Madinah]. You have only marched to protect your trade caravan and your property. Now that it is safe by God's help, you have no further purpose." He tried to persuade the Quraysh to go back, but they refused. Abū Jahl said: "We will not go back, but we shall march on to Badr, where we shall stay

9. That was the incident in which the expedition led by 'Abdullāh ibn Jaḥsh was involved.

10. As mentioned earlier, they were only 30–40 men according to Ibn Isḥāq's report.

> for three days to celebrate. We shall slaughter camels for food, feed whoever cares to come to us, drink wine in abundance and be entertained by singers and dancers. The whole of Arabia shall hear about us and hold us in awe for the rest of time."[11]

Qays went back to Abū Sufyān and told him that the Quraysh army marched on. He said: "Woe to my people! This is all the work of ʿAmr ibn Hishām [i.e. Abū Jahl]. He does not want to go back because he assumed leadership and went too far. Excess spells a bad omen. If Muḥammad gets the upper hand, we will be humiliated."[12]

Muḥammad ibn Isḥāq reports:

> Al-Akhnas ibn Sharīq, who was an ally of the Zuhrah clan, said to his people: "God has saved your property and spared your tribesman, Makhramah ibn Nawfal. You have mobilized to save him and his property. Put the blame on me if you are accused of cowardice, and let us go back. There is no need for you to go on a fighting course for nothing. Do not listen to what this man [meaning Abū Jahl] says." They accepted his advice and went back home. Not a single man from Zuhrah took part in the Battle of Badr. The rest of the Quraysh clans succumbed to the pressure and had some of their men participating, except for the clan of ʿAdiy ibn Kaʿb. Moreover, Ṭālib ibn Abī Ṭālib was with the Quraysh army, but some people said to him: "We know you, the Hāshimites, well. Even though you may come with us, your sympathy is with Muḥammad." Therefore, he went back home without continuing with the marchers.
>
> Meanwhile, the Prophet marched with his Companions in the month of Ramaḍān. They had only 70 camels which they rode in turns. The Prophet, ʿAlī ibn Abī Ṭālib and Marthad al-Ghanawī shared one camel. Ḥamzah ibn ʿAbd al-Muṭṭalib, Zayd ibn Ḥārithah, and the two servants of the Prophet, Abū Kabshah and Anasah had one camel to share, while Abū Bakr, ʿUmar and ʿAbd al-Raḥmān ibn ʿAwf shared another.[13]

---

11. Al-Maqrīzī, Aḥmad ibn ʿAlī, *Imtāʿ al-Asmāʿ*, Dār al-Kutub al-ʿIlmiyyah, Beirut, 1999, Vol. 1, pp. 85–89
12. Ibn Sayyid al-Nās, *ʿUyūn al-Āthār,* Dār al-Turāth, Madinah, Vol. I, p. 389
13. Ibn Hishām, *Al-Sīrah al-Nabawiyyah*, Dār al-Qalam, Beirut, Vol. II, pp. 264–270

In *Imtā' al-Asmā'*, al-Maqrīzī reports:

The Prophet marched on until he approached Badr when he received intelligence of the march of the Quraysh army. He consulted his Companions. Abū Bakr was the first to speak, and his words were reassuring to the Prophet. 'Umar was next, and he spoke in the same vein, before adding: "Messenger of God! It is indeed the Quraysh defending its honour. They have never been humiliated since they achieved their present honourable position, and they have never believed ever since they sunk into disbelief. By God, they would never compromise their position of honour and they will most certainly fight you. Hence, you had better be prepared."

Al-Miqdād ibn 'Amr, the next to speak, said: "Messenger of God! Go ahead and do whatever you feel is best. We will never say to you as the Israelites said to Moses: 'Go with your Lord and fight the enemy while we stay behind!' What we will say is: 'Go with your Lord and fight the enemy and we will fight alongside you.' By Him who has sent you with the message of truth, if you ask us to march with you to Bark al-Ghimād [a remote place in Yemen] we will fight with you anyone who stands in your way until you have got there." The Prophet thanked him and prayed for him.

But the Prophet continued to say to his Companions: "Give me your advice." He particularly wanted to hear from the *Anṣār*, because he felt they might think that they were only bound to defend him against those who attacked him in Madinah when they pledged to protect him as they protected their women and children.[14] Sa'd ibn Mu'ādh stood up and said: "I will answer for the *Anṣār*. You seem to want to know our opinion, Messenger of God?" When the Prophet indicated that it was so, Sa'd said: "It seems to me that you might have set out for a certain objective and then you received revelations concerning something different! We have declared our faith in you and accepted your message as the message of truth. We have made firm pledges to you that we will always do as you tell us. Go ahead, therefore, Messenger of God, and do whatever you wish, and we go with you. By Him who has sent you with the message of truth, if you take us right

14. That pledge was given at the time of the second 'Aqabah commitment, which was the basis of the migration to Madinah by the Prophet and his Companions.– Editor's Note

to the sea, we will ride with you. None of us shall stay behind. Make peace with whomever you will and cut relations with whomever you will, and take from our wealth and property what you may. Whatever you take is better placed than what you leave. By Him who holds my soul in His hand, I have never come this way, and I do not know it. Yet we have no qualms about encountering our enemy tomorrow. We fight hard and with strong determination when war breaks out. We pray to God to enable us to show you what would please you. You march, then with God's blessings."

Another report mentions that Sa'd said to the Prophet: "We have left behind some of our people who love and obey you as much as we do; but they did not turn up because they thought it was only the trade caravan. Shall we erect for you a shed to stay in, and we will have your mount ready? We will then fight our enemy. If we win by God's grace, then that is what we want. If it is the other eventuality, then you will ride your horse to join the rest of our people." The Prophet said some kind words to him and added: "Or God may will something better."

The Prophet then said to his Companions: "March on, with God's blessings. God has promised me one of the two hosts. By God, it is as if I can see the place where some of them will be killed." As they heard these words, the Prophet's Companions realized that they would be involved in a battle, and that the trade caravan would manage to escape. As they heard the Prophet's words, they hoped for victory. The Prophet assigned banners to three people, one he gave to Muṣ'ab ibn 'Umayr, and two black ones were given to 'Alī and a man from the *Anṣār*, [said to be Sa'd ibn Mu'ādh]. He put out the weapons. When the Prophet left Madinah, he had no banner holder.

The Prophet arrived at the bottom of the Badr plain on Friday night, 17 Ramaḍān. He later sent 'Alī, al-Zubayr, Sa'd ibn Abī Waqqāṣ and Basbas ibn 'Amr to gather intelligence around water wells. He pointed out a knoll and said: "You may get some news there." They found there a number of camels for carrying water, belonging to the Quraysh. Most of the men with the camels fled. One of them called 'Ujayr shouted to the Quraysh: "Your man [meaning the Prophet] has taken your water carriers. This sent an air of disturbance among them. Rain was pouring over them. That night, they took with them Abū Yasār, a slave belonging to ʿUbaydah ibn Saʿīd ibn al-ʿĀṣ, Aslam who belonged to Munabbih ibn al-Ḥajjāj and Abū Rāfiʿ who belonged to Umayyah ibn Khalaf. All three were brought to the Prophet when he was praying. They declared that they were responsible for fetching water to the Quraysh, but the Prophet's Companions disliked that and beat them. So, they said that they were travelling with Abū Sufyān and his caravan. So they left them and waited. As the Prophet finished his prayer, he said to his Companions: "If they tell you the truth, you beat them; and if they lie, you leave them alone!" He then asked the captives about the Quraysh, and they told him that they were beyond the hill, and that they slaughtered nine or ten camels every day for food, and named some of those who were in the army. The Prophet said: "The host is between 900 and 1,000 strong. Makkah has sent you its dearest children."

The Prophet consulted his Companions about the place to encamp. Al-Ḥubāb ibn al-Mundhir ibn al-Jamūḥ said: "Take us forward, right to the nearest well to the enemy. I know this place and its wells. One of its wells is plentiful in fine water, where we can encamp, make a basin and throw in our containers. We will thus have water to drink when we fight. We will also close the rest of the wells." The Prophet said to him: "You have given good counsel."[15] He rose and marched on to encamp at the well indicated by al-Ḥubāb.

The Prophet spent that night, Friday 17 Ramaḍān, praying with his face turned towards the stem of a felled tree. There was a rainfall, but it was light where the Muslims were, making the ground firm but not difficult to walk on, but the rain was much heavier where the Quraysh were, although the two hosts were not far apart. Indeed the rain was a blessing for the believers and a real adversity for the unbelievers. That night the Muslims experienced

15. This exchange is reported somewhat differently by Ibn Isḥāq. According to him, al-Ḥubāb asked the Prophet: "Are we encamping here because God has told you to do so and we are not to move forward or backward from here? Or is it your own judgement that this is the right place to gain advantage against the enemy?" The Prophet answered that it was the latter. Therefore, al-Ḥubāb said that it was not the right place, and gave the Prophet his advice as reported in the text. – Editor's Note

deep slumber, so much so that a man might have his head on his chest and not feel it until he fell to one side. A young man, Rifāʿah ibn Rāfiʿ ibn Mālik had a wet dream and managed to bathe before the night was out. The Prophet sent ʿAmmār ibn Yāsir and ʿAbdullāh ibn Masʿūd to go around the place where the Quraysh encamped. When they came back, they told him that the unbelievers were in fear and it was pouring with rain.

A shed was erected for the Prophet near the well, and Saʿd ibn Muʿādh stood at the door with his sword in his hand. The Prophet went around the area where the battle was to take place, and pointed out certain places to his Companions, saying this person will be killed here and that person will be killed there. None of the ones he named was killed beyond the place the Prophet indicated. The Prophet marshalled his Companions and went back to the shed with Abū Bakr.[16]

Rejecting Wise Counsel

Ibn Isḥāq reports:

> The Quraysh marched on in the morning to draw near to the Muslims. When the Prophet saw them coming into the valley, he said: "My Lord, this is the Quraysh demonstrating all its conceit to contend against You and call Your Messenger a liar. My Lord, grant me the victory You have promised me. My Lord, destroy them today." The Prophet saw ʿUtbah ibn Rabīʿah riding a red camel, and said: "If any of these people has some wisdom, it is the man with the red camel. If they obey him, they will follow good counsel."
>
> Khufāf ibn Aymāʾ ibn Raḥḍah al-Ghifārī, or his father, sent to the Quraysh some slaughtered animals he had prepared for them as a gift as they passed close to his quarters. He also sent them a message that he was ready to support them with men and arms. They sent him a message of thanks, and added: "You have done more than your duty. If we are fighting men like us, we are more than a match for them, but if we are fighting God, as Muḥammad says, then no one can stand up to God."

16. Al-Maqrīzī, Ibid, pp. 93–98

When the Quraysh encamped, some of their men, including Ḥakīm ibn Ḥizām, came up to the Prophet's basin and the Prophet ordered his Companions to let them do what they wanted. Every one of them who drank from the basin was killed in Badr, except for Ḥakīm ibn Ḥizām who later became a good Muslim. Subsequently, if he wished to swear very firmly, he would say: "By Him who saved me on Badr day."

When the Quraysh had encamped, they sent 'Umayr ibn Wahb of Jumaḥ to make a good guess at the number of Muslim troops. He went around the troops on his horse before returning to his people to say: "They are three hundred, give or take a few. But hold on a while and I will see if they have any hidden support." He went far into the valley, but found nothing. He came back with this report: "I have found no hidden support, but I can see a catastrophe and much killing. They simply have no protection apart from their swords. I think that we will not kill any one of them without him killing one of us first. Should they be able to kill their number from our side, life would not be worth living. You make your own decision."

When Ḥakīm ibn Ḥizām heard that, he went to 'Utbah ibn Rabī'ah and said to him: "You are the honourable man of the Quraysh and its obeyed master. Shall I tell you something which would bring you high praise for the rest of time?" When 'Utbah showed his interest, Ḥakīm said: "Tell the Quraysh to go back and you will pay the indemnity for the death of Ibn al-Ḥaḍramī, for he was your ally. You also bear the loss of his looted caravan." Recognizing the great advantages of this course of action 'Utbah immediately accepted and asked Ḥakīm to act as his witness. He also said to him: "Go to Ibn al-Ḥanẓaliyyah [meaning Abū Jahl], because I fear that he is the only one to oppose that."

'Utbah then stood up and addressed the Quraysh, saying: "Take it from me and do not fight this man [meaning the Prophet] and his Companions. You will gain nothing by fighting them. Should you win, many a man among us will look around and see the killer of his father or brother. This will lead to much enmity and hostility in our ranks. Go back and leave Muḥammad to the rest of the Arabs. If they kill him, they will have done what you want.

If they do not, you will meet him without having such barrier of enmity."

Ḥakīm reports: "I went up to Abū Jahl and I found him preparing a spear. I said to him: 'Abū al-Ḥakam, 'Utbah has sent me with this message to you.' And I told him what 'Utbah said. He said: 'His cowardice has surfaced now that he has seen Muḥammad and his Companions. We shall not go back until God has judged between our two parties. 'Utbah does not believe what he says. It is simply that having seen that they are few in number and that his son is among them, he fears that his son may be killed.'"

Abū Jahl also sent a message to 'Āmir ibn al-Ḥaḍramī, saying: "Your ally is trying to take the people back now that you have the chance to get your revenge. Stand up and appeal to the Quraysh by your brother's blood to get your revenge." 'Āmir did that and shouted, 'Woe to 'Amr'. Thus, the air was one of war, and people were more determined to fight. Abū Jahl frustrated the good counsel 'Utbah had given. When 'Utbah was told what Abū Jahl had said, he answered: "This woman-like person will soon know whose cowardice has surfaced: mine or his."

As the army moved, one of its number, al-Aswad ibn 'Abd al-Asad of the Makhzūm clan, a vulgar ill-bred man, sprang out from the ranks, saying: "I pledge to God to drink from their reservoir, or I will pull it down, or I will die in my attempt." Ḥamzah ibn 'Abd al-Muṭṭalib, the Prophet's uncle struck him with his sword, chopping off his leg. Al-Aswad, however, continued to crawl towards the reservoir and Ḥamzah followed him until he killed him at the reservoir.

'Utbah ibn Rabī'ah, his brother Shaybah and his son al-Walīd came out of the Quraysh army and offered a six-man duel. Three young men from the *Anṣār*, 'Awf ibn al-Ḥārith and his brother Mu'awwadh and a third man said to be 'Abdullāh ibn Rawāḥah, answered the challenge. The challengers asked them who they were, and when they told them that they were from the *Anṣār*, they said that they had no business with them. It is said that 'Utbah said to them: "You are honourable equals, but we only want some of our own people." One of them shouted: "Muḥammad, let our equals come out for a duel." The Prophet sent out three of his own relatives: Ḥamzah, his uncle, and his two cousins ʿAlī and ʿUbaydah ibn al-Ḥārith. ʿUbaydah, the eldest of the three fought ʿUtbah, Ḥamzah fought Shaybah and ʿAlī fought al-Walīd. In no time, Ḥamzah and ʿAlī succeeded in killing their two opponents, while ʿUtbah and ʿUbaydah struck each other at the same time. Both fell to the ground wounded. Ḥamzah and ʿAlī then made sure that ʿUtbah was killed, and carried ʿUbaydah with them to the Prophet.

The two armies began to draw near to each other. The Prophet ordered his companions not to move forward until he had given them the order. "When they approach, try to repel them with your arrows." He then marshalled them and went to his shed with Abū Bakr. His prayers included: "My Lord, I appeal to you for the fulfilment of Your promise to me. Should this company of believers be overrun, You will not be worshipped again on earth." Abū Bakr said to him: "Messenger of God! Not so hard with your appeal to Your Lord. He will surely grant you what He has promised you."[17]

Al-Maqrīzī mentions in *Imtāʿ al-Asmāʿ*:

ʿAbdullāh ibn Rawāḥah said to the Prophet: "Messenger of God! I counsel you – knowing that God's Messenger is far greater and more knowledgeable than to need counsel – that God is too great in His majesty to be appealed to for the fulfilment of His promise." The Prophet said to him: "Should I not appeal to God to fulfil His promise? God never fails to fulfil a promise."[18]

Ibn Isḥāq continues:

The Prophet was momentarily overtaken by sleep. When he woke up he was markedly cheerful. He said to his companion: "Rejoice, Abū Bakr. Victory is certainly coming from God. This is the Angel Gabriel holding the rein of his horse with dust all over it."

Mahjaʿ, a slave belonging to ʿUmar ibn al-Khaṭṭāb, was killed when he was hit by an arrow, and thus he was the first casualty

17. Ibn Hishām, Ibid, pp. 191–195
18. Al-Maqrīzī, Ibid, p.103

among the Muslims. Ḥārithah ibn Surāqah, from the Najjār clan was also hit in his neck by an arrow as he was drinking from the reservoir, and he died.

The Prophet went on encouraging his Companions, saying: "By Him who holds Muḥammad's soul in His hand, anyone who is killed fighting these people, dedicating his life for the cause of God, moving forward not backward, shall be admitted by God into heaven." On hearing this, ʿUmayr ibn al-Ḥamām from the Salamah clan, said as he held a few dates in his hand and was eating them: "Well, Well! All that separates me from heaven is that these people should kill me!"

ʿAwf ibn al-Ḥārith asked the Prophet: "What would make God smile at a servant of His?" The Prophet said: "His determined fight without protection." He took off his body armour and threw it away, picking up his sword and fighting until he was killed.

As the two armies drew closer, Abū Jahl said: "Lord! Let the side which severs relations of kinship, and invents falsehood, be destroyed today." His was a prayer to ensure his own ruin.

The Prophet took a handful of dust and said: "Let these faces be hung down." He then blew the dust at the Quraysh. He then ordered his Companions to fight hard, and they did to ensure the defeat of the Quraysh. God caused the killing and capture of so many of the Quraysh's nobility.

When the Muslims started to take enemy prisoners, the Prophet, who was in his shed with Saʿd ibn Muʿādh and a group of the *Anṣār* standing at the door, swords in hands, guarding him, the Prophet noticed that Saʿd looked displeased. He said to him: "You do not seem to be pleased with what our people are doing?" He said: "Indeed. This is the first defeat God has inflicted on the idolaters. I would have preferred killing their men rather than sparing them."

At one point the Prophet said to his Companions: "I have come to know that a few men from the Hāshim clan and others have been made to join the army against their will. They have no quarrel with us. Any one of you who meets any Hāshimite should not kill him. If you come across Abū al-Bakhtarī ibn Hishām, do not kill him. If you meet al-ʿAbbās ibn ʿAbd al-Muṭṭalib, do not kill him. He came out against his will." Abū Hudhayfah ibn ʿUtbah ibn Rabīʿah said on hearing this: "Are we to kill our fathers, sons, brothers and tribesmen and let al-ʿAbbās alone? By God, if I see him, I will certainly hit him with my sword." The Prophet said to ʿUmar ibn al-Khaṭṭāb: "Abū Ḥafṣ![19] Is God's Messenger's uncle to be hit with the sword in his face?" ʿUmar said: "Messenger of God! Allow me to kill him, for he is a hypocrite."[20] Abū Hudhayfah used to say afterwards: "I am always worried about what I said that day, and fear that it may condemn me, unless it is atoned if I gain martyrdom." He was to die a martyr in the Battle of al-Yamāmah.

The Prophet singled out Abū al-Bakhtarī ibn Hishām, ordering that he should not be killed, because he was the most moderate among the Quraysh in his attitude towards the Prophet. Never did he try to harm the Prophet, or say something against him. Besides, he was one of the five men who successfully mounted the campaign to end the three-year boycott of the Prophet's clan by the rest of the Quraysh.[21]

ʿAbd al-Raḥmān ibn ʿAwf reports: "Umayyah ibn Khalaf was a friend of mine when we were in Makkah. My name at the time was ʿAbd ʿAmr, but when I became a Muslim, I changed my name to ʿAbd al-Raḥmān. He said to me once when we were still in Makkah: 'ʿAbd ʿAmr! Do you reject a name given to you by your father?' I confirmed that. He said: 'I do not know who is al-Raḥmān. Let us agree on a name I call you by, so that you do not reply to me if I call you by your original name and I do not call you by what I do not know.' Afterwards, if he called me ʿAbd

19. ʿUmar comments as he reports on this incident that it was the first time the Prophet called him Abū Ḥafṣ, following the Arabian tradition of calling a man as the father of his child, with Abū meaning father and Hafs a short version of his daughter's name.

20. The Prophet refused ʿUmar's request, as he refused to allow any killing of people that professed to be Muslims, even though they were known to be hypocrites. Abū Hudhayfah might have said this after seeing his father, brother and uncle being killed at the start of the battle, but he was a good Companion of the Prophet. May God be pleased with him.

21. Abū al-Bakhtārī was nevertheless killed in this battle, because he refused to be taken prisoner.

ʿAmr, I would not reply. Then I said to him: 'Abū ʿAlī, you choose whatever you are comfortable with.' He said: 'I will call you ʿAbd al-Ilāh [another name of God].' I agreed. After that, when I passed by him, he would call me ʿAbd al-Ilāh, and I would respond and have some conversation with him.

On the Day of Badr, I passed by him as he was standing with his son ʿAlī, holding his hand. I was carrying some body armour which I had looted. When he saw me, he called me ʿAbd ʿAmr, and I did not respond. He called me again ʿAbd al-Ilāh and I responded. He said: 'Would you rather have me, for I am a better gain for you than this body armour.' I agreed and told him to come with me, and threw the body armour away. I took him and his son prisoners and walked away. He said: 'I have never seen a day like this! Do you not need milk?'[22] I proceeded leading them away.

Umayyah asked me as I walked between him and his son, holding both their hands: 'ʿAbd al-Ilāh, who is the man in your host who has an ostrich feather on his chest?' I told him that he was Ḥamzah ibn ʿAbd al-Muṭṭalib. He said: 'He is the one who has done us a great deal of harm.' Then, as I was leading them away, Bilāl saw him with me. It was Umayyah who used to torture Bilāl in Makkah to force him to abandon Islam. He would take him out to the sandy area when it was extremely hot, and cause him to lie back on the sand, and place a large rock on his chest, telling him that he would remain so until he abandoned Muḥammad's faith. Bilāl's reply was always: 'He is One! He is One!' Now, when Bilāl saw him, he shouted: 'Umayyah, head of idolatry, may I perish if he survives!' I said to him: 'Bilāl! Would you kill my two prisoners?' He said: 'May I perish if he survives.' I said: 'Do you hear me, you son of a black woman!' He repeated his words. Bilāl appealed to the *Anṣār*: 'Supporters of God's cause! Here is Umayyah, head of idolatry. May I perish if he survives.' A group of the *Anṣār* surrounded us forming a circle and I was trying to defend him, but one of the men struck Umayyah's son's leg and

22. What he meant was that if he was taken prisoner, he would then buy his freedom by several camels that would produce much milk.

he fell down. Umayyah uttered a loud cry, the like of which I never heard before. I said to him: 'Try to escape, but there seems to be no escape for you. By God, I cannot defend you.' They soon killed both of them." 'Abd al-Raḥmān used to say afterwards: 'May God forgive Bilāl! I lost my loot and he killed my two prisoners.'[23]

Ibn Ishaq later adds:

When the battle was over, the Prophet instructed some people to look for Abū Jahl among the dead. The first man to meet Abū Jahl in the battle was Muā'dh ibn 'Amr ibn al-Jamūḥ of the Salamah clan. He reports: "I noticed a group of men standing around him like a siege, saying to one another: 'Abū al-Ḥakam[24] shall not be reached.' When I heard them saying that, I resolved to get to him. I made a determined attack towards him and when he was within my reach I struck him with my sword once, which was enough to send half his leg high into the air, as a date stone flies from underneath the date-stone crusher. His son, 'Ikrimah, struck back at me and cut off my arm, which remained attached to my body by a thin piece of my skin. I was prevented by the raging battle from coming back on him. I, however, kept on fighting for the rest of the day, pulling my arm behind me. When it became too troublesome I bent down and put my hand under my foot and stood up to cut off my arm."

As Abū Jahl was wounded, Mu'awwadh ibn al-Ḥārith passed by him and hit him hard until he could not get up. He then left him, not quite dead. Mu'awwadh went on fighting until he was killed.

When the Prophet ordered a search for Abū Jahl among the dead, 'Abdullāh ibn Mas'ūd found him. The Prophet had told his Companions: 'If you cannot identify him among the dead, look for a cut on his knee. When we were young, he and I pushed each other when we were attending a banquet held by 'Abdullāh ibn

---

23. Ibn Hishām, Ibid, pp. 196–199

24. Abū al-Ḥakam was Abū Jahl's name among the Quraysh, and it has the opposite meaning of the nickname given to him by the Muslims, i.e. Abū Jahl, which means 'the father of ignorance.' – Editor's note.

Jud'ān. I was a little thinner than him. When I pushed him, he fell on his knees, badly injuring one of them.' 'Abdullāh ibn Mas'ūd reports: "I found him at his last breath. When I recognized him, I put my foot over his neck. Once in Makkah he had attacked and hurt me. Now I said to him: 'You enemy of God, haven't you been humiliated?' He said: 'How? Am I not a man of merit you have killed? Tell me, who is victorious today?' I said: 'God and His Messenger.'" Some people from Abū Jahl's clan of Makhzūm later claimed that Ibn Mas'ūd mentioned that Abū Jahl said to him as he put his foot over his neck: 'You have climbed high, you little shepherd.'[25] 'Abdullāh ibn Mas'ūd continues his report: "I chopped off his head and took it to the Prophet and said: 'Messenger of God! This is the head of Abū Jahl, God's enemy.' He said: 'God is One. There is no deity other than Him.' I put his head before the Prophet and he praised God."[26]

Ibn Hishām says:

It is reported that 'Umar ibn al-Khaṭṭāb said to Sa'īd ibn al-'Āṣ when he passed by him: 'I see that you harbour some feelings and that you may think that I killed your father. Had I killed him, I would not apologize to you; but I killed my uncle al-'Āṣ ibn Hishām ibn al-Mughīrah. As for your father, I passed by him as he was searching like a bull with his horns and I sidestepped him. His cousin 'Alī went to him and killed him.'[27]

Ibn Isḥāq reports on the authority of 'Ā'ishah, the Prophet's wife:

When the Prophet ordered that the killed be buried, they were all buried in one grave except for Umayyah ibn Khalaf, whose body swelled inside his armour. When they tried to remove it, his flesh was cut. So, they left it on him and buried him. When they were all buried, the Prophet stood at the grave and said to them: 'People in the grave! Have you found out that what your Lord has promised you to be true? I have found that His promise to me

25. This is a reference to 'Abdullāh ibn Mas'ūd's background who was a small man working as a shepherd in Makkah.

26. Ibn Hishām, Ibid, pp. 201–202

27. Ibn Hishām, Ibid, p. 202

has come true.' Some of his Companions asked him: 'Messenger of God! Do you speak to dead people?' He said: 'They have known that what God has promised is true.' Some people mention that he said, 'They hear what I say to them.' But the Prophet only said, 'They have known.'" ...

When the Prophet ordered that they should be buried, the body of 'Utbah ibn Rabī'ah was drawn towards the grave. The Prophet looked at his son Abū Hudhayfah and saw that he was sad. He asked him: "Abū Hudhayfah! You may be experiencing some misgivings concerning what happened to your father." He said: "No, Messenger of God. I have no doubt about my father and his death. But I knew him to be a sagacious and honourable man and I hoped that this would guide him to accept Islam. When I saw what happened to him and remembered that he died an unbeliever, I felt sad." The Prophet prayed for Abū Hudhayfah and said some kind words...

The Prophet then ordered that all the booty picked up by the Muslims be collected together. As it was collected, people differed concerning it. Those who picked up the booty claimed it, while those who were fighting and chasing the enemy said to them: "Had it not been for us, you would not have picked it up. We kept the people preoccupied while you took it away." A third group providing a guard to the Prophet said: "You do not have a claim stronger than ours. We had the booty close to us, and we could have picked it up, but we feared that the enemy would attack the Prophet and kept guarding him."

Asked about *Sūrah* al-Anfāl, or The Spoils of War, 'Ubādah ibn al-Ṣāmit answered: "It was revealed concerning us, the people of Badr, when we disputed about the booty and were impolite about it. God removed it from us and gave it up to His Messenger who divided it equally among the Muslims." ...

When the Prophet arrived in Madinah, he assigned the prisoners to various groups of his Companions and said to them: "Look after the prisoners well." Among the prisoners was Abū 'Azīz ibn 'Umayr ibn Hāshim. He reports that his brother, Muṣ'ab passed by him as he was being taken captive by a man from the *Anṣār*. Muṣ'ab said to the *Anṣārī* man: "Hold tight to him. His mother is rich and she might give a good ransom for him." Abū 'Azīz says: "I was assigned to a group of the *Anṣār*. When they laid out their lunch or dinner, they would give me the bread while they themselves ate dates without bread.[28] This was because of the Prophet's instructions to them. Every time any one of them had a piece of bread he would give it to me. Sometimes I felt embarrassed by their hospitality and I gave the bread to any one of them who was around. He would return it without taking a single bite."

Ibn Hishām explains: Abū 'Azīz was the holder of the banner of the unbelievers in Badr, next to al-Naḍr ibn al-Ḥārith. When his brother Muṣ'ab ibn 'Umayr said this to Abū al-Yusr, the man who held him captive took hold of him tightly, whilst Abū 'Azīz remonstrated with him: "Is this what you recommend about me?" Muṣ'ab said: "He is my brother, ahead of you." His mother asked what the highest ransom paid for a man from the Quraysh was, and she was told that it was 4000 dirhams. She sent that amount as his ransom. Then the Quraysh sent ransom for other prisoners.[29]

Qur'ānic Comments

It was in comment on the Battle of Badr, of which we have given a brief outline, that this *sūrah* was revealed. It portrays the obvious events of this battle, and also shows the ultimate power behind the events and how God determined the sequence of events. Beyond that, it shows the line followed throughout human history. It describes all this in the unique language of the Qur'ān and its inimitable style. We will speak about all these in detail as we discuss the text. Here we will only highlight the main lines of the *sūrah*.

A particular event reported by Ibn Isḥāq on the authority of 'Ubādah ibn al-Ṣāmit, the Prophet's Companion who says in reference to this *sūrah*: "It was revealed concerning us, the people of Badr, when we disputed about the booty and were impolite about it. God removed it from us and gave it up to His Messenger who divided it equally among the Muslims."

---

28. Dates were the most common food in Madinah, while bread was not always available. Bread is also filling; thus someone who ate bread would not feel the pangs of hunger like someone who ate only dates. – Editor's note.

29. Ibn Hisham, Ibid, pp.204–209

This event sheds ample light on the opening of the *sūrah* and the line it takes. The Prophet's Companions disputed over the little booty they gained in a battle that God considered a landmark in human history for the rest of time. But God wanted to teach them, and all humanity in succeeding generations, some highly important facts.

The first thing He wanted them to understand was that this battle was far more important than the spoils of war over which they were in dispute. Therefore, He called the day that witnessed it "*the day when the true was distinguished from the false, the day when the two hosts met in battle.*" (Verse 41)

He also wanted them to know that this greatly important event was accomplished by God's will and planning, in every step and every move. He had a purpose which He wished to accomplish. This means that they had nothing to do with the planning and accomplishment of this great victory or with its outcome and consequences. Both its small booty and great consequences were the result of God's will and design. He only put the believers, by His grace, through a fair test of His own making.

He wanted to show them the great gulf between what they wished for themselves, which was to take the caravan, and what He wanted for them, and for all humanity, through the escape of the caravan and the encounter with the Quraysh army.

The *sūrah* starts with recording their questions about the spoils of war, and explains God's ruling concerning them. It gives the spoils of war to God and His Messenger, calling on the believers to remain God-fearing and set to right their internal relations, after they were impolite concerning the booty, as 'Ubādah ibn al-Ṣāmit, the Prophet's Companion describes. They are further called upon to obey God and His Messenger, reminding them of their faith which requires them to be so obedient. Furthermore, right at the outset, the *sūrah* paints a highly inspiring and awesome picture of the believers: "*They ask you about the spoils of war. Say: The spoils of war belong to God and the Messenger. So, have fear of God and set to right your internal relations. Obey God and His Messenger, if you are true believers. True believers are only those whose hearts are filled with awe whenever God is mentioned, and whose faith is strengthened whenever His revelations are recited to them. In their Lord do they place their trust. They attend regularly to their prayers and spend on others some of what We have provided them with. It is those who are truly believers. They shall be given high ranks with their Lord, and forgiveness of sins and generous provisions.*" (Verses 1–4)

This is followed by a reminder of what they wished and hoped for themselves and what God wanted for them. It describes what they see of what is happening on earth and God's unlimited power beyond them and the events they see. (Verses 5–8) This is followed by a further reminder of the support God had given them, the victory He facilitated for them, and the reward He has, by His grace, set for them. (Verses 9–14)

Thus the *sūrah* proceeds, recording that the whole battle was fought by God's will and under His direction, with His help and support. It is all by His will, and for His sake and to serve His cause. Thus, the fighters have no claim to the spoils of war, as they belong to God and His Messenger. Thus, when God gives them back the spoils of war, this becomes an act of His grace. They must be purged of any desire to gain such booty, so that their *jihād* and struggle is undertaken purely for God's sake. (Verses 17–18, 26, 41–44)

Why Believers Fight

Since every battle believers fight is of God's own planning, under His command and for His cause, the *sūrah* mentions time and again the need to remain steadfast, prepare well for it remembering that God's support is certain to come, guard against the lure that keeps believers away from it, including property and offspring. They have to observe all values related to it, and guard against any element of showing off. The Prophet is ordered to encourage the believers to fight it. (Verses 15–16, 24, 27–28, 45–47, 60, 65)

While orders are given to remain steadfast and stand firm in battle, the *sūrah* provides clarifications of different aspects of the Islamic faith, strengthening its roots, making it the source of every commandment and every judgement. Thus, orders are not left as individual and unrelated items; they are seen to be stemming from the same clear, consistent and profound source.

1. On the question of the spoils of war, the believers are reminded of the need to remain God-fearing, to feel their hearts filled with awe when He is mentioned, and of the close and permanent manifestation of faith by obedience to God and

His Messenger: "*They ask you about the spoils of war. Say: The spoils of war belong to God and the Messenger. So, have fear of God and set to right your internal relations. Obey God and His Messenger, if you are true believers. True believers are only those whose hearts are filled with awe whenever God is mentioned, and whose faith is strengthened whenever His revelations are recited to them. In their Lord do they place their trust. They attend regularly to their prayers and spend on others some of what We have provided them with. It is those who are truly believers. They shall be given high ranks with their Lord, and forgiveness of sins and generous provisions.*" (Verses 1–4)

2. On the battle strategy, they are reminded of God's will, power and planning. It is He who intervened to direct every stage: "*[Remember the day] when you were at the near end of the valley and they were at the farthest end, with the caravan down below you. If you had made prior arrangements to meet there, you would have differed on the exact timing and location. But it was all brought about so that God might accomplish something He willed to be done.*" (Verse 42)

3. On the events and results of the battle, they are reminded of God's leadership, help and support: "*It was not you who slew them, but it was God who slew them. When you threw [a handful of dust], it was not your act, but God's, so that He might put the believers through a fair test of His own making.*" (Verse 17)

4. When the order is given to the believers to remain steadfast, they are reminded of the fact that God wants them to have a true and worthy life, and that He is able to stand between a man and his heart. It is He who guarantees victory to those who place their trust in Him alone: "*Believers, respond to the call of God and the Messenger when he calls you to that which will give you life, and know that God comes in between a man and his heart, and that to Him you shall all be gathered.*" (Verse 24) "*Believers, when you meet an enemy force, be firm, and remember God often, so that you may be successful.*" (Verse 45)

5. Defining the ultimate objective of the battle, God commands: "*Fight them until there is no more oppression, and all submission is made to God alone.*" (Verse 39) "*It does not behove a Prophet to have captives unless he has battled strenuously in the land.*" (Verse 67) "*God promised you that one of the two hosts would fall to you. It was your wish that the one which was not powerful to be yours, but it was God's will to establish the truth in accordance with His words and to wipe out the unbelievers. Thus He would certainly establish the truth firmly and show falsehood to be false, however hateful this might be to the evildoers.*" (Verses 7–8)
6. On the organization of the Muslim community's international relations, faith is seen as the basis of the community and its distinctive character. It is faith values that determine position and loyalty. (Verses 72–75)

In this *sūrah*, the line that is seen to be clearly prominent, side by side with the line of faith, is that of *jihād*. It is given its high value both in concept and in strategy. It is also purged of all personal elements. Its essential justification is clarified so that it is well understood by all those who fight for God's cause at any time. They reiterate this justification with confidence, reassurance and pride. Overall, the *sūrah* gives this impression, but we may refer to some verses that are particularly relevant and will elaborate upon it when we discuss them. These are verses 15–16, 55–57, 60, 65, 67, 74.

The *sūrah* also sets the Muslim community's international relations on the basis of faith, as we have already stated. It outlines the rules that form the basis of such relations with other communities in times of war and peace, up to the time when this *sūrah* was revealed. It details rulings on the distribution of the spoils of war; and also on international treaties, providing fundamental principles that govern all these areas. (Verses 1, 15–16, 20–21, 24, 27, 38–39, 41, 45–47, 55–62, 64–71, 72–75)

To Sum up

Such are the main lines of the *sūrah*. When we remember that it was revealed to comment on the Battle of Badr, we can appreciate some aspects of the method the Qur'ān follows in the education of the

Muslim community, preparing it for the leadership of humanity. We can also recognize how Islam looks at what happens on earth and in human life, in order to give Muslims the right perception.

Badr was the first major battle when the Muslims inflicted a very heavy defeat on their idolater enemies. But the Muslims did not leave their homes for this purpose or with this intention. They only marched to intercept a trade caravan belonging to the Quraysh, the tribe that confiscated all their homes and property. They wanted to regain some of their losses, but God wanted something else. He wanted the caravan to escape and the Muslims to meet in battle their most hardened enemies who were able to place Islam under siege in Makkah. They further plotted to kill God's Messenger [peace be upon him] after they had mounted an uncompromising campaign of persecution against his companions.

God willed that this battle would be the criterion that separates the truth from falsehood, and that it be a landmark in the line of Islamic history and, consequently in human history. He willed that this battle should show the great gulf between what people may plan for themselves, believing it to serve their best interests, and what God chooses for them, even though they may think little of it at first sight. He wanted the emerging Muslim community to properly learn the factors that bring victory and those that bring defeat, receiving these directly in the battlefield, from none other than God, their Lord and protector.

The *sūrah* includes highly inspiring directives pointing to these highly important issues, as well as much of the rules that govern states of peace and war, captives and booty, treaties and pacts, and what ensures victory or defeat. All these are given in the most enlightening and instructive style of the Qur'ān which begins by expounding the faith and its main concepts, making it the prime mover in all human activity. This is characteristic of the Qur'ānic method of looking at events and evaluating them.

The *sūrah* also portrays scenes of the battles and images of thoughts and feelings before, during and after the battle. These scenes and images are so vivid and lifelike that they enable the reader and the listener to interact with them.

At times, the *sūrah* gives glimpses of the life the Prophet and his companions lived in Makkah, when they were few in number, weak, fearing that others may do away with them. Now when they remember what their life was like then, they will realize the extent of God's grace in giving them this great victory. They know that they can only achieve victory with God's help, and by following the faith they preferred to their own life and property. The *sūrah* also portrays some images of the life of the unbelievers before and after the Prophet's migration to Madinah, as well as images of the doom suffered by earlier unbelievers such as Pharaoh and his people. These are given in order to establish the law that never fails, which gives victory to believers and defeat to God's enemies.

The second half of the *sūrah* mirrors the first, beginning with a definitive ruling on the sharing out of the spoils of war, coupled with a call to believe in God and His revelations. It expounds on God's planning in this battle that gave the Muslims such spoils of war, portraying images of what actually took place in the battle. We clearly see that the believers were only a means through which God accomplished His purpose. Believers are then urged to always remain steadfast when they meet their enemy in battle, remembering to glorify God, obey Him and His Messenger, and steer away from internal conflict, lest they weaken and be defeated. They must also guard against showing off and against being deceived by Satan's wicked schemes. They must always place their full trust in God who alone can bring them victory. It tells them of the rule God has established in punishing unbelievers for their sins.

In the first half, the *sūrah* mentioned how the angels were ordered to support the believers and strike the unbelievers' necks and hands. Here in the second half, we see them striking the unbelievers on their faces and backs. The description of the unbelievers as the worst of all animals which occurs in the first half is repeated in the second in the context of their violation of every treaty or promise they make. This leads to the rules defined by God for the conduct of international relations by the Muslim community, both with those who take a hostile attitude and those who wish to live in peace with it. Some of these rules are provisional and some final.

Up to this point, the nature and sequence of issues discussed in the second half of the *sūrah* mirror the first half, with some more details on rules governing relations with other communities. As the *sūrah* draws to its close, it adds certain issues and rules to complete the picture.

God reminds His Messenger and the believers of His favour of bringing about unity of their hearts, which could not have been accomplished except through God's will and grace. The Prophet and the believers are also reassured that God will protect them. God then commands His messenger to encourage his followers to fight, making it clear that, with their faith and if they remain steadfast, they are a good match to a force of unbelievers ten times their number, because the unbelievers are devoid of understanding, since they do not believe. When they are at their weakest, the believers are equal to twice their number, provided they remain steadfast. God is sure to support those who are steadfast in the defence of His cause.

God then takes issue with the believers because of their taking ransom from their prisoners of war, in return for their release, when the Muslims had not yet fought hard to irretrievably weaken their enemy and establish their own authority. Thus the policy of the Islamic movement in different stages and conditions is established and shown to be flexible, looking at every stage and what responses are suitable for it. The *sūrah* tells the believers how to treat prisoners of war, and how to present the Islamic faith to them in a fair manner to encourage them to embrace it. God makes it clear to the prisoners of war that to resort to treachery again is futile. It was God who gave the believers mastery over them when they played false to Him by refusing to believe in Him and His Messenger. Should they try to play false to the Prophet, God will most certainly hand them over to him.

The final passage in the *sūrah* organizes internal relations within the Muslim community, and its relations with groups that embrace Islam but remain away from the land of Islam. It also regulates relations between the Muslim community and unbelievers in certain cases, and in general. These rules clearly show the nature of the Muslim community and the Islamic approach to its relations with others. It is absolutely manifest that Islam will always exist in a positive, forward-looking and proactive community. All the rules governing its internal and external relations are based on this fact. It is simply not possible to separate the faith and the law from the positive, proactive approach and the sound structure of the Muslim community.

I

Different Types of Victory

Al-Anfāl (The Spoils of War)

سُورَةُ الأَنفَالِ

In the Name of God, the Merciful, the Beneficent

بِسْمِ ٱللَّهِ ٱلرَّحْمَٰنِ ٱلرَّحِيمِ

They ask you about the spoils of war. Say: The spoils of war belong to God and the Messenger. So, have fear of God and set right your internal relations. Obey God and His Messenger, if you are true believers. (1)

يَسْـَٔلُونَكَ عَنِ ٱلْأَنفَالِ ۖ قُلِ ٱلْأَنفَالُ لِلَّهِ
وَٱلرَّسُولِ ۖ فَٱتَّقُوا۟ ٱللَّهَ وَأَصْلِحُوا۟ ذَاتَ
بَيْنِكُمْ ۖ وَأَطِيعُوا۟ ٱللَّهَ وَرَسُولَهُۥٓ إِن
كُنتُم مُّؤْمِنِينَ ﴿١﴾

True believers are only those whose hearts are filled with awe whenever God is mentioned, and whose faith is strengthened whenever His revelations are recited to them. In their Lord do they place their trust. (2)

إِنَّمَا ٱلْمُؤْمِنُونَ ٱلَّذِينَ إِذَا ذُكِرَ ٱللَّهُ
وَجِلَتْ قُلُوبُهُمْ وَإِذَا تُلِيَتْ عَلَيْهِمْ
ءَايَٰتُهُۥ زَادَتْهُمْ إِيمَٰنًا وَعَلَىٰ رَبِّهِمْ
يَتَوَكَّلُونَ ﴿٢﴾

They attend regularly to their prayers and spend on others some of what We have provided them with. (3)

ٱلَّذِينَ يُقِيمُونَ ٱلصَّلَوٰةَ وَمِمَّا
رَزَقْنَٰهُمْ يُنفِقُونَ ﴿٣﴾

It is those who are truly believers. They shall be given high ranks with their Lord, and forgiveness of sins and generous provisions. (4)

أُوْلَـٰٓئِكَ هُمُ ٱلْمُؤْمِنُونَ حَقًّا لَّهُمْ دَرَجَـٰتٌ عِندَ رَبِّهِمْ وَمَغْفِرَةٌ وَرِزْقٌ كَرِيمٌ ٤

Just as your Lord brought you forth from your home for the truth, even though some of the believers were averse to it. (5)

كَمَآ أَخْرَجَكَ رَبُّكَ مِنۢ بَيْتِكَ بِٱلْحَقِّ وَإِنَّ فَرِيقًا مِّنَ ٱلْمُؤْمِنِينَ لَكَـٰرِهُونَ ٥

They would argue with you about the truth even after it had become manifest, just as if they were being driven to certain death and saw it with their very eyes. (6)

يُجَـٰدِلُونَكَ فِى ٱلْحَقِّ بَعْدَمَا تَبَيَّنَ كَأَنَّمَا يُسَاقُونَ إِلَى ٱلْمَوْتِ وَهُمْ يَنظُرُونَ ٦

God promised you that one of the two hosts would fall to you. It was your wish that the one which was not powerful to be yours, but it was God's will to establish the truth in accordance with His words and to wipe out the unbelievers. (7)

وَإِذْ يَعِدُكُمُ ٱللَّهُ إِحْدَى ٱلطَّآئِفَتَيْنِ أَنَّهَا لَكُمْ وَتَوَدُّونَ أَنَّ غَيْرَ ذَاتِ ٱلشَّوْكَةِ تَكُونُ لَكُمْ وَيُرِيدُ ٱللَّهُ أَن يُحِقَّ ٱلْحَقَّ بِكَلِمَـٰتِهِۦ وَيَقْطَعَ دَابِرَ ٱلْكَـٰفِرِينَ ٧

Thus He would certainly establish the truth firmly and show false-hood to be false, however hateful this might be to the evildoers. (8)

لِيُحِقَّ ٱلْحَقَّ وَيُبْطِلَ ٱلْبَـٰطِلَ وَلَوْ كَرِهَ ٱلْمُجْرِمُونَ ٨

When you implored your Lord for help, He answered: 'I will reinforce you with a thousand angels advancing in ranks.' (9)

إِذْ تَسْتَغِيثُونَ رَبَّكُمْ فَٱسْتَجَابَ لَكُمْ أَنِّى مُمِدُّكُم بِأَلْفٍ مِّنَ ٱلْمَلَـٰٓئِكَةِ مُرْدِفِينَ ٩

God made this only as good news with which to reassure your hearts, for victory comes only from God. Indeed, God is Almighty, Wise. (10)

وَمَا جَعَلَهُ ٱللَّهُ إِلَّا بُشْرَىٰ وَلِتَطْمَئِنَّ
بِهِۦ قُلُوبُكُمْ ۚ وَمَا ٱلنَّصْرُ إِلَّا مِنْ عِندِ
ٱللَّهِ ۚ إِنَّ ٱللَّهَ عَزِيزٌ حَكِيمٌ ﴿١٠﴾

He made slumber fall upon you, as an assurance from Him, and He sent down water from the sky to cleanse you and to remove from you Satan's filth, to strengthen your hearts and steady your footsteps. (11)

إِذْ يُغَشِّيكُمُ ٱلنُّعَاسَ أَمَنَةً مِّنْهُ وَيُنَزِّلُ
عَلَيْكُم مِّنَ ٱلسَّمَآءِ مَآءً لِّيُطَهِّرَكُم بِهِۦ
وَيُذْهِبَ عَنكُمْ رِجْزَ ٱلشَّيْطَٰنِ وَلِيَرْبِطَ
عَلَىٰ قُلُوبِكُمْ وَيُثَبِّتَ بِهِ ٱلْأَقْدَامَ ﴿١١﴾

Your Lord inspired the angels, saying: 'I am with you. So, give courage to the believers. I shall cast terror into the hearts of the unbelievers. Strike, then, their necks and strike off their every fingertip.' (12)

إِذْ يُوحِى رَبُّكَ إِلَى ٱلْمَلَٰٓئِكَةِ أَنِّى مَعَكُمْ
فَثَبِّتُوا۟ ٱلَّذِينَ ءَامَنُوا۟ ۚ سَأُلْقِى فِى قُلُوبِ
ٱلَّذِينَ كَفَرُوا۟ ٱلرُّعْبَ فَٱضْرِبُوا۟
فَوْقَ ٱلْأَعْنَاقِ وَٱضْرِبُوا۟ مِنْهُمْ كُلَّ
بَنَانٍ ﴿١٢﴾

This is because they have defied God and His Messenger. Whoever defies God and His Messenger [will find out that] God is severe in retribution. (13)

ذَٰلِكَ بِأَنَّهُمْ شَآقُّوا۟ ٱللَّهَ وَرَسُولَهُۥ ۚ
وَمَن يُشَاقِقِ ٱللَّهَ وَرَسُولَهُۥ فَإِنَّ
ٱللَّهَ شَدِيدُ ٱلْعِقَابِ ﴿١٣﴾

This is for you, [enemies of God]! Taste it, then. The unbelievers shall be made to suffer the torment of fire. (14)

ذَٰلِكُمْ فَذُوقُوهُ وَأَنَّ لِلْكَٰفِرِينَ
عَذَابَ ٱلنَّارِ ﴿١٤﴾

Believers, when you meet in battle those who disbelieve, do not turn your backs to them in flight. (15)

يَٰٓأَيُّهَا ٱلَّذِينَ ءَامَنُوٓاْ إِذَا لَقِيتُمُ ٱلَّذِينَ
كَفَرُواْ زَحْفًا فَلَا تُوَلُّوهُمُ ٱلْأَدْبَارَ ﴿١٥﴾

Anyone who turns his back to them on that day, except when manoeuvring for battle or in an endeavour to join another troop, shall incur God's wrath, and hell shall be his abode: how vile a journey's end. (16)

وَمَن يُوَلِّهِمْ يَوْمَئِذٍ دُبُرَهُۥٓ إِلَّا مُتَحَرِّفًا
لِّقِتَالٍ أَوْ مُتَحَيِّزًا إِلَىٰ فِئَةٍ فَقَدْ بَآءَ
بِغَضَبٍ مِّنَ ٱللَّهِ وَمَأْوَىٰهُ جَهَنَّمُ
وَبِئْسَ ٱلْمَصِيرُ ﴿١٦﴾

It was not you who slew them, but it was God who slew them. When you threw [a handful of dust], it was not your act, but God's, so that He might put the believers through a fair test of His own making. Indeed, God hears all and knows all. (17)

فَلَمْ تَقْتُلُوهُمْ وَلَٰكِنَّ ٱللَّهَ قَتَلَهُمْ وَمَا
رَمَيْتَ إِذْ رَمَيْتَ وَلَٰكِنَّ ٱللَّهَ رَمَىٰ
وَلِيُبْلِىَ ٱلْمُؤْمِنِينَ مِنْهُ بَلَآءً حَسَنًا
إِنَّ ٱللَّهَ سَمِيعٌ عَلِيمٌ ﴿١٧﴾

That is so; it is God who shall make feeble the schemes of the unbelievers. (18)

ذَٰلِكُمْ وَأَنَّ ٱللَّهَ مُوهِنُ كَيْدِ
ٱلْكَٰفِرِينَ ﴿١٨﴾

If you were seeking a judgement, then a judgement has come to you. If you desist, it will be best for you; and if you revert to your erring ways, We will also be back [with Our punishment]. Your host, numerous as it may be, shall avail you nothing; for God is with the believers. (19)

إِن تَسْتَفْتِحُواْ فَقَدْ جَآءَكُمُ ٱلْفَتْحُ
وَإِن تَنتَهُواْ فَهُوَ خَيْرٌ لَّكُمْ وَإِن تَعُودُواْ
نَعُدْ وَلَن تُغْنِىَ عَنكُمْ فِئَتُكُمْ شَيْـًٔا وَلَوْ
كَثُرَتْ وَأَنَّ ٱللَّهَ مَعَ ٱلْمُؤْمِنِينَ ﴿١٩﴾

Believers, obey God and His Messenger, and do not turn away from him now that you have heard [his message]. (20)

يَٰٓأَيُّهَا ٱلَّذِينَ ءَامَنُوٓا۟ أَطِيعُوا۟ ٱللَّهَ
وَرَسُولَهُۥ وَلَا تَوَلَّوْا۟ عَنْهُ وَأَنتُمْ
تَسْمَعُونَ ﴿٢٠﴾

Do not be like those who say: 'We have heard,' while they do not listen. (21)

وَلَا تَكُونُوا۟ كَٱلَّذِينَ قَالُوا۟ سَمِعْنَا
وَهُمْ لَا يَسْمَعُونَ ﴿٢١﴾

Indeed, the worst of all creatures, in God's sight, are the deaf and dumb who are devoid of reason. (22)

إِنَّ شَرَّ ٱلدَّوَآبِّ عِندَ ٱللَّهِ ٱلصُّمُّ ٱلْبُكْمُ
ٱلَّذِينَ لَا يَعْقِلُونَ ﴿٢٢﴾

If God had known of any good in them, He would certainly have made them hear. But even if He were to make them hear, they would have turned away and refused to listen. (23)

وَلَوْ عَلِمَ ٱللَّهُ فِيهِمْ خَيْرًا لَّأَسْمَعَهُمْ ۖ وَلَوْ
أَسْمَعَهُمْ لَتَوَلَّوا۟ وَّهُم مُّعْرِضُونَ ﴿٢٣﴾

Believers, respond to the call of God and the Messenger when he calls you to that which will give you life, and know that God comes in between a man and his heart, and that to Him you shall all be gathered. (24)

يَٰٓأَيُّهَا ٱلَّذِينَ ءَامَنُوا۟ ٱسْتَجِيبُوا۟ لِلَّهِ
وَلِلرَّسُولِ إِذَا دَعَاكُمْ لِمَا يُحْيِيكُمْ ۖ
وَٱعْلَمُوٓا۟ أَنَّ ٱللَّهَ يَحُولُ بَيْنَ ٱلْمَرْءِ
وَقَلْبِهِۦ وَأَنَّهُۥٓ إِلَيْهِ تُحْشَرُونَ ﴿٢٤﴾

Beware of temptation that does not lure only those among you who are wrongdoers. Know that God is severe in retribution. (25)

وَٱتَّقُوا۟ فِتْنَةً لَّا تُصِيبَنَّ ٱلَّذِينَ ظَلَمُوا۟
مِنكُمْ خَآصَّةً ۖ وَٱعْلَمُوٓا۟ أَنَّ ٱللَّهَ
شَدِيدُ ٱلْعِقَابِ ﴿٢٥﴾

Remember when you were few and helpless in the land, fearful lest people do away with you: how He sheltered you, strengthened you with His support and provided you with many good things so that you might be grateful. (26)

وَٱذْكُرُوٓا۟ إِذْ أَنتُمْ قَلِيلٌ مُّسْتَضْعَفُونَ
فِى ٱلْأَرْضِ تَخَافُونَ أَن يَتَخَطَّفَكُمُ ٱلنَّاسُ
فَـَٔاوَىٰكُمْ وَأَيَّدَكُم بِنَصْرِهِۦ وَرَزَقَكُم مِّنَ
ٱلطَّيِّبَٰتِ لَعَلَّكُمْ تَشْكُرُونَ ﴿٢٦﴾

Believers, do not betray God and the Messenger, nor knowingly betray the trust that has been reposed in you. (27)

يَٰٓأَيُّهَا ٱلَّذِينَ ءَامَنُوا۟ لَا تَخُونُوا۟ ٱللَّهَ
وَٱلرَّسُولَ وَتَخُونُوٓا۟ أَمَٰنَٰتِكُمْ وَأَنتُمْ
تَعْلَمُونَ ﴿٢٧﴾

Know that your worldly goods and your children are but a trial, and that with God there is a great reward. (28)

وَٱعْلَمُوٓا۟ أَنَّمَآ أَمْوَٰلُكُمْ وَأَوْلَٰدُكُمْ
فِتْنَةٌ وَأَنَّ ٱللَّهَ عِندَهُۥٓ أَجْرٌ عَظِيمٌ ﴿٢٨﴾

Believers, if you remain God-fearing, He will give you a standard by which to discern the true from the false, and will wipe off your bad deeds, and forgive you. God's bounty is great indeed. (29)

يَٰٓأَيُّهَا ٱلَّذِينَ ءَامَنُوٓا۟ إِن تَتَّقُوا۟ ٱللَّهَ
يَجْعَل لَّكُمْ فُرْقَانًا وَيُكَفِّرْ عَنكُمْ
سَيِّـَٔاتِكُمْ وَيَغْفِرْ لَكُمْ ۗ وَٱللَّهُ ذُو
ٱلْفَضْلِ ٱلْعَظِيمِ ﴿٢٩﴾

Overview

This opening passage of the *sūrah* provides God's ruling over the booty that Muslims may gain in their campaigns to serve God's cause. Those who fought in the first major battle that took place at Badr between the newly-established Muslim state and the pagan Arabs disputed among themselves over its distribution. God gives here His ruling and reminds them of their need to fear and obey Him, and also obey His Messenger. He reminds them of their faith and that they need to live up to its values.

God also reminds them that they had hoped to gain a trade caravan, but God wanted something much better for them: strength and victory. He further puts before their eyes the factors that made the battle go in their favour when they were facing an enemy who was far superior to them in numerical strength and equipment. They were given support by angels. Rain gave them water to drink, and made the terrain firmer so that they were not impeded by a sandy battleground. Slumber overwhelmed them to give them calmness and reassurance. Their enemies were overwhelmed with fear, and ended up suffering stern punishment.

The believers are commanded to remain steadfast in every battle, no matter how strong and unassailable their enemies may initially appear to be. It is God who plans, acts and kills. They are merely a means with which He accomplishes His will. He may do with them what He pleases.

The *sūrah* then ridicules the unbelievers who, before the battle, were keen to precipitate God's will, appealing to God to bring about the defeat of the party which was far more astray and ready to sever relations of kinship. He tells them that their appeal is granted. It also warns the believers against behaving like the hypocrites who hear God's message but do not listen or respond to it.

The passage concludes with appeals to the believers to respond to God and His Messenger when he calls on them to follow the path that gives them life, although it may appear at first sight to involve death and being killed in battle. It reminds them of the days when they were few in number, oppressed, living in fear, but God gave them shelter and granted them support and victory. It promises them that God will give them a clear criterion if they continue to fear Him. That will be in addition to forgiveness of their sins and abounding grace that makes all spoils of war appear petty and trivial.

Dispute Over the Spoils of War

They ask you about the spoils of war. Say: The spoils of war belong to God and the Messenger. So, have fear of God and set right your internal relations. Obey God and His Messenger, if you are true believers. True believers are only those whose hearts are filled with

> *awe whenever God is mentioned, and whose faith is strengthened whenever His revelations are recited to them. In their Lord do they place their trust. They attend regularly to their prayers and spend on others some of what We have provided them with. It is those who are truly believers. They shall be given high ranks with their Lord, and forgiveness of sins and generous provisions.* (Verses 1–4)

We mentioned in the Prologue a number of reports speaking about the reasons for the revelation of these verses. It is useful to add here some more reports in order to be fully aware of the prevailing atmosphere at the time when the *sūrah* was revealed, particularly those verses that speak of the spoils of war. This will give us a clear view of the actual situation of the Muslim community after its first major battle since the establishment of the Muslim state in Madinah.

In his commentary on the Qur'ān, Ibn Kathīr quotes a report related by Abū Dāwūd, al-Nasā'ī and others on the authority of Ibn 'Abbās who says: "On the day of the Battle of Badr, the Prophet said: 'Whoever does this or that shall have so and so.' The young ones among the Muslims fought hard to establish their claims, while the older people held the banners. When it was time to distribute the booty, they pressed their claims. The older people said: 'Do not take it all for yourselves, for we were providing you with support. Had you suffered a setback, you would have needed our cover.' There was a dispute over the matter between them. So God revealed the opening verse of the *sūrah*."

Another report by Ibn 'Abbās goes as follows: "On the day of Badr, the Prophet said: 'Whoever kills an enemy soldier shall have this and that, and whoever brings a prisoner shall have so and so.' A man called Abū al-Yasīr brought two men he had taken prisoner and said: 'Messenger of God, you have promised us.' Sa'd ibn 'Ubādah said: 'Messenger of God, if you were to give only to these people, nothing will be left for your Companions. We did not stay behind because we thought little of the reward or out of cowardice. We only stayed behind to provide you with protection, should the enemy attack you from behind.' A dispute broke out, and the first verse of the *sūrah* was revealed. God also revealed Verse 41 which outlines the distribution of the spoils of war.

Imām Aḥmad relates on the authority of Sa'd ibn Abī Waqqāṣ: "On the day of the Battle of Badr, my brother, 'Umayr, was killed. However,

I managed to kill Sa'īd ibn al-'Āṣ and took his sword which was called Dhu'l-Kuthayfah. I brought it to the Prophet, but he said: 'Go and put it with the rest of the booty.' As I went back, only God could know how distressed I was as a result of the killing of my brother and being deprived of my gain. I walked only a short distance before the *sūrah* entitled al-Anfāl was revealed. God's Messenger said to me: 'Go and claim your gain.'"

Imām Aḥmad also relates a different version on the authority of Sa'd himself who says: "I said to the Prophet: 'Messenger of God, by God's grace I have taken my revenge against the unbelievers. Grant me this sword.' He said: 'This sword belongs neither to you nor to me. Put it down.' I did, and went away saying to myself that he may give the sword to someone who might not have fought as hard as I did. A voice was then calling me from behind. I said: 'Has God revealed something concerning me?' He said: 'You asked me to give you the sword when it was not mine. Now it has been given to me, and I gift it to you.' He added that it was then that the opening verse of the *sūrah* was revealed."

These reports describe the general atmosphere that prevailed at that time. Some of us may wonder at the fighters at Badr disputing over the spoils. These fighters were the followers of Islam in its very early days. They belonged either to the *Muhājirīn*, who migrated from Makkah, their hometown, leaving behind all their possessions for no reason other than to serve God's cause, or to the *Anṣār* of Madinah who received the *Muhājirīn* and shared with them their homes and property, denying them nothing. These were the ones who are described by God in the Qur'ān as ones "*who love those who have come over to them; they harbour in their hearts no grudge for whatever the others have been given, but rather give them preference over themselves, even though poverty be their lot.*" (59: 9) But these reports give us part of the answer. Being given something of the spoils of war was in itself a testimony for having fought hard. Those people were keen to have such a testimony from God's Messenger and from God Himself, in the first major battle which saw them triumph over the unbelievers. That keenness overshadowed something of great importance, namely, to maintain kindly relations and to promote bonds of brotherhood among themselves. When these verses were revealed, they recognized their fault. 'Ubādah ibn al-Ṣāmit says: "These verses speak about us, the people of Badr, when we disputed over the spoils of war and behaved in an unbecoming way. God took it away from us and gave it to His Messenger (peace be upon him)."

God gives them a verbal and practical lesson. The whole question of dividing the spoils of war was taken away from them and given to the Prophet himself. Then He revealed His verdict on how all spoils of war should be shared out. It was no longer the right over which they might dispute. It was something that was given to them by God's grace, and the Prophet would divide it among them in accordance with his Lord's instructions. In addition to this edifying experience, they were given directives that begin with this opening verse: "*They ask you about the spoils of war. Say: The spoils of war belong to God and the Messenger. So, have fear of God and set right your internal relations. Obey God and His Messenger, if you are true believers.*" (Verse 1)

Essential Qualities of Believers

Thus, the opening verse of the *sūrah* reminds the hearts of those who disputed over the booty that they should maintain fear of God. Glory be to the Creator who knows all hearts' secrets. It is only the fear of God and the desire to earn His pleasure in this life, as well as in the life to come, that turns human hearts away from valuing the riches and pleasures of this world and disputing over them, even though such a dispute should also have an overtone of having a testimony for fighting hard to serve God's cause. A heart that does not turn in its totality to God, fearing to incur His anger and seeking to earn His pleasure, will never be able to get rid of the temptation of worldly comforts and riches. Fearing God is what makes people's hearts willing to be guided with ease and humility so that they can maintain friendly relations and promote bonds of brotherhood between them: "*So, have fear of God and set right your internal relations.*" (Verse 1) It is through fearing God that they are led to total obedience of God and His Messenger: "*Obey God and His Messenger, if you are true believers.*" (Verse 1)

The first aspect of obedience in this connection is to submit to His ruling over the spoils of war. It no longer belonged to any one of the fighters. The entire booty belongs to God and His Messenger, and they have sole discretion over its use. Those believers could only submit to God's ruling and the Prophet's division of the booty with easy hearts and happy minds. They also needed to maintain their brotherly relationship which nothing could weaken, provided that "*you are true believers*". (Verse 1)

Faith must have a practical example to testify to its applicability and to demonstrate how it works. The Prophet says: "Faith does not come about through wishful thinking or maintaining appearances. True faith is that which establishes roots in people's hearts and to which action gives credence." This is the reason for frequently repeating this final phrase in the Qur'ān in order to stress the meaning of faith outlined by the Prophet. It thus becomes a practical definition of faith so that it is no longer thought to be a mere verbal statement that has no practical correlative.

This is followed by an outline of the qualities of true faith, as God wants it to be: "*True believers are only those whose hearts are filled with awe whenever God is mentioned, and whose faith is strengthened whenever His revelations are recited to them. In their Lord do they place their trust. They attend regularly to their prayers and spend on others some of what We have provided them with. It is those who are truly believers. They shall be given high ranks with their Lord, and forgiveness of sins and generous provisions.*" (Verses 2–4)

The Qur'ānic style is extremely accurate in its choice of words, in order to provide a very clear statement of the meaning it wants to impart. Here we have the phrase "only those" in order to limit the meaning of having faith to those who have these qualities. When we have such a limiting expression, no one could try to give a subjective interpretation of these qualities, claiming for example that they refer to 'people with complete faith'. Had God meant it that way He would have said it. What we have here is a highly definitive statement which tells us that only the people who have such qualities and who act and feel in this way are believers. Those who do not have all these qualities are not believers. At the end of these opening verses, a repeat statement is given to re-emphasize this fact: "*It is those who are truly believers.*" (Verse 4) People who are not 'truly' believers do not believe at all. Qur'ānic expressions and statements interpret one another. God says elsewhere in the Qur'ān: "*What may differ with the truth other than error.*" Hence, only error stands opposite to the truth. Those who do not belong to the 'truly believers' cannot be described as 'having faith, though it may be less than complete'. A definitive Qur'ānic statement cannot be interpreted at will in such an ambiguous manner.

The early Muslims realized that a person who does not have such qualities and whose actions do not conform to these descriptions is not a believer at all. Commenting on the Qur'ānic verse that states, '*True believers are only those whose hearts are filled with awe whenever God is mentioned,*' Ibn 'Abbās says: "When hypocrites perform worship duties, nothing touches their hearts as they mention God. They do not believe in any of God's signs, and they do not rely on Him. When they are alone, they neither pray nor pay *zakāt*. Hence, God describes them as unbelievers, and then He describes the believers, saying: "*True believers are only those whose hearts are filled with awe whenever God is mentioned.*" Hence, they do the duties He requires them to do. "*And whose faith is strengthened whenever His revelations are recited to them.*" They feel the truth of these revelations as they listen to them. "*In their Lord do they place their trust.*" They rely only on Him, seeking nothing from anyone else."

As we proceed with our commentary, we will see clearly that without such qualities, faith does not exist. It is not a matter of having complete or less than complete faith, but whether faith exists or not.

"*True believers are only those whose hearts are filled with awe whenever God is mentioned.*" (Verse 2) It is a feeling of awe that fills a believer's heart when God's name is mentioned in connection with any duty. The believer feels God's greatness and majesty, and he remembers God's greatness and how imperfect his own attitude is. All this provides strong motivation for him to act. Or it may be described in the words of Umm al-Dardā', a lady Companion of the Prophet who said: "A feeling of awe is similar to a burning sensation that causes you to tremble. When you experience that, then pray to God, for such prayer is sure to give you comfort." It is a situation that leaves its effect on people's hearts, and they need to appeal to God for comfort. This is exactly what a believer experiences when he is reminded of God in connection with any order. He will then do what he is bid and refrain from what he is forbidden.

"*And whose faith is strengthened whenever His revelations are recited to them.*" (Verse 2) A believing heart is sure to find in the Qur'ānic verses what gives him strength of faith and reassurance. The Qur'ān deals directly with human hearts, without any intermediary. Only disbelief can place a barrier between human hearts and the Qur'ān. When the barrier is removed by faith, a believing heart will begin to appreciate the Qur'ān and watch his faith grow stronger until he finds complete reassurance. Just as the Qur'ānic effect strengthens the faith of a believer, a believing heart is the only one to appreciate the Qur'ānic directives. Hence, this fact is often stressed in statements like: "*Surely, in this there are signs for believers.*" And "*Certainly, in this there are signs for people who believe.*" This is succinctly expressed by one of the Prophet's Companions who describes their community as one which was given faith before it was given the Qur'ān.

Practising What We Preach

The Prophet's Companions were indeed models of true believers. The Qur'ān had a special effect on them, enhanced by the general atmosphere in their community in which people tried their best to practically live by the Qur'ān and not confine themselves to an intellectual appreciation of its meaning. We have mentioned certain reports that relate the incident leading to the revelation of the opening verse of the *sūrah*. These reports speak of Sa'd ibn Mālik[1] who requested the Prophet to give him a particular sword before the revelation that gave the Prophet complete control over the spoils of war and how they were to be distributed. The Prophet said to him: "This sword belongs neither to you nor to me. Put it down." When Sa'd complied with this instruction and went away, and was then called back, he feared that his request might have been answered by revelation. Quoting Sa'd, the report goes on: "I said: Has God revealed something concerning me?" The Prophet told him: "You asked me to give you this sword when it was not mine. Now it has been given to me, and I gift it to you." Thus did they live with their Lord and with the Qur'ān which was being revealed. That was great indeed, taking place in a remarkable period of human history. Those Companions of the Prophet were thus able to appreciate the Qur'ān in their own exemplary way. The fact that they conducted their own practical affairs, guided by the Qur'ānic directives made their own appreciation of the Qur'ān both practical and highly effective. While no repeat of the first aspect is possible in the sense that no human community could receive the Qur'ān directly anymore, yet the type

1. Mālik is also known as Abū Waqqāṣ. Therefore Sa'd is often referred to as Sa'd ibn Abī Waqqāṣ.

of interaction with the Qur'ān that characterized the community of the Prophet's Companions can certainly be repeated. It only requires a community of believers to try to establish this religion of Islam in practical life just like the first Muslim community did. Such a community of believers will certainly have the same type of appreciation of the Qur'ān and will have their faith increased whenever it is recited, because, to start with, it is a believing community. For them, true faith requires that they take action to establish this religion in practice after *jāhiliyyah* had regained control over the whole world. To them, faith is not confined to wishful thinking, but it means something that is deeply rooted in one's heart and to which credence is given through action.

"*In their Lord do they place their trust.*" (Verse 2) The way this statement is phrased signifies that they rely on God alone, associating no one with Him from whom to request help. Ibn Kathīr explains the significance of this statement fully as he says: "They place their hopes in none other than Him, turn to no one other than Him, seek no one else's protection, address their appeals only to Him and turn for help to no one other than Him. They know that whatever He wishes will be accomplished and what He does not will never take place. They also know that He alone has complete control over the whole universe, with no one needed to endorse, ratify, or confirm His judgement. He is also fast in reckoning. For this reason, Sa'īd ibn Jubayr says: "True reliance on God is the net sum of faith."

This is the practical meaning of pure faith in God's oneness, addressing all worship completely and purely to Him alone. It is not possible for any person to have true faith in God as the only Lord in the universe and yet rely on someone other than Him. Those who find themselves relying on someone other than God must first of all search in their own hearts to discover whether they truly believe in God.

To rely on God alone does not prevent anyone from taking action or precaution. A believer takes precautions against any eventuality as a sign of believing in God and obeying Him, as He has ordered us to do so. But a true believer does not consider his actions and precautions as the only causes to give the effects they produce, to the extent that he relies only on such actions and precautions. What produces these effects, and indeed brings their causes into being, is God's will. In a believer's heart, the cause and effect relationship is not self-enforcing. A believer takes action in order to obey God. But the results and effects come about by God's own will which is totally independent from the causes leading to it. Such will is determined by God alone. In this way, a believer does not feel controlled by such actions and causes. Nevertheless, he tries his best to take every precaution hoping that he will be rewarded for doing so in obedience to God.

Modern *jāhiliyyah* which describes itself as 'scientific' has tried hard to emphasize the "inevitability of natural laws", in order to deny God's will and whatever God has chosen not to make known to us. All its attempts and the manipulation of all means at its disposal have shown it to be powerless in the face of God's will. It was eventually forced to admit its inability to make future predictions with any degree of certainty or inevitability. It then resorted to what it terms 'the theory of probabilities' in the material world. Whatever used to be 'inevitable' in its lexicon has come to be considered only 'probable'. *Ghayb,* which is the Qur'ānic term for what lies beyond the reach of human perception, remains a sealed secret. Furthermore, God's will remains the only true certainty. The only inevitable law is that expressed in the Qur'ānic statement: "*You never know but God may well cause something new to come about.*" (65: 1) This statement refers to the fact that God's will is free, unrestrained. It lies behind the natural laws which God has set into operation to control the universe according to His will.

Sir James Jeans, a renowned British physicist says:

> The old science had confidently proclaimed that nature could follow only one road, the road which was mapped out from the beginning of time to its end by the continuous chain of cause and effect; state A was inevitably succeeded by state B. So far the new science has only been able to say that state A may be followed by state B or C or D or by innumerable other states. It can, it is true, say that B is more likely than C, C than D, and so on; it can even specify the relative probabilities of states B, C and D. But, just because it has to speak in terms of probabilities, it cannot predict with certainty which state will follow which; this is a matter which lies on the knees of the gods – whatever gods there be.[2]

---

2. Sir James Jeans, *The Mysterious Universe*, Cambridge University Press, 1931, pp. 18–19.

When a person has rid his mind of the pressure of apparent causes, it is left with the only alternative of relying completely on God. It realizes that God's will is the only cause for all that happens, and that this is the only true certainty. Apparent causes produce only probabilities. With this truth, Islamic faith enables the human mind to bridge a great gulf. Modern *jāhiliyyah* has spent three centuries in order to arrive at the first intellectual stage in bridging that gulf. But it has not made any progress towards bridging it in as far as beliefs are concerned, or with regard to the far-reaching practical effects that result from it, in accepting God's will and dealing with it as apparent causes and forces. Bridging that gulf means the total liberation of mankind, intellectually, politically, socially and morally and, above all, in matters of faith. It is not possible for man to achieve this freedom if he were to remain under the yoke of 'inevitabilities' that would undoubtedly lead him to submission to the will of human beings or the will of nature. Any inevitability other than that of God's will serves as a basis for submission to something else. Hence, the Qur'ān emphasizes the need to rely on God alone, making it an essential condition of faith. In Islam, the basic concept of belief is a complete whole. It must interact as such in the practical model which this religion of Islam provides for human life.

"*They attend regularly to their prayers.*" (Verse 3) In this quality we find a visible aspect of faith, after we had seen some of its invisible ones. Faith is defined as that which is deeply rooted in one's heart and to which credence is given through action. Action is, therefore, the practical aspect of faith which appears to all people signifying that the person who takes such action is a person of faith. Regular attendance to prayer does not signify its mere performance. It is the performance which befits a servant standing in the presence of his Master (limitless is He in His glory). It is not the mere recitation, movement, bowing and prostration when one's mind is totally oblivious to what one is actually doing. In its proper performance, prayer is a true evidence of faith.

"*And [they] spend on others some of what We have provided them with.*" (Verse 3) This applies to *zakāt* and other forms of charity. These people spend on others 'some of what We have provided them with.' It is God who is the provider, and whatever they donate is part of His provision. Qur'ānic statements are always rich in their connotations and the impressions they leave. Those people have not created their wealth. It is only part of the countless abundance which God has provided for them.

Whatever they may spend is only part of it. They retain the rest; for whatever they have has been provided for them by God alone.

These are the qualities God mentions here as signifying faith. They include believing in God's oneness, responding to the mentioning of His name, being influenced by His revelations, placing one's trust only in Him, offering prayer to Him alone and donating to others some of what He has provided for them. These qualities do not represent the details of faith as they have been explained elsewhere in the Qur'ān; but they deal with a certain situation when the Prophet's companions disputed with one another over the spoils of war, allowing ill feelings to develop between themselves. Hence, only those qualities of the believers which are particularly relevant to dealing with such a situation are mentioned here. At the same time, they outline certain essential qualities of proper faith. If all these qualities are lacking, a person cannot be a true believer. It is not necessary to enlist all the qualities of faith here. The Qur'ānic method of cultivating the finer human qualities with the Qur'ān tackles only those aspects and provides only those directives that are useful in dealing with certain practical situations. Besides, the Qur'ān provides a practical method for human life, not a mere theory that it wishes to present. Hence, the final comment on these qualities is as follows: "*It is those who are truly believers. They shall be given high ranks with their Lord, and forgiveness of sins and generous provisions.*" (Verse 4)

Here we find highlighted those qualities of true believers which are particularly relevant to the situation prevailing at the time of their revelation. Those companions of the Prophet were keen to attain martyrdom through fighting hard for God's cause. A clear reference to this is given in the fact that those whose qualities are such "*shall be given high ranks with their Lord.*" (Verse 4) We also have a reference to what 'Ubādah ibn al-Ṣāmit describes as bad manners and unbrotherly relations being clearly apparent. The passage tells us that those believers who have all these qualities shall be given forgiveness by their Lord. The *sūrah* also refers to the dispute over the spoils of war that took place after the battle, stating that people with such qualities of true believers shall have 'generous provisions' given to them by their Lord. Thus, all aspects of the situation are covered, whether they appeared in practical attitudes or were confined to feelings only. At the same time, this passage makes it very clear that a person who does not have any of these qualities is certainly not a true believer.

"*It is those who are truly believers.*" (Verse 4) The first Muslim community was being taught that faith has an essence which must be felt by every believer. Faith is not merely a claim or a verbal statement, or wishful thinking. In an authentic *ḥadīth*, a man from the *Anṣār* named al-Ḥārith ibn Mālik is reported to have met the Prophet who asked him: "How do you feel this morning, Ḥārith?" The man said: "I feel myself to be a true believer." The Prophet said: "Reflect on what you say, for everything has an essence. What is the essence of your faith?" He answered: "This world is no longer of much appeal to me. Therefore, I am staying up at night and enduring thirst by day. (This means that he spent much of his nights in worship and he frequently fasted voluntarily.) I feel as though I am looking at my Lord's throne in full view. I almost see the dwellers of heaven visiting one another there, and the people of hell uttering cries of anguish. "The Prophet said: "Ḥārith, you have come to know the facts, so maintain your attitude." He repeated his advice three times.

This Companion of the Prophet deserved the Prophet's testimony that he was in full knowledge of the facts. Yet, when he answered the Prophet's question he not only mentioned his feelings, but the type of action he did in response to his knowledge. A person who can almost see his Lord's throne in full view, and the dwellers of heaven visiting one another, and the people of hell making their cries of anguish will not merely look at these scenes. They leave very strong impressions on him that generate powerful feelings characterizing every move and action he makes. It is because of what he has experienced that he spends so much of his time in night worship and he fasts frequently, trying to refine his nature.

True faith must be taken very seriously. It is not a mere word that people say while practice remains in conflict with what is said. Taking true faith seriously and approaching it with determination are highly important, particularly for any community of believers who try to re-establish the faith of Islam in practice after *jāhiliyyah* has imparted its ugly colour to human life everywhere.

Better than the Believer's Desire

Now that the *sūrah* has established at the outset the nature of true faith, it refers to the battle which allowed the Muslim community to gain the spoils of war that became the subject of their dispute to the extent that their behaviour was not all that becoming, as the Prophet's Companion, 'Ubādah ibn al-Ṣāmit, candidly states. The *sūrah* refers in a general way to the various events that took place, and how the Prophet's companions felt and behaved in response. This reference makes it clear that the Prophet's Companions were merely the means through which God's will was accomplished. It is clear that all those events, and the situation that arose from them, including the spoils of war over which they disputed, were only made possible through God's will, His planning and the help He gave to those believers. What they had hoped to achieve from this battle was only a small, limited gain. It could not be compared to what God wanted for them, to be the ones through whom the great divide between truth and falsehood is established in the heavens and on earth. It is this great criterion which is the main preoccupation of the Supreme Society in heaven as well as the preoccupation of the people on earth and human history generally. The *sūrah* reminds them that a group of them went into the battle against their preferred choice. Another party did not like that the spoils of war should be divided among them. Now God wanted them to realize that what they had preferred is not to be compared with what God prefers or what He chooses to accomplish. He knows the results of all matters.

> *Just as your Lord brought you forth from your home for the truth, even though some of the believers were averse to it. They would argue with you about the truth even after it had become manifest, just as if they were being driven to certain death and saw it with their very eyes. God promised you that one of the two hosts would fall to you. It was your wish that the one which was not powerful to be yours, but it was God's will to establish the truth in accordance with His words and to wipe out the unbelievers. Thus He would certainly establish the truth firmly and show falsehood to be false, however hateful this might be to the evildoers. When you implored your Lord for help, He answered: 'I will reinforce you with a thousand angels advancing in ranks.' God made this only as good news with which to reassure your hearts, for victory comes only from God. Indeed, God is Almighty, Wise. He made slumber fall upon you, as an assurance from Him, and He sent down water from the sky to cleanse you and to remove from you Satan's filth, to strengthen your hearts and steady your footsteps. Your Lord inspired the angels, saying: 'I am with you. So, give courage to the believers. I shall cast terror into*

the hearts of the unbelievers. Strike, then, their necks and strike off their every fingertip.' This is because they have defied God and His Messenger. Whoever defies God and His Messenger [will find out that] God is severe in retribution. This is for you, [enemies of God]! Taste it, then. The unbelievers shall be made to suffer the torment of fire. (Verses 5–14)

God willed that the spoils of war be totally left to God and His Messenger, so that the Messenger (peace be upon him) would distribute them equally among them after retaining one-fifth which would be spent in a way to be outlined later in the *sūrah*. That would ensure that the community of believers would no longer entertain any thoughts about the spoils of war, which would mean that no dispute would ever arise over them. The Prophet would have complete authority over their distribution, in accordance with what God taught him. Thus, those who actually took the spoils of war and found themselves receiving the same shares as others would not entertain any ill feeling.

God gives them this example of what they wanted for themselves and what He wanted for them, and accomplished through them. Thus, they know now that God's choice is best for them, whether it relates to the spoils of war or to anything else. People know only what they have in front of them. Their knowledge does not stretch far beyond their own immediate world. The example given is taken from their practical situation, the battle that gave them their booty. What did they hope for when they went into battle? What did God want to establish for and through them? How do the two compare? The gulf between the two eventualities is wide indeed, stretching far beyond what human beings can visualize.

Just as your Lord brought you forth from your home for the truth, even though some of the believers were averse to it. They would argue with you about the truth even after it had become manifest, just as if they were being driven to certain death and saw it with their very eyes. (Verses 5–6)

Giving authority over the spoils of war to God and His Messenger, their subsequent distribution equally among all soldiers, despite expressed reservations by some of them is similar in a sense to the fact that God brought His Messenger forth from his home to fight the well-armed host when some of the believers were very reluctant to go into such a battle.

In our narration of the events of the battle, as related in history books, we mentioned that Abū Bakr and ʿUmar spoke well and the Prophet consulted his companions after the trade caravan of the Quraysh was able to slip away and evade its pursuers. The battle looked imminent after it was known that the Quraysh had raised a large, well-equipped army. Al-Miqdād ibn ʿAmr also spoke well, saying: "Messenger of God, go ahead and do whatever you feel is best. We will never say to you as the Israelites had said to Moses: 'Go with your Lord and fight the enemy while we stay behind!' What we will say is: go with your Lord and fight the enemy and we will fight alongside you." We also mentioned that all this determination was expressed by people from among the *Muhājirīn*. When the Prophet asked again for the views of his Companions, the *Anṣār* recognized that he wanted to hear their view. Saʿd ibn Muʿādh spoke out in a very decisive and highly assuring manner.

But all that was said by Abū Bakr, ʿUmar, al-Miqdād and Saʿd ibn Muʿādh (may God be pleased with them all) was not shared by all those who came out of Madinah with the Prophet. Some of them were very reluctant to fight. They did not have the necessary equipment and did not have the necessary preparation for a major battle. They came out chasing a trade caravan, expecting to confront only a relatively small band that guarded it. When they learned that the Quraysh had mobilized its forces and brought forth its best fighters, they strongly disliked the prospect of confronting that army. Their dislike is described so vividly in the inimitable style of the Qur'ān: "*Just as your Lord brought you forth from your home for the truth, even though some of the believers were averse to it. They would argue with you about the truth even after it had become manifest, just as if they were being driven to certain death and saw it with their very eyes.*" (Verses 5–6)

A report by Abū Ayyūb al-Anṣārī runs as follows: "God's Messenger said to us when we were in Madinah: 'I have been told that the great caravan led by Abū Sufyān is on its way. What would you say to going out to intercept it? It may be that God will gift it to us.' We agreed and went out with him. After we had marched for a day or two, he said to us: 'What do you say to fighting the enemy? They have been told about you coming out to intercept the caravan.' We said most firmly that we were not a match for the enemy, and that we wanted the trade caravan. He then repeated the same question, asking us what we would say to fighting the enemy. We repeated the same answer. Al-Miqdād ibn 'Amr, however, said: 'We will not say to you, Messenger of God, what Moses was told by his people when they said, "Go with your Lord and fight while we stay behind." We, the *Anṣār*, wished that we had said the same as al-Miqdād ibn 'Amr. That would have been far more preferable to us than being in great wealth.'" God then revealed to His Messenger the verses starting with: "*Just as your Lord brought you forth from your home for the truth, even though some of the believers were averse to it.*" (Verse 5)

Such, then, were the feelings of some Muslims. To them fighting was unwelcome. The Qur'ān describes their attitude in these words: "*As if they were being driven to certain death and saw it with their very eyes.*" (Verse 6) That was the situation when the truth was clearly manifest, and when they knew that God had promised them that one of the two enemy hosts would fall to them. They realized that they had no choice left after one host, the trade caravan, had escaped them. Their only choice was to confront the other host, the Quraysh army, which God willed to fall to them, regardless of the disparity between the two parties in terms of fighters and military equipment.

This is a situation where human weakness is exposed in the face of imminent danger. Here we see the effect of actual confrontation, despite firm conviction. The picture the Qur'ān paints should make us more realistic when we assess the requirements of conviction in the face of practical pressures. We must not overlook human ability at the time of confrontation. We must not despair when people generally, including our own group, shake as they face danger, although they are true believers at heart. It is sufficient that people proceed along the proper way and face up to the danger, making a solid stand after the initial hesitation. Those people were the ones who fought the Battle of Badr and concerning whom the Prophet said: "How can you tell? It may be that God has looked at the people of Badr and said: 'Do as you please, for I have forgiven you all.'" That is all that may be said here.

An Aim Superior to All Human Hopes

The Muslim group continued to wish that they would have to face the less powerful host, rather than the Quraysh army. "*God promised you that one of the two hosts would fall to you. It was your wish that the one which was not powerful to be yours.*" (Verse 7) This was their wish, but God wanted a different prospect for them. He wanted to accomplish a different purpose through them: "*But it was God's will to establish the truth in accordance with His words and to wipe out the unbelievers. Thus He would certainly establish the truth firmly and show falsehood to be false, however hateful this might be to the evildoers.*" (Verses 7–8)

By His grace, God did not want the encounter to be one that brings materialistic gains. He wanted it to be a full-fledged battle between truth and falsehood, so that the truth could triumph and be well established, and falsehood be proven and seen as false. He wanted the unbelievers to be routed, suffering heavy losses and many of them to be taken captive. Thus, they would be humiliated and their power greatly weakened while the banner of Islam would remain hoisted high and God's will enforced. In this way, God gives power to the Muslim community which implements the code of living God has revealed. Through such implementation, the principle of God's oneness is firmly established, while tyranny and falsehood are completely shattered. God wanted all this to be earned and merited through endeavour and hard struggle both in practical life and on the battlefield, not to be a gift granted haphazardly, for God does not do anything haphazardly.

Yes, God willed that this Muslim community should become a nation and a state having power and authority. He wanted it to measure its true power against that of its enemies, and to gain the upper hand using only a portion of its power. Thus, it would learn that victory is not guaranteed by numerical strength, heavy armament, material power or wealth. True victory is guaranteed by the strength of the bond that links believers' hearts and minds with God's might which overpowers everything. God's will was such that all this should come through practical experience, and not be limited to a conceptual belief. Such an experience would give the small Muslim community a guiding line for its whole future. Every Muslim group, whenever and wherever it lives, can be certain that it can overcome its enemies, no matter how greatly superior they may be in numbers and equipment. This fact could not have been so profoundly impressed on the believers' minds without that experience of a decisive battle between faith and tyranny.

Anyone can see at any time the vast gulf between what that small Muslim community wanted for itself and what it thought to be of benefit on the one hand, and the much better outcome God willed for it on the other. As he appreciates the difference, he knows how mistaken people are when they think that they can choose for themselves better than what God chooses for them, or when they are deeply hurt by taking some small risks or experiencing minor harm to which God may expose them, while it is calculated to bring them unthinkable and immeasurable benefit.

How do the hopes of that Muslim community compare with what God willed and chose for them? Had they been given the trade caravan, or the band with little power, their encounter would have been nothing more than a small raid that gained them a caravan. The Battle of Badr, on the other hand, remains and will always be remembered in history as a story of faith, a profound victory that distinguishes truth from falsehood. It is the story of the triumph of truth, supported by a small, poorly equipped host over enemies that boasted great superiority in numbers and equipment. It is the story of the triumph of hearts that have been purged from their own weakness and that have established a firm bond with God. Not only so, but it is the story of the triumph of a small band of hearts that included quite a few who were reluctant to fight. As these hearts still had firm conviction of the soundness of the values of the message they believed in and were certain where true power lay, they were able to triumph first over their own desires. They went into the battle when every indication showed the side of falsehood to be overpowering, but through faith that community overturned the scales and the truth was triumphant.

In all its particular circumstances, the Battle of Badr sets a great example in human history, setting out the law that brings victory or defeat and revealing the true factors of each. It is an open book to be read by all generations at all times and in all places, giving the same message that remains always true. It speaks of a law that God willed to remain operative as long as the heavens and the earth remain in existence. The Muslim community that struggles today for the rebirth of Islam on earth, after the whole world has succumbed to *jāhiliyyah*, should reflect deeply on Badr and the decisive values it presents. This community must reflect on the great difference between what human beings may wish for themselves and what God may will for them: "*God promised you that one of the two hosts would fall to you. It was your wish that the one which was not powerful to be yours, but it was God's will to establish the truth in accordance with His words and to wipe out the unbelievers. Thus He would certainly establish the truth firmly and show falsehood to be false, however hateful this might be to the evildoers.*" (Verses 7–8)

The Muslim community which tries today to re-establish Islam in human life may not have attained the standard of that small Muslim community that fought the Battle of Badr. However, the standards, values and general directives that applied to Badr, its circumstances and outcome, as well as the Qur'ānic comments on that Battle, remain applicable to it. They point out the attitude the Muslim community should adopt at every stage, because those standards, values and directives remain valid as long as life continues in the heavens and on earth, and as long as there remains on this planet a Muslim community facing up to *jāhiliyyah* and trying to re-establish Islam in practice.

An Appeal and a Response

At this point, the *sūrah* recalls the atmosphere of the Battle of Badr, the circumstances leading to it and the attitudes adopted prior to the Battle and during it. It paints a complete picture of the conditions that the Muslims were in, what God planned for them and how the victory they attained was part of His planning. In the inimitable style of the Qur'ān, the whole situation is brought back to them with its different scenes, events, feelings and reactions so that they could relive it, but this time in the light of Qur'ānic directives. Thus they are able to appreciate its true dimensions that go far beyond Badr, the Arabian Peninsula and the whole earth to stretch across the universe and reach up to the Highest Society. It also goes beyond the day of Badr, Arabian and human history in general, and beyond this life to reach to the time of reckoning in the life to come and the perfect reward. The Muslim community is thus enabled to appreciate its value in God's sight, and how He values the moves and actions of individuals and communities in the service of their faith.

> *When you implored your Lord for help, He answered: 'I will reinforce you with a thousand angels advancing in ranks.' God made this only as good news with which to reassure your hearts, for victory comes only from God. Indeed, God is Almighty, Wise. He made slumber fall upon you, as an assurance from Him, and He sent down water from the sky to cleanse you and to remove from you Satan's*

filth, to strengthen your hearts and steady your footsteps. Your Lord inspired the angels, saying: 'I am with you. So, give courage to the believers. I shall cast terror into the hearts of the unbelievers. Strike, then, their necks and strike off their every fingertip.' This is because they have defied God and His Messenger. Whoever defies God and His Messenger [will find out that] God is severe in retribution. This is for you, [enemies of God]! Taste it, then. The unbelievers shall be made to suffer the torment of fire. (Verses 9–14)

The whole battle is conducted by God's will and according to His careful planning. The actors are God's soldiers whom He directs and commands. The whole scene is painted so vividly through the Qur'ānic expressions that bring it alive as if it is happening here and now.

As for the appeal for God's help, Imām Aḥmad relates on 'Umar ibn al-Khaṭṭāb's authority: "On the Day of Badr, the Prophet looked at his Companions who numbered a little over three hundred, and he looked at the unbelievers who were over one thousand. The Prophet turned his face towards the *qiblah* (i.e. the direction faced by Muslims in prayer), wearing both his garments and prayed earnestly, saying: 'My Lord, fulfil Your promise to me. My Lord, if this group of believers are left to perish, You will not be worshipped on earth.' He continued his imploring prayer until his top garment fell off his shoulders. Abū Bakr took his garment and put it back on him. He held him from behind and said: 'Messenger of God, not so hard in your appeal to your Lord. He will surely grant you what He has promised you.' The verse was then revealed which says: '*When you implored your Lord for help, He answered: I will reinforce you with a thousand angels advancing in ranks.*'" (Verse 9)

There are numerous detailed reports that mention the angels who came to support the Muslims on the day of Badr, their number, how they took part in the battle, what they said to reassure the believers and what they said to dishearten the unbelievers. Following our method in this work, we confine ourselves in all matters that relate to the realm that lies beyond the reach of human perception only to the authentic statements in the Qur'ān and the *ḥadīth*. The Qur'ānic text in this connection gives us enough information: "*When you implored your Lord for help, He answered: 'I will reinforce you with a thousand angels advancing in ranks.'*" (Verse 9) This is then the angels' number. "*Your Lord inspired the angels, saying: 'I am with you. So, give courage to the believers. I shall cast terror into the hearts of the unbelievers. Strike, then, their necks and strike off their every fingertip.*" (Verse 12) Such is, then, the task assigned to them. We need not go into any details beyond this statement. It is sufficient for our purposes that we should know that God did not abandon the Muslim community to their own devices on that day, when they were much inferior in number to their enemies. The Highest Society played an active part in the determination of what happened to the Muslim army and to Islam, along the lines described by God Himself in the Qur'ān.

In a chapter entitled, The Angels' Presence at Badr, al-Bukhārī relates on the authority of Rifā'ah ibn Rāfi': "Gabriel came to the Prophet (peace be upon him) and said: 'What status do you assign to the people of Badr among you?' He answered: 'They are among the best Muslims', or he might have said something similar. Gabriel said: 'And so do we count the angels who were present at Badr.'" [Related by al-Bukhārī].

"*When you implored your Lord for help, He answered: 'I will reinforce you with a thousand angels advancing in ranks.' God made this only as good news with which to reassure your hearts, for victory comes only from God. Indeed, God is Almighty, Wise.*" (Verses 9–10) Their Lord, then, answered their appeal and informed them that He had decided to reinforce them with a thousand angels moving in close ranks. Greatly significant as this decision is, indicating the great value assigned by God to those believers and the faith of Islam, God does not want the Muslims to understand that there is a mechanical process of a direct cause leading to a definite effect. The whole matter is referred back to Him so that the Muslims maintain the right beliefs and concepts. This whole response, enforcement, and the revelation announcing it were merely given as happy news to reassure the believers' hearts. Victory itself comes only from God. This is a basic fact of faith restated here so that Muslims do not attach undue importance to any particular cause or factor.

It was sufficient that the Muslims should do their best and exert their maximum effort, overcoming the initial shock some of them experienced as they found themselves facing real danger. All they needed to do was to actually proceed in obedience of God, assured of His support. In other words, they needed to fulfil their part and leave the rest to God's will. It is He who plans matters for them and dictates the final outcome of their efforts. The rest was merely a piece of happy news, giving reassurance to the believers to calm their hearts and enable them to face up to the real danger. A community of believers does not need more than to feel that they are supported by God's soldiers for their hearts to be set at rest and to go into battle with courage and perseverance. Victory then comes from God, who alone can grant it. He is, mighty indeed, able to accomplish His purpose, and He is wise, putting everyone and everything in the proper place.

> *He made slumber fall upon you, as an assurance from Him, and He sent down water from the sky to cleanse you and to remove from you Satan's filth, to strengthen your hearts and steady your footsteps.* (Verse 11)

This slumber that overcame the believers before the battle is a manifestation of a remarkable state that can only take place by God's will. The Muslims were shaken when they saw themselves facing a much superior force and taking a risk they had not reckoned with and for which they had not prepared themselves. Slumber momentarily falls upon them and they presently wake to find themselves in complete reassurance, with their hearts set at rest.

The same took place at the Battle of Uḥud when the Muslims experienced fear. The same condition of slumber was repeated and the same reassurance was given. I used to read these verses mentioning this slumber, and I used to understand it as an event reported to us by God who alone knows its secret. I then experienced a hard situation when I went through a period of stifling stress and worried apprehension. It was around sunset when I was overtaken by slumber that lasted only for a few moments. I woke up to find myself a totally different man, reassured, at peace with everything around me. It was a profound feeling that set me at ease. I simply cannot tell how it all happened, or how this whole transformation took place. After this experience, I have come to appreciate what happened at Badr and Uḥud, not merely mentally, but by my whole being. I go through this whole experience again, not merely visualize it. I see in it God's hand at work, and I am reassured.

God's Support in All Forms

This slumber and reassurance were part of the reinforcement God granted to the Muslim host at Badr. "*He made slumber fall upon you, as an assurance from Him.*" (Verse 11) The wording here is very significant; "fall upon you", "slumber", "assurance" are all words that impart a feeling of confidence and friendliness. The *sūrah* paints the complete picture and highlights the great value of that moment which separated two opposite situations experienced by the Muslim host.

The water or the rain was, then, another form of support given to the Muslim fighters. A report by ʿAbdullāh ibn ʿAbbās tells the story as follows: "When the Prophet marched towards Badr, he and his Companions stopped at a barren area with the unbelievers closer to the wells. The Muslims were apparently exhausted. Satan began to whisper into their ears trying to create doubts and suspicions. He said: 'How can you claim that God is your patron and His Messenger is among you, when the idolaters have beaten you to the water to the extent that you now offer your prayers when you are in the state of ceremonial impurity?' God sent rain pouring down which enabled the Muslims to drink and cleanse themselves. God thus removed Satan's filth from them. The sandy area where they were became much firmer to enable people and animals to walk easily. They marched towards their enemies. God then supported His Messenger with one thousand angels, with the angel Gabriel leading five hundred of them on one side, and the angel Michael leading another five hundred on the other side."

This was before the Prophet carried out the advice given him by his Companion, al-Ḥubāb ibn al-Mundhir, who suggested that they should encamp right at the main well of Badr and that they should dump the other wells. Ibn Kathīr reports: "It is well known that when the Prophet arrived at Badr, he encamped at the nearest well he found. Al-Ḥubāb ibn al-Mundhir came forward and asked him: 'Messenger of God, has God ordered you to encamp here so that we are not allowed to move further, or have you chosen this place as part of your strategy for the battle?' The Prophet told him that it was his own choice and strategy. Al-Ḥubāb then said: 'Messenger of God, this is not the proper place to encamp. Take us forward until we reach the source of water closest to them, and then we dump all the other wells. We can also fill the reservoirs so that we have water while they do not.' The Prophet acted on his advice."

On that night, then, and before al-Ḥubāb ibn al-Mundhir gave his advice, the Muslims were in this situation of which they are here reminded. The support they received was of a material and spiritual nature. In the desert, water is the source of life and a means to achieve victory. An army without water in the desert is bound to be demoralized even before the battle starts. Besides, there was this psychological uncertainty that came as a result of Satan's whispering, with the believers feeling uneasy about praying when they were in a state of ceremonial impurity and had no water to wash themselves. At that time, they had not been granted the concession of dry ablution, or *tayammum*. That concession was given in a later battle they fought in the fifth year of the Islamic calendar. In such a situation, worries and uncertainties abound. Satan may try to go through the door of faith in order to increase such worries. When people go into a battle experiencing worry and doubt of this type, they can easily be defeated. At this moment, support is very timely: "*He sent down water from the sky to cleanse you and to remove from you Satan's filth, to strengthen your hearts and steady your footsteps.*" (Verse 11) Thus, the spiritual support comes together with the material one. The worry is removed as water becomes abundant, and uncertainty is replaced by assurance after they had cleansed themselves. Their march is steadier as the land becomes firmer.

In addition to this, God inspired the angels to encourage the believers and promised to strike fear in the hearts of the unbelievers. He also commanded the angels to take an active part in the battle: "*Your Lord inspired the angels, saying: 'I am with you. So, give courage to the believers. I shall cast terror into the hearts of the unbelievers. Strike, then, their necks and strike off their every fingertip.'*" (Verse 12)

This is indeed the greatest aspect of this whole battle. It is the fact that God Almighty was with the angels in this battle, and the angels took part in it alongside the Muslim army. We must not lose sight of the importance of this fact by trying to find out how the angels took part. How many enemy soldiers did they kill? Or how they killed them? The great fact is that when the Muslim community takes action to establish God's faith in the land, their action is valued so highly as to deserve God's presence with the angels in battle and the angels' participation in it.

We believe that among God's creation there is a type called the angels. We know of their nature only what God, their Creator, has told us. We cannot fathom how they participated in the Muslim victory at Badr except in as far as the fact is stated in the Qur'ān. Their Lord inspired them saying that He was with them and commanded them to encourage the believers. They complied, because they always do what they are commanded. We, however, do not know how they fulfilled this task. God also ordered them to strike the unbelievers over their necks and strike off their fingertips. So they did all this, but in a fashion unknown to us. Knowledge of all this is merely a detail of knowing the nature of the angels, but we know of this nature only what God has chosen to tell us. Furthermore, God promised to strike terror in the hearts of the unbelievers, and this was certainly the case because God always fulfils His promises. However, we do not know how this was done. It is God who is the Creator, and He knows His creation. Indeed, God may cause a split between a person and his heart, and He is closer to any person than his own jugular vein.

To try to go into the details of all these matters is contrary to the serious nature of this faith and its practical approach. But these questions have featured prominently among the concerns of different Muslim schools and scholastic theology generally in later generations when people were no longer seriously interested in this faith. Instead, they pursued intellectual luxury. Reflection on the great significance of God's presence with the angels in the battle and the active participation of the angels in the battle itself is much more beneficial.

At the end we have a statement clarifying the reality beyond the battle and the rule that shapes events to bring about victory or defeat: "*This is because they have defied God and His Messenger. Whoever defies God and His Messenger [will find out that] God is severe in retribution.*" (Verse 13) It is not by mere coincidence that God has granted support to the Muslim army and has stricken terror into the hearts of its enemies and commanded the angels to fight them in support of the Muslims. All this took place because they had defied God and His Messenger, adopting a line of action and an attitude that was in opposition to those of God and His Messenger, trying to prevent the code of living God had revealed from being established.

"*Whoever defies God and His Messenger [will find out that] God is severe in retribution.*" (Verse 13) He is certainly able to punish severely those who defy Him and His Messenger. They are too weak to show any resistance.

This is an established rule, not merely a coincidence. Whenever a Muslim community takes active steps to establish the principle of God's oneness and to implement His message, it will be granted victory against any enemy that opposes it in defiance of God and His Messenger. Terror will be stricken in the hearts of those engaged in such defiance, and they will end up in defeat as long as the Muslim community holds on to its principles, relying totally on God, certain of His support.

At the end of the scene, the unbelievers who defied God and His Messenger are told directly that the terror they felt and the defeat they experienced were not all. The whole question of this faith, its implementation, and the opposition to it are not of the concerns of this world alone. It goes further, extending to the life to come. Its dimensions go far beyond our immediate world: "*This is for you, [enemies of God]! Taste it, then. The unbelievers shall be made to suffer the torment of fire.*" (Verse 14) This is the real end. That torment is incomparable to what they had already experienced of terror, defeat and the striking off of their necks and their fingertips.

Thus far, the *sūrah* has reminded the Muslims of the conditions in which the Battle of Badr took place, showing them different scenes of the battle itself and what preceded it. It makes clear to them that at every step, it was God who dictated events and moved them in the direction He wanted, in order to accomplish His purpose.

Except for Tactical Reasons

Now that the decisive victory has been attributed to its true factors: God's planning, support, the believers' reliance on Him alone and acceptance of whatever eventuality He determines – now with all minds visualizing the whole event, and all hearts ready for the best response, the believers are given an order to remain steady whenever they meet unbelievers in battle. They must never run away, since victory or defeat are determined by God's will and the factors contributing to either of them are different from the factors people may see. The whole battle and all its events are of God's own making and planning: "*Believers, when you meet in battle those who disbelieve, do not turn your backs to them in flight. Anyone who turns his back to them on that day, except when manoeuvring for battle or in an endeavour to join another troop, shall incur God's wrath, and hell shall be his abode: how vile a journey's end.*" (Verses 15–16)

These verses begin with a strong warning, a fearsome threat. Should the believers face their enemies who may in essence present themselves in a great show of power, they must not, under any circumstances, turn away, except for tactical reasons. These may include choosing a better position, carrying out a more effective plan, joining another group of believers, or moving to another Muslim stronghold in order to resume the fight. Deserters and people who turn away in flight deserve the most terrible double punishment of incurring God's wrath and being thrown into hell.

Some scholars have expressed the view that this ruling applies only to the people of Badr, or to a battle in which the Prophet himself took part. But the overwhelming majority of scholars have emphasized its general application. They consider fleeing from battle as one of the gravest sins. In the two *Ṣaḥīḥ*, the most authentic collections of the Prophet's *ḥadīth*, al-Bukhārī and Muslim relate, on the authority of Abū Hurayrah, that God's Messenger says: "Steer away from the seven ruining sins." When he was asked which these were, the Prophet answered: "Associating partners with God, black magic, killing a human being except for a legitimate cause, devouring usury, pilfering an orphan's property, running away from battle and falsely accusing chaste believing women of adultery."

In his scholarly work, *Aḥkām al-Qur'ān* or Qur'ānic Rulings, al-Jaṣṣāṣ, a leading Ḥanafī scholar, explains in detail the different views on this point. It is useful to quote here what he says:

> God says: "*Anyone who turns his back to them on that day, except when manoeuvring for battle or in an endeavour to join another troop...*" (Verse 16) Abū Naḍrah mentions that this statement applies only to the Battle of Badr. Abū Naḍrah argues that had they turned away on that day, they could only have joined the unbelievers, because there were no other Muslims on that day. But this statement is not particularly accurate, because there were numerous Muslims in Madinah who were not ordered by the Prophet to join the army. They had not gone out with the Prophet because they believed that no battle was imminent and the whole affair would merely be a case of intercepting a trade caravan. The Prophet was joined by those who were ready and quick to move out with him in the circumstances. Hence, Abū Naḍrah's view that there were no other Muslims at that time and that they would have only joined the unbelievers is wrong.
>
> It has also been said that they were not permitted to join any other group on that day because the Prophet was with them and they were not allowed to leave him, as God says in the Qur'ān: "*It is not open for the people of Madinah and those Bedouins living*

nearby to hold back from following God's Messenger or to care for their own selves more than for him." (9: 120) This shows that they could not let God's Messenger down or abandon him, even though God had taken it upon Himself to protect him as He clearly states in the Qur'ān: "*God will protect you from all men.*" (5: 67) That was imperative on them, whether their enemies were small or large in number. Moreover, the Prophet himself was the rallying force for the Muslims on that day. Anyone turning away could only do so for tactical reasons, in an endeavour to join a company of believers. On the day of Badr, they could only join the Prophet. Ibn 'Umar reports: "I was with an army when we had a quick round before returning to Madinah. People accused us of fleeing, but the Prophet said: 'I am your group.' This means that a person who is in a position away from the Prophet and wants to turn away from the unbelievers could only do so in order to join the Prophet. If the Prophet was in the army, then there was no group other than his. In such a case, no turning away was possible. Al-Ḥasan says that this verse, beginning with "*Anyone who turns his back to them*", defined the situation for the people of Badr. God says in the Qur'ān: "*Those of you who turned away on the day when the two hosts met in battle, Satan caused them to slip only in consequence of something that they themselves had done.*" (3: 155) This is due to the fact that they turned away leaving the Prophet in battle. Similarly, on the day of Ḥunayn, they deserved God's punishment for leaving the Prophet and turning away: "*On the Day of Ḥunayn, when you took pride in your great numbers and they proved of no avail whatever to you. The earth, despite its vastness, became too narrow for you and you turned back, retreating.*" (9: 25) This was then the ruling applicable when they were with the Prophet fighting any enemy that mustered small or large forces.

In another verse, God says: "*Prophet, urge the believers to fight. If there are twenty steadfast men among you, they will overcome two hundred, and if there are a hundred of you, they will defeat a thousand of those who disbelieve, for those are devoid of understanding.*" (Verse 65) This applied perhaps – and God knows best – to a situation when the Prophet was with them. A company of twenty had to fight two hundred, remaining steadfast. If the hostile force was greater than that, then they were allowed to try to join another group in order to resume the fight. But this was later abrogated by the Qur'ānic statement: "*Now God has lightened your burden, for He knows that you are weak. So, if there are a hundred steadfast men among you, they will overcome two hundred, and if there are a thousand of you they will, by God's will, defeat two thousand.*" (Verse 66)

According to Ibn ʿAbbās: It was a commandment that one man must not turn away in flight if he was facing ten enemy soldiers. This was then reduced by the Qur'ānic verse, "*God has lightened your burden, for He knows that you are weak.*" You are now commanded that one hundred may not flee from two hundred unbelievers. Ibn ʿAbbās states: "If one man runs away from two enemy soldiers, then he is a deserter. If he flees when he faces three, he is not." Desertion refers to turning away in flight as mentioned in the Qur'ānic verse.

The verse makes it compulsory for a Muslim soldier to fight when he faces two unbelievers. If they are more than two, then it is permissible for a single soldier to try to join a company of Muslims that may give him support. If he wants to join a group of Muslims who will not support him in the fight, he is under the threat mentioned in the Qur'ānic verse: "*Anyone who turns his back to them on that day, except when manoeuvering for battle or in an endeavour to join another troop, shall incur God's wrath.*" (Verse 16) For this reason the Prophet says: "I am company to every Muslim." When ʿUmar ibn al-Khaṭṭāb heard that Abū ʿUbayd ibn Masʿūd fought hard without thinking of retreat until he was killed, ʿUmar said: "May God have mercy on Abū ʿUbayd. Had he joined me, I would have been company for him." When Abū ʿUbayd's fellow soldiers arrived, ʿUmar said to them: "I am your company." He did not take issue with them over their retreat.

This ruling is confirmed in our school of law, [i.e. the Ḥanafī school], and it remains in force unless the Muslim army is 12,000 in number, in which case they may not flee from a force which is more than double their size, except for tactical reasons. They may move to a position where they can engage their enemy better, or may take a different step that does not constitute fleeing from battle, or join a group of Muslims who will fight with them. Muḥammad ibn al-Ḥasan (a leading Ḥanafī scholar) mentions

> that if a Muslim army is 12,000 in number, they may not turn away in flight, although their enemy may be much greater. There is no difference among our scholars (i.e. Ḥanafī scholars) on this point. In support of this view, a *ḥadīth* reported by Ibn ʿAbbās is cited in which the Prophet is quoted as saying: "The best group of friends is four, and the best expedition is 400, and the best host is 4,000. An army of 12,000 shall not suffer on account of inferior numbers, and shall not be defeated." In another version: "An army of 12,000 shall not be defeated if they are truly united." Mālik was asked: "Is it open for us not to join a battle against those abandoning God's law in favour of a different law?" Mālik answered: "If you have 12,000 with you, you may not stay behind. Otherwise, staying behind is permissible." The person who put the question to him was ʿAbdullāh ibn ʿUmar ibn ʿAbd al-ʿAzīz ibn ʿAbdullāh ibn ʿUmar. This confirms what is stated by Muḥammad ibn al-Ḥasan. The authentic reports attributed to the Prophet with regard to an army of 12,000 constitute a basic principle in this respect. An army of such numbers may not turn away in flight from any enemy, even though that enemy may be several times their number, because the Prophet says: "If they are truly united." God has commanded believers to be always truly united.[3]

Ibn al-ʿArabī also comments on this difference of views. He writes in his book bearing the same title, *Aḥkām al-Qur'ān* or Qur'ānic Rulings:

> People have disputed whether the turning away in flight applies only to the Battle of Badr or to all battles Muslims may fight at any time until the Day of Judgement. Abū Saʿīd al-Khudrī reports that this order applies only to the Battle of Badr, when the Muslims had no other company or troop other than God's Messenger. This view is supported by Nāfiʿ, al-Ḥasan, Qatādah, Yazīd ibn Ḥabīb and al-Ḍaḥḥāk. Ibn ʿAbbās and all other scholars are of the view that this Qur'ānic verse applies at all times until the Day of Judgement. Those who have taken a different view, saying that it

3. Al-Jaṣṣāṣ, Aḥmad Ibn ʿAlī, *Aḥkām al-Qur'ān*. Dār al-Kitāb al-ʿArabī, Beirut, Vol. III, pp. 47–48

> applies to Badr only have misinterpreted the statement, "*Anyone who turns his back to them on that day*," making the phrase 'on that day' a reference to the Day of Badr only. But this is not so. It refers to the day of battle whenever a battle takes place. In evidence we take the fact that this Qur'ānic verse was revealed after the Battle of Badr was over with all that it involved. The Prophet is authentically quoted to list fleeing from battle as one of the worst cardinal sins. In itself, this *ḥadīth* should settle all disputes and make the ruling absolutely clear. We have clarified how the confusion arose that led some scholars to think that it applied to Badr only.[4]

For our part, we support Ibn 'Abbās's view and all other scholars as reported by Ibn al-'Arabī. To flee from battle deserves such condemnation because of the magnitude of its serious consequences on the one hand, and because it has a bearing on the very question of having faith. A believer should be firm and resolute, able to resist any force on earth, since he believes that God's power can overcome all powers. If a believer's heart experiences a tremor at a moment of danger, such a tremor should not go as far as making him flee from battle. The moment of anyone's death is determined by God alone. Hence, no believer may flee from battle fearing for his life. This should not constitute too much of a burden for anyone. A believer is a human being who encounters an enemy, who, in turn, is a human being. Hence, they are of the same nature. The believer, however, has the advantage of relying on the overpowering might of God Himself. Moreover, he is under God's care while he is alive, and he entrusts himself to God's care if he attains martyrdom. This means that in all situations he is stronger than his enemy who defies God and His Messenger. Hence this absolute ruling: "*Anyone who turns his back to them on that day, except when manoeuvering for battle or in an endeavour to join another troop, shall incur God's wrath, and hell shall be his abode: how vile a journey's end.*" (Verse 16)

We should reflect a little here on the mode of expression and its remarkable connotations. The statements, "*Do not turn your backs to*

4. Ibn al-'Arabī, Muḥammad Ibn 'Abdullāh, *Aḥkām al-Qur'ān*. Dār al-Ma'rifah, Beirut, Vol. II, pp. 843–844

them in flight", and, "*Anyone who turns his back to them on that day*", portray a sense of defeat as it manifests itself physically. They also add a strong condemnation as the whole action is shown to be repugnant, particularly the image of turning one's back to one's enemies. Then we have the expression, "*shall incur God's wrath.*" In the Arabic text, there is a connotation that a defeated person is carrying with him God's wrath right to his abode in hell, which is an awful end to his journey. Thus these connotations add to the sense and effectiveness of the statement. Together they spread a feeling of abhorrence of the very act of fleeing from battle.

God's Planning and Human Implementation

The *sūrah* then moves on to show God's hand as He dictates events, killing the enemies of the believers, and throwing whatever is thrown. The believers, nevertheless, receive the reward, because God wants to perfect His grace on them, helping them to pass well the test He has set for them, and to reward them well for it: "*It was not you who slew them, but it was God who slew them. When you threw [a handful of dust], it was not your act, but God's, so that He might put the believers through a fair test of His own making. Indeed, God hears all and knows all.*" (Verse 17)

Many authentic reports explain that the throwing mentioned here refers to the handful of dust the Prophet threw in the direction of the unbelievers, saying "Ugly are those faces! Ugly are those faces!'" The dust hit the faces of those God had predetermined to be killed. But the Qur'ānic statement has a much wider import. It refers to God's planning of the whole affair, beyond the actions of the Prophet and his Companions. This is the reason for following it with God's words: "*So that He might put the believers through a fair test of His own making.*" (Verse 17) This means that God guides the believers to prove themselves by going through the test with great determination, so that He grants them victory through it and gives them reward for it. This is the sort of abounding grace that God bestows on His servants.

"*Indeed, God hears all and knows all.*" (Verse 17) He listens to your appeals and knows your situation. He makes of you a means to accomplish His purpose when He is certain that you are dedicated to His cause. He grants you victory and reward, just as He bestowed both on you at Badr.

"That is so; it is God who shall make feeble the schemes of the unbelievers." (Verse 18) This follows on the heels of the first aspect of grace. God's planning does not end by letting you kill your enemies with your own hands, hitting them with what His Messenger threw at them. Nor is it over with granting you strength to enable you to make a good showing in the test He set for you, and to reward you handsomely for it. He adds to all that the frustration of the designs of the unbelievers. There is no room, then, for fear or defeat. Nor is there any reason for the believers to turn their backs to the unbelievers in flight.

These statements are related to all the circumstances of the battle. Since it is God who killed the unbelievers, threw everything at them, helped the believers to put up this good show, and frustrated the designs of the unbelievers, then how come that they dispute over the spoils of war? The whole battle was conducted according to God's plan and by His will. Their role in it was merely to act as a manifestation of God's planning and His will.

Much Power, Little Avail

When the *sūrah* has clearly stated that God is certain to make feeble the unbelievers' scheming it directs its address to certain people among the unbelievers. Just before the start of battle, those unbelievers sought a divine judgement, praying that the party which they described as more astray, fabricating what was unheard of and severing ties of kinship should end in miserable defeat. That was exactly Abū Jahl's prayer, seeking God's judgement. Defeat was then the outcome of the unbelievers' endeavours. Now they are addressed directly and their prayer for a judgement is decried. They are assured that what happened at Badr was the rule not the exception. Their forces, numerous as they may be, will avail them of nothing, because it is a consistent rule that God will always be on the side of the believers: *"If you were seeking a judgement, then a judgement has come to you. If you desist, it will be best for you; and if you revert to your erring ways, We will also be back [with Our punishment]. Your host, numerous as it may be, shall avail you nothing; for God is with the believers."* (Verse 19)

You have sought God's judgement between the Muslims and yourselves, and you have prayed to Him to destroy the party which was in error and which severed ties of kinship. God has responded, and defeat was your lot, as you have requested. Now you know for certain which party is more erring and which severs ties of kinship.

With facts giving clear pointers, they are invited to abandon their rejection of the truth and their hostile attitude to Muslims, as well as their defiance of God and His Messenger: "*If you desist, it will be best for you.*" (Verse 19) These are words of persuasion coupled with a clear warning: "*And if you revert to your erring ways, We will also be back [with Our punishment].*" The outcome is well known and cannot be changed by any gathering of forces and equipment no matter how great these are: "*Your host, numerous as it may be, shall avail you nothing.*" (Verse 19) Of what use can any great force be, when God is decidedly on the side of the believers? "*For God is with the believers*". (Verse 19) Such a battle will never be even. On one side there will be the believers who have God Himself with them. On the other, there will be the unbelievers who have only human beings fighting with them. The outcome of such a battle is a foregone conclusion.

The unbelievers among the Arabs were well aware of these facts. Their knowledge of God was neither ambiguous nor superficial as those influenced by the generalizations of history books tend to think. Disbelief among the Arabs did not take the form of a denial of God's existence or total ignorance of the truth. It was mostly represented in the fact that they did not submit totally to Him and derived their laws and their code of living from sources other than Him. That was certainly inconsistent with their acknowledgement of God and their knowledge of Him as the Supreme Lord.

When the Quraysh army was moving across the desert, a man called Khufāf ibn Aymā' ibn Raḥḍah al-Ghifārī, or his father, sent them a gift consisting of a number of camels he had slaughtered for food. He also sent them a message that he was prepared to supply them with equipment and fighters. They only had to ask. They sent him this reply with his son: "You have done more than your duty and we are very grateful to you. If we are going to fight human beings, we are certainly a match for them. But if we are going to fight God, as Muḥammad alleges, then no force may stand up to God."

As we reported earlier (p. 43), al-Akhnas ibn Sharīq, an unbeliever, said to his clan of Zuhrah: "God has spared you the loss of your property and saved your man, Maḥraqah ibn Nawfal, etc." Likewise, Abū Jahl who is described by the Prophet as the Pharaoh of the Arabs, said: "Our Lord, destroy this day the party which is more guilty of severing ties of kinship and fabricating what is false." When 'Utbah ibn Rabī'ah sent him a man to persuade him not to fight, Abū Jahl, said: "No. By God we shall not return until God has made a judgement between us and Muḥammad."

These examples show their concept of God's nature and how it was present in their minds on all serious occasions. It was not a question of total ignorance of God or lack of awareness that He is overpowering or that He can make a complete judgement between the two parties. It was a question of associating partners with Him. This was represented initially through deriving their code of living and their laws from sources other than God. The same type of disbelief is practised today by people who think themselves to be Muslims, following the faith of the Prophet Muḥammad (peace be upon him). Indeed, the non-believers of Makkah thought that they were following the faith of the Prophet Abraham. It was that misguided belief which prompted Abū Jahl himself to seek that judgement, praying to God to destroy the party which was deeper in error and more guilty of severing ties of kinship.

It is true that they worshipped idols, but they never attributed to those idols any concept of godhead similar to that which they recognized as belonging to God. The Qur'ān explains their concepts of such idols and the basis of their rituals of worship which they offered to them: "*Those who took for themselves patrons other than God (would say): We only worship them so that they may bring us closer to God.*'" (39: 3) This then was the basis of their idolatry: they felt that their idols could intercede with God on their behalf. But the essence of their polytheistic beliefs were not these. Nor was it enough for any of them to simply abandon such a concept of intercession by those idols in order to be a Muslim. Otherwise, the people known as *al-Ḥunafā'*, or the pure, who dissociated themselves from the worship of those idols and believed in God alone, would have been considered Muslims. But they were not. Islam comprises conceptual beliefs, the offering of worship to God and attributing all sovereignty to Him alone. Those who do not acknowledge Him as the overall sovereign, wherever and whenever they may happen to live, are polytheist, even though they acknowledge that there is no deity other than God and offer worship to Him. When they stop at that, they are the same as those people known as *al-Ḥunafā'* whom no one describes as Muslims. People become Muslims when they complete the circle and add to their concepts and worship the acknowledgement of God's sovereignty which entails a rejection of any law, set-up, value or tradition that is not derived from God. This is the only true meaning of Islam because it is the true import of the declaration that there is no deity other than God and that Muḥammad is His Messenger. Moreover, those people who have this understanding of the declaration must join a single movement under an Islamic leadership that separates itself from the society of *jāhiliyyah* and its leadership.

This must be fully understood by those people who want to be Muslims so that they are not deceived by the thought that they are Muslims in belief and practice. This is not sufficient for people to become Muslims unless they acknowledge that all sovereignty belongs to God alone. This is represented in practice by rejecting all claims that sovereignty belongs to anyone else and until they have no loyalty whatsoever to *jāhiliyyah* societies and their leaderships.

Many good-natured and well-meaning people who want to be true Muslims fall prey to this trick. It is important, therefore, that they make certain of the only true form of Islam. They should also know that the idolatrous Arabs were no different from them. They knew who God was and made of their idols partners who could intercede with Him on their behalf. Thus, their true disbelief centred around sovereignty and to whom it belonged.

Moreover, the Muslim community which strives to re-establish this religion in daily life must be fully and clearly aware of this fact. They must also make it decisively clear to all people. This is the starting point. If an Islamic movement deviates from this fact at any moment, it is bound to go astray, even though it may have abundance of sincerity, perseverance, and determination to fulfil its duties.

Response to a Call to Life

Earlier, the *sūrah* mentioned the believers making it clear that God is on their side. Now they are addressed repeatedly to encourage them to obey God and His Messenger and to warn them against turning away from Him. Should they do so they will be in the same position as those who hear God's revelations being recited and who pay no heed to them. They are deaf and dumb although they may have ears to hear with and tongues to speak with. These are the vilest of all creatures on earth because they are not guided by what they hear.

Believers, obey God and His Messenger, and do not turn away from him now that you have heard [his message]. Do not be like those who say: 'We have heard,' while they do not listen. Indeed, the worst of all creatures, in God's sight, are the deaf and dumb who are devoid of reason. If God had known of any good in them, He would certainly have made them hear. But even if He were to make them hear, they would have turned away and refused to listen. (Verses 20–23)

The believers are asked to obey God and His Messenger and not to turn away when they listen to His revelations. This address follows a number of inspiring introductions and an account of the events of the battle in which God's hand was clearly seen at work as He determined the course of events and provided help and support. All this reassured the believers that God was with them and He was certain to foil the schemes of the unbelievers. Thereafter the only proper course of action was for them to listen and obey. To turn away from God's Messenger and pay no heed to his orders after all that had happened would clearly be seen as totally unbecoming of anyone who has a mind to think and reflect.

The mention of animals occurs at its appropriate place. The Arabic term used here to refer to animals includes human beings because this is derived from the act of walking. Human beings also walk on earth. However, the term used here is most commonly used for quadruped animals. Hence, its usage gives clear connotations so as to make those who are 'deaf, dumb and devoid of reason' appear like animals. Indeed, they are the worst type of animals. Animals do have ears, but they only hear unintelligible words, and they have tongues but they can only make unintelligible noises. Yet by their nature, animals are guided to what is needed for their lives. Those humans, on the other hand, do not make use of their faculty of understanding. As such, they are fittingly described in the Qur'ānic verse: "*The worst of all creatures, in God's sight, are the deaf and dumb who are devoid of reason.*" (Verse 22)

If God had known of any good in them, He would certainly have made them hear. (Verse 23)

This means that He would have made their minds receive well what they hear with their ears. But He – limitless is He in His Glory – does not know of any goodness in them or any desire to follow proper guidance. They have perverted their natural receptive faculty. Therefore, God does not open their hearts which they have shut down or repair their nature which they have perverted. Even if God made them understand the truth of what is being presented to them, they would not open their hearts to it and they would not respond to what they understood. "*But even if He were to make them hear, they would have turned away and refused to listen.*" (Verse 23) A person may understand something with his mind, but he may still keep his heart closed, unresponsive. Even if God were to make these people understand, they would turn away and refuse to respond. A positive response is the outcome of proper listening. Many are those who may understand or choose to keep their hearts closed, unresponsive.

A further address is made to the believers calling on them to respond to God and His Messenger, providing encouragement for a positive response and warning them against turning away. They are reminded of God's blessings which they have enjoyed when they responded to God and His Messenger. "*Believers, respond to the call of God and the Messenger when he calls you to that which will give you life, and know that God comes in between a man and his heart, and that to Him you shall all be gathered. Beware of temptation that does not lure only those among you who are wrongdoers. Know that God is severe in retribution.*" (Verses 24–25)

God's Messenger (peace be upon him) calls on them to follow what would certainly give them life. It is a call to life in its fullness, with all its connotations. He calls on them to believe in a faith that keeps hearts and minds alive, free from the restrictions of *jāhiliyyah*, ignorance and superstition, the pressures of legends, misconceptions and submission to superficial causes and inevitabilities. It is a faith that frees them from submission to anyone other than God and from being humiliated or subjugated by human beings or desires.

God's Messenger also calls on them to implement a divine law that proclaims man's freedom. In itself, this imparts a great honour to man because he will then believe in something that comes from God directly, and before which all human beings are equal. There is no room for the tyranny of a single person over a whole community, or a race or nation over another. All human beings are made free, enjoying equal status before the law that has been formulated and laid down by God, for the benefit of mankind. God's Messenger also calls on them to adopt a code of living and a set of thoughts and beliefs that set them free from every bondage other than checks of nature established by God. It is He who created man and knows what He has created. These checks are meant to preserve the constructive potential of man and make the best use of it, without wasting any part of it or deviating from its constructive operation.

He also calls on them to have power and to feel exalted through their faith and constitution, having full confidence in their religion and their reward. This will enable them to fulfil their duty, to take appropriate initiative aiming at the liberation of the human race as a whole, breaking the chains of submission to creatures in order to acknowledge submission to God alone. Thus the honoured position of man which tyrants have taken away will be retrieved and re-established.

God's Messenger further calls on them to strive for God's cause so that the position of God as the Supreme Lord in this world and in human life will be re-established. All claims to Godhead would thus be refuted. Usurpers of God's authority, sovereignty and power would be chased away, until they have submitted to God's sovereignty. When this takes place all submission is acknowledged to God alone. If believers die when they strive in this way, they achieve martyrdom. A new life is thus imparted to them.

This is in a nutshell what God's Messenger calls on them to do. This is indeed a call to life in the full sense of the word. This religion is a complete way of living, not a mere concept of belief. It is a practical method that allows life to flourish and prosper. Hence, it is a call to life in all its connotations, forms and aspects. The Qur'ān sums up all this in a few inspiring words: "*Believers, respond to the call of God and the Messenger when he calls you to that which will give you life.*" (Verse 24) Make this response willingly, with obedience. After all, God is able to force you to follow His guidance if He so desires.

"*Know that God comes in between a man and his heart.*" (Verse 24) This is an awesome picture of God's power and its subtle operation.

He thus forces a split between a human being and his heart and mind, making that heart His property, so that He directs it wherever He wishes. The person himself will be totally unable to influence the heart that beats within him. This is certainly an awe-inspiring image that our hearts can contemplate as we listen to it in the Qur'ān. Human expression, however, cannot describe its effects on our hearts and how we respond to it. But the ultimate message of this statement should always keep us on the alert, so that we watch our feelings and guard against any tendency that may lead us to slip, or any fleeting thought that may push us along the way to disobedience of God. We must always be on guard so that we maintain the path that earns God's pleasure and not deviate from it during any moment of self-indulgence or negligence.

God's Messenger (peace be upon him) who was immune to sin often used to say in his supplication: "My Lord. You are the One who changes people's hearts. Make my heart constant in following Your faith." Compared to this, what should the attitude of ordinary people be when they are neither given a message, nor granted immunity to sinful temptation?

A believer is bound to feel his heart shiver as he contemplates this image, looking at his own heart placed in God's own hand, while he himself has no power to influence it in any way, although it remains inside him beating all the time.

This image is presented to the believers as they are called upon to respond to God and His Messenger when He calls on them to accept what will give them life. He is thus telling them that God can make them give the response He wants and force them to follow His guidance. But God honours them by giving them the choice and calling on them to respond willingly, so that they can earn a reward from Him, and exercise their own will which enhances their position and brings them up to the level worthy of God's trust. This is the trust of following God's guidance and exercising the role He has assigned to them on earth, as He placed them in charge of it. When people do this, they exercise their freedom of choice on the basis of clear knowledge and well-defined objectives.

"*To Him you shall all be gathered.*" (Verse 24) You cannot escape Him, either in this world or in the Hereafter, because your hearts are in His hands and to Him you shall all be gathered. Nevertheless, He calls on you to respond to Him by your free choice to earn His reward. A forced response is not worthy of man.

Victory Coming on the Heels of Hardship

They are then warned against adopting a negative attitude to *jihād*, or making a negative response to the call to life, or refraining from the fulfilment of their duty to change what is wrong, whatever form it may take: "*Beware of temptation that does not lure only those among you who are wrongdoers. Know that God is severe in retribution.*" (Verse 25) A community that allows a section of its members to be unjust will be guilty of injustice or wrongdoing. When a community does not stand up to wrongdoers, when it does not take any positive steps to punish transgressors, it deserves to share in the punishment of those wrongdoers and transgressors. It should be said that the worst type of wrongdoing is to abandon God's law which He has laid down to be implemented in human life. As a system, Islam has a serious outlook based on mutual help and solidarity within the community. Islam does not allow its followers to sit idle when injustice, corruption and wrongdoing continue on the rampage, let alone sees God's faith abandoned and His Godhead denied in order to be substituted by false claims. Such people cannot hope to be spared trial and temptation simply because they are good within themselves.

Since resistance to injustice and wrongdoing requires great sacrifices of lives and property, the Qur'ān reminds the first Muslim community of its own weakness, small numbers, the fear and persecution it endured. It also reminds those early Muslims of how God extended His shelter to them and granted them security and good provision. It must never, then, hesitate to respond to the type of life to which God's Messenger calls it, or to meet the responsibilities of this life that ensures its dignity, freedom and independence: "*Remember when you were few and helpless in the land, fearful lest people do away with you: how He sheltered you, strengthened you with His support and provided you with many good things so that you might be grateful.*" (Verse 26)

You must remember this in order to be absolutely certain that God's Messenger calls you to that which will give you life. Remember it so that you do not ever feel reluctant to resist injustice of any type or form. Remember the days when you were weak and afraid. These were the days before God instructed you to fight the unbelievers, and before His Messenger called on you to face the mighty host in spite of your reluctance. Reflect on your situation after you have responded to this call and how you are now enjoying victory, God's reward, and the many good things He has provided for you. When you reflect on all this, you will then express your gratitude and gain further reward for that gratitude.

The *sūrah* paints a very powerful image of their inferior numbers and strength, as well as their worry and fear: "*fearful lest people do away with you.*" (Verse 26) The Arabic expression emphasizes the connotations of worry, apprehension and fearful expectation that we can almost see their worried features, restless eyes and clear apprehension.

However, a transformation takes place and we have a scene of security, strength, victory and enjoyable provision, all granted by God who has extended His protection to them: "*How He sheltered you, strengthened you with His support and provided you with many good things.*" (Verse 26) Coupled with this is a directive to them to demonstrate their gratitude in order to earn more reward: "*So that you might be grateful.*" (Verse 26) Who can contemplate this great transformation and decline to respond to a call to a secure life that enjoys strength and affluence? This is the call of the noble Prophet who conveys God's message. Who can enjoy such a transformation without showing his gratitude to God for all His grace, when both scenes of weakness and strength, worry and security are held up in front of his eyes?

Yet those people actually lived both situations. They are reminded of their past and present. Hence they appreciated fully what the Qur'ān said.

The Muslim community which strives today to re-establish this faith in human life may not have gone through both stages or experienced both states. The Qur'ān, nevertheless, describes this transformation to this and every Muslim community. If a Muslim community finds itself in the stage of weakness such as that described in the Qur'ān: "*Remember when you were few and helpless in the land, fearful lest people do away with you,*" then it will do well to respond to the call to life conveyed by God's Messenger. It can await with certainty the fulfilment of God's promise. He fulfilled it to the first Muslim community and He has promised to fulfil it to every community that follows the same course of action and makes the required sacrifices. It can then look forward to a situation to which the same description applies: "*He sheltered you, strengthened you with His support and provided you with many good things so that you might be grateful.*" (Verse 26) In all this, a Muslim community is actually dealing with God and His promise that will always come true. They need be in no doubt of that.

A Reassuring Criterion

Another address to the believers follows. God knows that property and children may discourage people from giving the proper response to such a call as they tend to enhance traits of fear and miserliness. Therefore, the Qur'ān highlights the fact that property and children may be the subject of a trial and warns against weaknesses that may cause people to fail in such a trial. They may feel too reluctant to respond to the call of *jihād*, or to shoulder the responsibilities of the trust God placed in them and the pledges of loyalty they have given. To refrain from the fulfilment of such duties is a betrayal of God and His Messenger, and a betrayal of the trust God has assigned to the Muslim community on earth. This trust requires the Muslim community to strive to make God's word triumphant, establish His Godhead as absolute, and maintain truth and justice. Coupled with this warning is a reminder of the great reward that God has in store for them which outweighs by far the value of property and children: "*Believers, do not betray God and the Messenger, nor knowingly betray the trust that has been reposed in you. Know that your worldly goods and your children are but a trial, and that with God there is a great reward.*" (Verses 27–28)

To abandon the duties God has assigned to the Muslim community is a betrayal of God and His Messenger. The basic issue in the Islamic faith is that of attributing Godhead purely and solely to God alone, following only what has been conveyed to us by His Messenger, the Prophet Muḥammad (peace be upon him). Throughout human history, people did not deny God altogether, but they mostly associated partners with Him. On a few occasions, this took the form of beliefs and worship, but the form of attributing sovereignty and authority to others beside Him was much more common. Therefore, the basic issue is not to make people believe in God, but to make such a belief pure of all distortion. The declaration that "there is no deity other than God" means that He is the sovereign over their life on earth, as they acknowledge His sovereignty in the universe. This is embodied in the Qur'ānic statement: "*It is He alone who is God in heaven and God on earth.*" (43: 84) This basic issue also entails that God's Messenger is the only source to convey what God wants of human beings, and this means that they must follow all his orders and directives. As this includes both conviction and action, the Muslim community, which has declared its belief in God, is warned against abandoning this whole issue. To do so is equal to betraying God and His Messenger.

Believers are also warned against betraying the trust they have accepted when they pledged their loyalty to God's Messenger and declared their acceptance of Islam. Islam means submission to God. This is not merely a verbal statement, but a complete code of living that must be implemented, even though such implementation faces numerous obstacles and difficulties. It is a code that aims to build human life on the basis of the declaration that there is no deity other than God. This means that people should submit only to their true Lord, and the whole community should accept His sovereignty and implement His law. The usurpers who tyrannize people and claim sovereignty for themselves must be taken to task. Right and justice must be maintained for all people. Human life must be built entirely on the basis of the divine constitution. All these are aspects of the trust God has placed in the Muslim community. Those who do not fulfil their trust actually betray their pledges to God and His Messenger.

Such tasks require sacrifices, perseverance and endurance. They also need freedom from the lure of property and children, so that people look up to the reward God has promised to those of His servants who are true to their trust. These are the ones who persevere in the face of adversity: "*Know that your worldly goods and your children are but a trial, and that with God there is a great reward.*" (Verse 28)

The Qur'ān addresses human beings on the basis of God's knowledge of their constitution, thoughts and action. He knows the human points of weakness, most prominent among which is love of property and children. Therefore, He reminds them that God has given them such worldly goods and children as a trial. They represent the strongest temptation in life. Hence, they are made the subject of a trial so that people can prove themselves and show whether they thank God well enough for His grace, or whether they give all their attention to their property and children and neglect their duty towards God: "*We test you all with evil and good by way of trial.*" (21: 35) This means that a trial may not be limited to difficulties and deprivation. It may take the form of affluence and blessings which may include property and children.

Their attentions are firstly drawn to this trial: "*Know that your worldly goods and children are but a trial.*" (Verse 28) When their hearts recognize the sort of test to which they are subjected, they are able to be on their guard so that they can pass the test easily. But God does not leave them without support or compensation. Although a human being may be alert, he or she may feel too weak to render the great sacrifices they may be called upon to make, particularly when such sacrifices involve one's property and children. Hence, we are promised what is greater and more everlasting, so that we are better able to endure the trial: "*With God there is a great reward.*" (Verse 28) It is He who has granted human beings their properties and children. But He has a reward much greater than these which He keeps in store for those who are able to rise above the lure of property and children. Therefore, no one should slacken in the fulfilment of their trust or in meeting the requirements of *jihād*. The promise of this reward is the type of support man is given, because God knows his weakness: "*Man has been created weak.*" (4: 28)

It is, then, a fully integrated code that comprises concepts of beliefs, directives and education, as well as duties and responsibilities. It is a code that has been devised by God who knows what suits man, because it is He who has created man: "*Does He not know what He has created when He is fully aware of all things?*" (67: 14)

The last address to the believers in this passage of the *sūrah* requires them to remain God-fearing. People cannot fulfil such heavy responsibilities unless they are fully aware of their true position, equipped with light that clears all misunderstandings and a determination that steadies their footsteps along the road they have to traverse. They can only have that when they have the sensitivity imparted by fearing God and benefit by the light He provides: "*Believers, if you remain God-fearing, He will give you a standard by which to discern the true from the false, and will wipe off your bad deeds, and forgive you. God's bounty is great indeed.*" (Verse 29)

This is, then, the equipment needed along the road. It is the sense of fearing God which makes people's hearts alive and keeps them fully alert. With God's light they can see clearly; their vision is not clouded by anything. Besides, fearing God is the proper equipment which ensures forgiveness for errors and sinful deeds. It provides reassurance and security, as well as great hope for a great bounty from God on the Day of Judgement when people discover that their actions have fallen short of expectation.

It is a fact of life that fearing God provides people with a standard to distinguish truth from falsehood. Like all facts of faith, however, this can only be appreciated by those who have experienced it. Description cannot begin to give a feeling of this fact to those who have no experience of it. Matters remain intermingled in people's minds and thoughts, and falsehood tries to always cling to the truth, particularly at points of divergence. Argument may silence objections, but cannot provide conviction, and polemics remain futile unless people are equipped with a sense of fearing God. When such a God-fearing sense is present, minds are open to see the truth, and the way ahead is defined. Thus, people can enjoy security and reassurance, and walk along with steady steps.

The truth itself may not be lost to human nature because God has made this nature responsive to the truth. But people's desires may force a separation between the truth and human nature. It is such desires that becloud people's vision and cause them to lose their way. People's desires are not overcome by argument, but by a sense of fearing God. Hence, the standard to discern truth from falsehood is all important to enlighten the way to those who wish to follow it. It is a priceless gift from God. God's grace, however, does not stop at that. God adds to it the forgiveness of sins as well as a great bounty. This can only be provided by the Lord whose grace is great, limitless, unceasing.

2

In Defiance of the Truth

Remember how the unbelievers were scheming against you, seeking to keep you in chains or have you slain or banished. Thus they plot and plan, but God also plans. God is above all schemers. (30)

وَإِذْ يَمْكُرُ بِكَ ٱلَّذِينَ كَفَرُوا۟ لِيُثْبِتُوكَ
أَوْ يَقْتُلُوكَ أَوْ يُخْرِجُوكَ ۚ وَيَمْكُرُونَ
وَيَمْكُرُ ٱللَّهُ ۖ وَٱللَّهُ خَيْرُ ٱلْمَٰكِرِينَ ﴿٣٠﴾

Whenever Our revelations are recited to them, they would say: 'We have heard them. If we wanted, we could certainly compose the like of this. This is nothing but fables of the ancients.' (31)

وَإِذَا تُتْلَىٰ عَلَيْهِمْ ءَايَٰتُنَا قَالُوا۟ قَدْ
سَمِعْنَا لَوْ نَشَآءُ لَقُلْنَا مِثْلَ هَٰذَآ ۙ
إِنْ هَٰذَآ إِلَّآ أَسَٰطِيرُ ٱلْأَوَّلِينَ ﴿٣١﴾

They would also say: 'God, if this be indeed Your revealed truth, then rain down upon us stones from the skies, or inflict grievous suffering on us.' (32)

وَإِذْ قَالُوا۟ ٱللَّهُمَّ إِن كَانَ هَٰذَا هُوَ
ٱلْحَقَّ مِنْ عِندِكَ فَأَمْطِرْ عَلَيْنَا
حِجَارَةً مِّنَ ٱلسَّمَآءِ أَوِ ٱئْتِنَا
بِعَذَابٍ أَلِيمٍ ﴿٣٢﴾

But God would not punish them while you were present in their midst, nor would God punish them when they may yet ask for forgiveness. (33)

وَمَا كَانَ ٱللَّهُ لِيُعَذِّبَهُمْ وَأَنتَ فِيهِمْ ۚ
وَمَا كَانَ ٱللَّهُ مُعَذِّبَهُمْ وَهُمْ
يَسْتَغْفِرُونَ ﴿٣٣﴾

What [plea] have they now that God should not punish them, when they debar other people from the Sacred Mosque, although they are not its rightful guardians? Its only guardians are those that fear God; but of this most of these [evildoers] are unaware. (34)

وَمَا لَهُمْ أَلَّا يُعَذِّبَهُمُ ٱللَّهُ وَهُمْ يَصُدُّونَ
عَنِ ٱلْمَسْجِدِ ٱلْحَرَامِ وَمَا كَانُوٓا۟
أَوْلِيَآءَهُۥٓ ۚ إِنْ أَوْلِيَآؤُهُۥٓ إِلَّا ٱلْمُتَّقُونَ
وَلَٰكِنَّ أَكْثَرَهُمْ لَا يَعْلَمُونَ ﴿٣٤﴾

Their prayers at the House are nothing but whistling and clapping of hands. Taste then this punishment in consequence of your disbelief. (35)

وَمَا كَانَ صَلَاتُهُمْ عِندَ ٱلْبَيْتِ
إِلَّا مُكَآءً وَتَصْدِيَةً ۚ فَذُوقُوا۟
ٱلْعَذَابَ بِمَا كُنتُمْ تَكْفُرُونَ ﴿٣٥﴾

The unbelievers spend their riches in order to turn people away from the path of God. They will go on spending them, and then this will become a source of intense regret for them; and then they shall be defeated. The unbelievers shall into hell be driven. (36)

إِنَّ ٱلَّذِينَ كَفَرُوا۟ يُنفِقُونَ أَمْوَٰلَهُمْ
لِيَصُدُّوا۟ عَن سَبِيلِ ٱللَّهِ ۚ فَسَيُنفِقُونَهَا
ثُمَّ تَكُونُ عَلَيْهِمْ حَسْرَةً ثُمَّ يُغْلَبُونَ ۗ
وَٱلَّذِينَ كَفَرُوٓا۟ إِلَىٰ جَهَنَّمَ
يُحْشَرُونَ ﴿٣٦﴾

God will separate the bad from the good. The bad He will place one upon another, so He may heap them all up together, and then cast them into hell. Those indeed are the losers. (37)

لِيَمِيزَ ٱللَّهُ ٱلْخَبِيثَ مِنَ ٱلطَّيِّبِ
وَيَجْعَلَ ٱلْخَبِيثَ بَعْضَهُۥ عَلَىٰ
بَعْضٍ فَيَرْكُمَهُۥ جَمِيعًا
فَيَجْعَلَهُۥ فِى جَهَنَّمَ ۚ أُو۟لَٰٓئِكَ
هُمُ ٱلْخَٰسِرُونَ ﴿٣٧﴾

Say to the unbelievers that if they desist, all that is past shall be forgiven them; but if they persist [in their erring ways], let them remember what happened to the like of them in former times. (38)

قُل لِّلَّذِينَ كَفَرُوٓا۟ إِن يَنتَهُوا۟ يُغْفَرْ
لَهُم مَّا قَدْ سَلَفَ وَإِن يَعُودُوا۟ فَقَدْ
مَضَتْ سُنَّتُ ٱلْأَوَّلِينَ ﴿٣٨﴾

Fight them until there is no more oppression, and all submission is made to God alone. If they desist, God is certainly aware of all they do. (39)

وَقَٰتِلُوهُمْ حَتَّىٰ لَا تَكُونَ فِتْنَةٌ
وَيَكُونَ ٱلدِّينُ كُلُّهُۥ لِلَّهِ ۚ فَإِنِ
ٱنتَهَوْا۟ فَإِنَّ ٱللَّهَ بِمَا يَعْمَلُونَ
بَصِيرٌ ﴿٣٩﴾

But if they turn away, know that God is your Lord Supreme. How splendid is this Lord Supreme, and how splendid is this giver of support. (40)

وَإِن تَوَلَّوْا۟ فَٱعْلَمُوٓا۟ أَنَّ ٱللَّهَ مَوْلَىٰكُمْ ۚ
نِعْمَ ٱلْمَوْلَىٰ وَنِعْمَ ٱلنَّصِيرُ ﴿٤٠﴾

Overview

The *sūrah* continues its address showing glimpses from the past and compares them with the present. It paints a scene showing a great gulf between the two situations for the benefit of the Muslim community which fought the battle and achieved a great victory. Thus Muslims are able to appreciate God's grace as manifested in what He had planned for them. Compared to that, all the spoils of war appear trivial and all sacrifices of little consequence.

The first passage described the general situation of the Muslims in Makkah, and also in Madinah before the battle. They were small in number, poor in equipment to the extent that they always feared their enemies could launch an onslaught against them. However, by God's grace all that was changed to a situation of strength, security and good provision. In the present passage, the *sūrah* describes the attitude of the unbelievers as they scheme against God's Messenger shortly before his departure to Madinah. They turn away from God's revelations, claiming that they could produce something similar if they so wished. Their attitude is so stubborn that they appeal for God's punishment to come sooner if Muḥammad's message from God is true. They prefer this to accepting it and following its guidance. The passage also includes a reference to the fact that they allocate their resources so as to turn people away from God's guidance and pool their money in order to launch an onslaught on God's Messenger. They are warned that all their efforts will end in total failure in this life, and then they will be driven to hell in the life to come. Loss in both worlds will be the result of their scheming and plotting.

Ultimately God directs the Prophet to confront the unbelievers with a choice between two alternatives. The first is that they stop their stubborn denial of the truth and their hostility to God and His Messenger, in which case God will forgive them all the sins and evil deeds they committed in the past. Alternatively, they continue with their attitude, in which case the fate that engulfed earlier communities will befall them too. They will then suffer the punishment God will determine for them.

God then commands the Muslims to fight them until all their power is destroyed. Thus, they will no longer be able to scheme against the Muslims and turn them away from their faith. The fight should continue until all Godhead is recognized throughout the earth as belonging to God alone, and all submission is made to Him. If they, then, give up and surrender, the Prophet (peace be upon him) will accept that from them. As for their thoughts and intentions, these are known to God. He will hold them accountable for these. However, if they turn away and continue with their campaign against the Muslim community, denying God's Lordship over the whole universe and refusing to submit to Him, the Muslims will then continue to fight them, trusting to God, their Master, who will provide them with His support.

A Scheme to Put an End to Islam

"*Remember how the unbelievers were scheming against you, seeking to keep you in chains or have you slain or banished. Thus they plot and plan, but God also plans. God is above all schemers.*" (Verse 30) This is a reminder of the situation in Makkah before things underwent a total transformation. This reminder serves also as a reassurance concerning the future, and draws attention to the wisdom behind the operation of God's will. Those Muslims who were the first to be addressed by the Qur'ān were fully aware of both situations, having experienced both. A reminder of their immediate past, as well as the fear and worry they experienced in those days, was sufficient to make them appreciate the safety and security of the present. They were aware of the unbelievers' scheming and what they planned to do with the Prophet. But not only their schemes were totally foiled; the unbelievers also suffered a humiliating defeat.

The unbelievers were considering alternatives: they thought of arresting God's Messenger and putting him in chains until he died, and they also considered killing him so that they could get rid of him once and for all. They also thought of driving him away, sending him into exile. Having considered the pros and cons of each of these alternatives, they chose to kill him, entrusting the task to a number of young men, each belonging to a different tribe, so that all tribes would share in his assassination. His own clan, Hāshim, would thus be unable to fight all the Arabs at once. They would then accept an offer of blood money and the whole matter would finish at that.

Commenting on this verse, Imām Aḥmad relates on the authority of 'Abdullāh ibn 'Abbās: "The Quraysh were in consultation one night in Makkah. Some of them suggested that the following morning they should put the Prophet in chains; but others suggested that they should kill him, while still others suggested that it was sufficient to have him banished. God revealed to the Prophet what they were scheming. That night, 'Alī slept in the Prophet's bed, while the Prophet (peace be upon him) moved out of the city until he reached the cave. The unbelievers spent the night watching 'Alī, but thinking him to be the Prophet. In the morning, they rushed to him, but instead they discovered 'Alī sleeping in his bed. They realized that their scheming had been foiled. They asked him: 'Where is your companion?' He answered: 'I do not know.' They traced his footsteps, but when they reached the mountain, they could no longer distinguish his trace. They climbed up the mountain and passed by the cave and saw that spiders had weaved their webs over its entrance. They thought that if he had gone into the cave, there would be no spider's web at the entrance. All in all he stayed in that cave three nights."

"*They plot and plan, but God also plans. God is above all schemers.*" (Verse 30) These words paint a picture that leaves a profound effect, particularly when we stretch our minds to imagine that meeting of Quraysh idolaters and how they held their consultations discussing alternatives, looking at the advantages and disadvantages of every suggestion that was put forward. Yet, God Almighty was fully aware of all they said and decided. He rendered their schemes futile, but they were totally unaware of His planning. The whole scene is full of acute irony. But it is at the same time an awe-inspiring scene. How could those human beings, weak and clumsy as they were, be compared to God? Could anything they devised be compared to His design, able as He is to accomplish every purpose of His? The Qur'ānic style paints this image in the same inimitable method of the Qur'ān, bringing it alive so that it shakes hearts and set minds thinking.

After this brief but highly suggestive reference to the scheming of the Quraysh and what they plotted against the Prophet, the *sūrah* moves on to describe the attitude of the unbelievers, their deeds, fabrications and claims. They went as far as claiming they were able to produce something similar to the Qur'ān, if only they chose to do so. At the same time, they described the Qur'ān as fables of the ancients. "*Whenever Our revelations are recited to them, they would say: 'We have heard them. If we wanted, we could certainly compose the like of this. This is nothing but fables of the ancients.*'" (Verse 31)

Feeble Manoeuvres

In his scholarly commentary on the Qur'ān, Ibn Kathīr mentions that the person who said this was al-Naḍr ibn al-Ḥārith:

> Al-Naḍr had been to the Persian Empire where he learnt Persian history and read accounts of past Persian kings, such as Rustam and Isfandayar. When he returned home, he saw God's Messenger (peace be upon him) after he had been entrusted with God's message, and he listened to him reciting the Qur'ān to people. When the Prophet finished talking to any group of people, al-Naḍr would sit with them and tell them stories of those ancient kings. He would then ask them: 'Tell me, by God, who tells better stories: I or Muḥammad?' Hence, when he fell captive on

the day of the Battle of Badr, the Prophet ordered that he should be executed. His order was carried out, thank God.[1]

The Prophet's Companion who had taken him prisoner was al-Miqdād ibn al-Aswad, as Ibn Jarīr al-Ṭabarī reports:

> The Prophet ordered the execution of ʿUqbah ibn Abī Muʿayṭ, Ṭuʿaymah ibn ʿAdiy and al-Naḍr ibn al-Ḥārith. When he ordered the killing of al-Naḍr, al-Miqdād, the Prophet's Companion who had taken him prisoner, said: 'Messenger of God, he is my prisoner!'[2] The Prophet said: 'He used to say things against God's book.' The Prophet again ordered al-Naḍr's execution. Al-Miqdād again said: 'Messenger of God, he is my prisoner!' The Prophet said: 'My Lord, enrich al-Miqdād with Your bounty.' Al-Miqdād commented that all he had hoped for was to have such a prayer by the Prophet.
>
> It was in reference to al-Naḍr and what he used to say about the Qur'ān that this verse was revealed: "*Whenever Our revelations are recited to them, they would say: 'We have heard them. If we wanted, we could certainly compose the like of this. This is nothing but fables of the ancients.*'" (Verse 31)[3]

The unbelievers' claims that the Qur'ān was nothing but the tales of ancient people is mentioned several times in the Qur'ān. In another *sūrah* we read: "*And they say: 'Fables of ancient times which he has caused to be written down, so that they might be read out to him in the morning and the evening.*'" (25: 5)

This was only one episode in a chain of manoeuvres which they attempted in order to resist the Qur'ān and stop its profound effect. They realized that the Qur'ān put its address to human nature, based on the truth implanted in its very constitution. Hence, its response was bound to be positive. It confronted minds with its overpowering authority and they yielded to its irrefutable logic. Therefore, the elders of the Quraysh concocted some manoeuvres which they knew to be without foundation. Nevertheless, they tried to find in the Qur'ān

---

1. Ibn Kathīr, *Tafsīr al-Qur'ān al-ʿAẓīm*, Beirut, Vol. II, p. 279

2. Al-Miqdād's words were meant as a reference to the ransom he would have collected in return for al-Naḍr's release. He was not objecting to the Prophet's order, but he hoped for something different as is clear from the report. – Editor's note.

3. Ibn Jarīr al-Ṭabarī, *Jāmiʿ al-Bayān*, Dār al-Fikr, Beirut, Vol. VI, pp. 231–232

something similar to the fables and legends of ancient communities in order to spread confusion among the masses. Their aim was simply to maintain their sway over those masses.

Those elders of the Quraysh recognized the nature of the Islamic message, because they were fully aware of the meaning of its terms and expressions in their language. They recognized that the declaration, 'there is no deity other than God, and Muḥammad is God's Messenger,' signified a rebellion against all human authority, a complete rejection of the sovereignty of human beings and an acknowledgement that all sovereignty belonged to God alone. It also signified that putting such submission into practice meant following the teachings of Prophet Muḥammad, God's Messenger, to the exclusion of all those who claimed to speak for God. They were aware that those of them who made that declaration rebelled immediately against the Quraysh's authority, leadership and sovereignty. Without hesitation, they joined the community led by the Prophet, acknowledging his authority. They no longer entertained any feeling of loyalty to family, clan, tribe, leadership or human authority. All their loyalty was given to this new leadership and the community under its care.

This is certainly the true significance of the declaration that there is no deity other than God and that Muḥammad is God's Messenger. This was a reality witnessed by the elders of the Quraysh who recognized the threat it constituted to their social, political, economic and religious set-up. The new Muslims' declaration did not have the hollow and feeble significance demonstrated by those who nowadays claim to be Muslims. They make such a claim only because they repeat this declaration verbally and offer some worship rituals. However, they pay little heed to the fact that God's Lordship no longer has any practical significance in human life, since human beings allow man-made laws and ignorant leadership to conduct and manage all society affairs.

It is true that in Makkah, Islam had neither a legal code to put forward nor a state to implement such a code, had it been there. However, those who made the declaration that brought them into the fold of Islam immediately acknowledged the leadership of the Prophet Muḥammad and gave all their loyalty to the Muslim community. They rebelled against the leadership of the Arabian *jāhiliyyah* society, and disclaimed any loyalty to family, clan, tribe, etc. Hence, their declaration had its true political significance.

This was indeed what worried the Quraysh's elders as they recognized the threat posed by Islam and the Qur'ān. In earlier days, they were not at all worried when some individuals of foresight disowned the beliefs and rituals of the unbelievers, declaring that they believed in God's oneness and worshipped Him alone. Those individuals disowned all idolatry, offering no worship ritual to any of the Arabian idols. If the whole matter is confined to this, those who wield authority in any *jāhiliyyah* society would not care, because they do not see any threat to their authority in mere beliefs and worship rituals. Unlike what some kind and sincere people who wish to be Muslims may think, Islam is not confined to this. Islam is a positive movement that accompanies this declaration. It requires its followers to dissociate themselves from *jāhiliyyah* society, its conceptual beliefs, values, leadership, laws and authority. It also requires its followers to acknowledge loyalty only to the Muslim leadership which wants to bring Islam into practice. This was extremely worrying to the elders of the Quraysh, so they tried to resist it by various means, including their false claim that the Qur'ān was nothing but fables of the ancients, and that they could produce something similar to it. They certainly had no power to do so. The Qur'ān has challenged them time and again to produce even one *sūrah* similar to it. Every time they tried, their attempts ended in miserable failure.

A Sophisticated Version of an Old Ploy

A fable is an old tale that includes some superstitious beliefs about deities and the supernatural courage of legendary heroes. It speaks of imaginary events that involve so much superstition.

Those Quraysh elders referred to the accounts given in the Qur'ān of earlier nations and communities, the miracles shown to them and to the Qur'ānic descriptions of how God destroyed the unbelievers and saved the believers and said to the masses that such accounts were only fables of ancient people. They alleged that Muḥammad had it all written down in order to relate the same to the Arabs in Makkah, claiming that they had been revealed to him by God. Al-Naḍr ibn al-Ḥārith would take the Prophet's place after he had finished speaking to people, and would relate to them fables and legends which he had learnt on his travels in Persia. At times, al-Naḍr would even have a group of people in a circle sitting next to the group addressed by the

Prophet. He would then say to his audience: "These legends are similar to the fables related by Muḥammad, but I do not claim to be a Prophet or to receive any revelations. His are all fables and legends of the same type."

Such claims must, no doubt, have created some confusion among people, particularly at the beginning, before those legends were clearly seen as totally different from the Qur'ān. Hence, we appreciate why the Prophet issued an announcement before the Battle of Badr that al-Naḍr ibn al-Ḥārith should be killed. Then, when he was taken prisoner, the Prophet ordered his execution along with a couple of other prisoners for whom the Prophet was not prepared to accept ransom.

However, such matters did not last long in Makkah. These ploys were seen for what they really were. With its overpowering logic and profound truth that directly appealed to human nature, the Qur'ān could easily overcome all such ploys and manoeuvres. Nothing of them was able to resist the Qur'ān in any way. Hence, the elders of the Quraysh were in terrible fear and called on all their followers: "*Do not listen to this Qur'ān. Cut short its recitation with booing and laughter, so that you may gain the upper hand.*" (41: 26) But their leaders, such as Abū Sufyān, Abū Jahl and al-Akhnas ibn Sharīq went secretly at night, each on his own, to listen to the Qur'ān being recited. None of them could bring himself to refrain from being there night after night, to listen to the Prophet as he recited God's revelations. Each one of them thought he was totally alone. When they discovered each other, they made a firm pledge of honour not to do it again. They feared that they would be seen by young people who would then listen to the Qur'ān and accept the Islamic faith.

Al-Naḍr's attempt to attract people's attention to his stories in order to turn them away from the Qur'ān was not the last of its kind. It was repeated in different shapes and forms, and it will continue to be repeated. In our present times, the enemies of this faith have also tried to turn people's attentions away from the Qur'ān. But when they realize that all their attempts end in failure, they try to reduce the Qur'ān to a collection of hymns that reciters sing to enchant their audience. They also make of it charms and talismans which people wear or put in their pockets or under their pillows. When people do so, they imagine that they are Muslims and they think that they have paid the Qur'ān all its due respect.

The Qur'ān is no longer the guideline for human life. The enemies of this religion have managed to provide flimsy substitutes for it to which people refer for directives concerning all matters of life. Indeed, it is from such flimsy alternatives that people derive their concepts, laws, values and standards. These enemies then tell the masses that religion is held in a position of respect and that the Qur'ān is intact. It is being recited for you morning and evening, and at all times. You may listen to such recitations and be enchanted with them. What else do you want the Qur'ān to do for you? As for your concepts, systems, laws, constitutions, values and standards, you may refer to other things which are the authority for all that.

It is the same ploy as employed by al-Naḍr ibn al-Ḥārith, but with more sophistication to suit modern life with all its complexities. Indeed, it is just one of numerous forms. Throughout its history, this religion of Islam has never been short of enemies scheming against it.

What is remarkable about the Qur'ān is that it remains overpowering, despite the ever more sophisticated schemes that seek to undermine it. This divine book has such remarkable characteristics and such great appeal to human nature that it is able to overcome all the scheming of the forces of evil on earth, as well as the scheming of the Zionist Jews and imperialists, with all the international centres of power they erect everywhere and at all times. This book continues to crush its enemies the world over, forcing them to allocate a slot for it on all radio stations addressing the Muslim world. We listen to it being broadcast from Jewish and Christian radio stations as well as those controlled by their agents who falsely claim to be Muslims.

It is true that they broadcast it only after they have succeeded in reducing it in the minds of the Muslim masses to little more than hymns and recitals, or charms and talismans. They have also succeeded in dislocating it in the minds of the Muslim masses, so that it is no longer their guideline for life. They have replaced it with other sources of guidance. Nevertheless, this book continues to do so and there will continue to be a Muslim community that assigns to the Qur'ān its proper position, making it its only source of guidance. This community awaits the fulfilment of God's promise of victory so that they can re-establish Islam on earth. This had happened once and will certainly happen again, despite all persecution and extermination attempts to which the Muslim community is being subjected in many areas of the world.

No Limit to Human Folly

The *sūrah* goes on to describe an attitude of most amazing stubbornness by the unbelievers. They try to wrestle with the truth and they are defeated. Pride, however, prevents them from acknowledging the truth and its authority or submitting to it. Hence, they appeal to God to rain down stones over them or to smite them with grievous suffering, if the Qur'ān were the truth revealed by Him. Instead of praying to God to guide them to the truth and enable them to follow it, they pray for their own undoing: "*They would also say: 'God, if this be indeed Your revealed truth, then rain down upon us stones from the skies, or inflict grievous suffering on us.*'" (Verse 32)

This is certainly a very strange appeal which betrays a state of unwavering stubbornness that prefers total ruin to yielding to the truth, even when it is the absolute truth. When sound human nature experiences doubt, it prays to God to show it the truth and guide it to it. Sound human nature does not find that at all demeaning. But when it is corrupted by uncontrolled pride, arrogance drives it into sin to the extent that it prefers suffering and ruin to acknowledging the truth when it becomes clear, irrefutable. It is with this type of obstinacy that the unbelievers in Makkah resisted the Prophet's message. But this message was victorious in the end, despite such persistent obstinacy.

The *sūrah* makes it clear that they certainly deserved that stones be rained on them from the skies, or that painful suffering be inflicted on them, just as they had prayed for. Nevertheless, God willed not to inflict on them the type of extermination He had inflicted on earlier communities. This is because God's Messenger was still in their midst, calling on them to follow His guidance. Nor would God punish them for their sins if they continued to seek forgiveness after committing them.

It is untrue that their punishment was postponed because they were the guardians of the Sacred Mosque. Indeed, they were not its true guardians, because its rightful guardians are those who fear God: "*But God would not punish them while you were present in their midst, nor would God punish them when they may yet ask for forgiveness. What [plea] have they now that God should not punish them, when they debar other people from the Sacred Mosque, although they are not its rightful guardians? Its only guardians are those that fear God; but of this most of these [evildoers] are unaware. Their prayers at the House are nothing but whistling and clapping of hands. Taste then this punishment in consequence of your disbelief.*" (Verses 33–35)

It is, then, through God's grace that they are not punished for their arrogance and obstinacy, or for turning people away from the Sacred Mosque. They were indeed debarring Muslims from offering pilgrimage to the Sacred Mosque, the while they did not prevent anyone else from visiting the Mosque. It is through God's grace that they were given respite, so that, perchance, some of them might on a later date find faith creeping into their hearts and that they might follow divine guidance. As long as God's Messenger remained among them, calling on them to believe in God, then the possibility that some would have a positive change of heart remained. Hence, the respite they are given is in honour of God's Messenger. The way remains open for them to avoid the punishment of extermination. They only have to give a positive response and seek God's forgiveness for what they have done in the past: "*But God would not punish them while you were present in their midst, nor would God punish them when they may yet ask for forgiveness.*" (Verse 33)

If God were to treat them on the basis of their present situation, they would certainly deserve to be punished: "*What [plea] have they now that God should not punish them, when they debar other people from the Sacred Mosque, although they are not its rightful guardians? Its only guardians are those that fear God; but of this most of these [evildoers] are unaware.*" (Verse 34)

What delays their punishment is not their claim that they are the heirs of Abraham and the custodians of the Sacred Mosque. This is merely a claim that has no substance or foundation. They are not the owners or the guardians of this House of worship, i.e. the Ka'bah. Indeed, they are its enemies. God's Sacred Mosque, the Ka'bah, is not a place of property which one generation inherits from its predecessor. It is God's own house which is inherited by those who fear God. False also is their claim that they are the heirs of the Prophet Abraham (peace be upon him). It is not through blood and lineage that Abraham's legacy is inherited. It is only inherited through faith and religion. Those who fear God are the only ones to inherit Abraham and the House he built for God's sake. But those unbelievers were turning away from it, its true guardians who believed in Abraham's faith. Hence, they could not be guardians of this Sacred Mosque, although they may offer their prayers there. Indeed, theirs was not a true prayer. It was no more than whistling and hand clapping. It involved much chaos that imparted no air of serenity or atmosphere of humility before God. It did not inspire any feeling of sacredness of that mosque.

'Abdullāh ibn 'Umar says: "They used to place their cheeks on the ground, whistling and clapping. This brings to mind the image of musicians who produce a great deal of noise, and who put their heads at the feet of those in high position in many countries which claim to be Muslim. This is no more than an aspect of *jāhiliyyah* that is highlighted here. It is shown here after a clear picture of *jāhiliyyah* has been raised, showing how people impose a sort of divine authority on earth, and claim sovereignty over people. When this type of *jāhiliyyah* occurs, all other forms and styles of *jāhiliyyah* may follow.

"*Taste then this punishment in consequence of your disbelief.*" (Verse 35) This refers to the suffering inflicted on them in the Battle of Badr at the hands of the Muslim community. As for the suffering they prayed for, which involves extermination, it is simply postponed by God's mercy, as a gesture of honour to God's Messenger and his great position. It may be that they will eventually repent what they have been doing and pray to God to forgive them.

Separating the Good from the Bad

It is a common characteristic of unbelievers that they spend their money to cooperate in turning people away from God's path. This they did on the day of the Battle of Badr. They did the same thing again after Badr to prepare for the next battle. God warns them that their purpose will be foiled and that they will come to rue the loss of their money. He promises them defeat in this life and the punishment of hell in the life to come: "*The unbelievers spend their riches in order to turn people away from the path of God. They will go on spending them, and then this will become a source of intense regret for them; and then they shall be defeated. The unbelievers shall into hell be driven. God will separate the bad from the good. The bad He will place one upon another, so He may heap them all up together, and then cast them into hell. Those indeed are the losers.*" (Verses 36–37)

Muḥammad ibn Isḥāq and others report:

> When the Quraysh suffered their major setback at the Battle of Badr, and their defeated army arrived back in Makkah, Abū Sufyān and his trade caravan had already returned there. 'Abdullāh ibn Rabī'ah, 'Ikrimah ibn Abī Jahl, Ṣafwān ibn Umayyah and a number of other people from the Quraysh who suffered the loss of their fathers, brothers or sons at Badr went to Abū Sufyān and his fellow merchants who had major shares in that trade caravan. They said to them: 'Elders of the Quraysh, Muḥammad has levelled a heavy blow on you and killed a number of the best people among you. Help us to fight him by donating this money to the war effort. This may enable us to secure revenge against him. All of them agreed. It is in comment on their action that God revealed this Qur'ānic verse: "*The unbelievers spend their riches in order to turn people away from the path of God. They will go on spending them, and then this will become a source of intense regret for them; and then they shall be defeated.*" (Verse 36)

What happened before and after Badr was only an example of this continuous effort by the enemies of this faith. They spend their money, concentrate their efforts and use all their ability to turn people away from the path of God. They set up obstacles to impede the progress of this religion and to suppress the Muslim community everywhere and at all times.

This war against Islam will not cease. Hostile forces will not leave this religion of Islam alone. They will not allow its advocates any time of peace and security. Hence, the method of this religion is to move forward to attack *jāhiliyyah*. It is the duty of its advocates to take pre-emptive measures to smash the ability of *jāhiliyyah* to wage aggression, and then to raise God's banner high, immune from attacks by its enemies.

God warns those unbelievers who spend their money to turn people away from His path that they will come to rue their actions. They allocate their resources for a futile purpose. They will eventually be defeated and the truth will be triumphant. They will suffer the fate of hell, where they will taste the greatest regret. All this has the purpose outlined in the following statement: "*God will separate the bad from the good. The bad He will place one upon another, so He may heap them all up together, and then cast them into hell. Those indeed are the losers.*" (Verse 37) But how will this come about?

The money and other resources that are so allocated enable evil to sustain its aggression. The truth counters such aggression with a determined struggle, i.e. *jihād*, and moves to smash the ability of evil and falsehood to sustain their aggression. In this hard fought battle, natures crystallize and the truth is separated from the evil, as are the advocates and supporters of each side. Indeed, such separation takes place even within the ranks that initially join the side of the truth, and this before it begins to endure trials and hardship. Those who are firm believers, determined fighters and unwavering in their support of the truth are distinguished. These deserve to be granted victory by God, because they are well able to undertake the trust of its message. They will not abandon it under any circumstances, no matter what pressures and trials they are made to endure.

At this stage, God groups all the evil ones together and casts them into hell, where they suffer the greatest loss. The Qur'ānic expression shows evil as a sizeable mass, as if it is nothing more than a huge heap of dirt which is cast in hell with little regard: "*The bad He will place one upon another, so He may heap them all up together, and then cast them into hell.*" (Verse 37) This image gives the expression a stronger impact on our minds, as is always the case with Qur'ānic imagery.

With this clear outline of the destiny of heaped evil and allied falsehood, the *sūrah* directs the Prophet to issue a final warning to the unbelievers. The Muslim front is also commanded to fight until there is no more oppression on earth and human beings are all free to submit to God alone. The Muslim fighters are reassured that they receive support from God, their protector. Hence, they will not be overcome by any force or devious ploy.

> *Say to the unbelievers that if they desist, all that is past shall be forgiven them; but if they persist [in their erring ways], let them remember what happened to the like of them in former times. Fight them until there is no more oppression, and all submission is made to God alone. If they desist, God is certainly aware of all they do. But if they turn away, know that God is your Lord Supreme. How splendid is this Lord Supreme, and how splendid is this giver of support.* (Verses 38–40)

The Prophet is ordered to make it clear to the unbelievers that they have an open chance to mend their ways, to stop forming alliances against Islam and its advocates, and allocating resources to turn people away from God's path. The way is open to them to turn to God in repentance. If they do, God promises to forgive them all their past actions. The adoption of Islam waives all that a person has done in his past. He is just as innocent as a new-born child. But if they revert to their erring ways and continue with their aggression and rejection of the faith, then the laws God has set in operation in the universe will have their effect. These laws brought God's punishment on the unbelievers of the past after they were warned and given clear proof of the truth. It is also God's law to grant victory to the believers and to establish them in a position of power. This law will never fail. The unbelievers may make their choice now that they are at the crossroads. Thus the address to the unbelievers is concluded.

A Positive Approach to Reality

The *sūrah* now addresses the believers: "*Fight them until there is no more oppression, and all submission is made to God alone. If they desist, God is certainly aware of all they do. But if they turn away, know that God is your Lord Supreme. How splendid is this Lord Supreme, and how splendid is this giver of support.*" (Verses 39–40)

This is the purpose and the limit of *jihād*, or struggle for God's cause, not only at a particular period in time, but at all times. The statements related to *jihād* and the laws of war and peace in this *sūrah* are not the final ones. The final version is that included in *Sūrah* 9, Repentance, or *al-Tawbah*. On the other hand, Islam is a positive movement which deals with human situations employing means that are suitable for different situations. Moreover, it is a well structured movement that uses fitting means and methods for every stage. Nevertheless, we have here a statement that lays down a permanent principle that defines the objectives of the confrontation between Islam and un-Islamic social set-ups. This is embodied in the verse which says: "*Fight them until there is no more oppression, and all submission is made to God alone.*" (Verse 39)

In our Prologue to this *sūrah* we mentioned that Islam is a general declaration of the liberation of man on earth from subjugation to other creatures, including his own desires, through the acknowledgement of

God's Lordship over the universe and all creation. We also pointed out that this declaration signifies a total revolution against assigning sovereignty to human beings, whatever forms, systems and situations such sovereignty may take. There are two essential prerequisites for the achievement of this great goal. The first is to put an end to all oppression and persecution which targets the followers of this religion who declare their own liberation from human sovereignty and submit themselves to God alone. This cannot take place unless a community of believers establish their own movement and their own leadership that tries to put this general declaration into practice. This movement will be ready to continue its struggle against every tyrant who persecutes the followers of this religion or uses force, pressure and oppression to turn people away from it.

The second prerequisite is the destruction of every force that is established on the basis of submission to human beings, in any shape or form. This will guarantee the achievement of the first goal and put into effect the declaration that all Godhead and Lordship on earth belong to God alone. Thus, there will be no submission to anyone other than God and no authority except His. We are talking here about submission to God's authority, not merely believing in Him.

We need to add here a point of clarification, because some people may feel uneasy about what we say, particularly in the light of the Qur'ānic verse: "*There shall be no compulsion in [matters of] religion. The right way is henceforth distinct from error.*" (2: 256) What we have mentioned about the nature of *jihād* in Islam, particularly what we have quoted from Mawdūdī's book *Jihād for God's Cause* is clear enough. Nevertheless, some further clarification is in order, because of the great fuss that has been made about it by the enemies of Islam.

The statement, '*all submission is made to God alone,*' means the removal of physical impediments to people's submission to God. These impediments take the form of tyrannical authorities that impose their will on individuals. When these physical impediments are removed, all authority on earth will belong to God and human beings will not be subjugated by any tyrannical authority. Human beings will then be able to make their individual choices of what faith to adopt, in total freedom, without any pressure. Any faith other than Islam that people may choose must not establish a grouping that acquires physical force to exercise pressure on others and prevent them from following divine guidance. It must never resort to oppression against those who dissociate themselves from any power other than that of God. As individuals, human beings are free to choose the faith they want. But they are not free to establish a tyrannical authority to subjugate other human beings. Every human being must be free to submit himself, or herself, to the Lord of mankind, the Lord of the universe.

Human beings will not achieve the position of honour God has guaranteed them, nor will mankind all over the earth be liberated unless submission is made to God alone, to the exclusion of anyone and anything else. It is for this noble objective that the Muslim community fights: "*Fight them until there is no more oppression, and all submission is made to God alone.*" (Verse 39) Whoever accepts this principle and abides by it will be at peace with the Muslims who will accept such a position, making no attempt to search into motives and intentions. They will leave all that to God. "*If they desist, God is certainly aware of all they do.*" (Verse 39) But whoever persists in opposing God's authority will be fought by the Muslims who rely on God's help: "*But if they turn away, know that God is your Lord Supreme. How splendid is this Lord Supreme, and how splendid is this giver of support.*" (Verse 40)

Such is the positive, practical and serious attitude of this religion of Islam as it moves to establish itself in practical life and ensure that Lordship is acknowledged to God alone by all mankind. This religion is not a theory that people learn from a book to enjoy its intellectual subtleties and to boast about their knowledge. Nor is it a negative faith that is confined to a relationship between human beings and their Lord. On the other hand, it is not merely a set of worship practices which people offer to their Lord. This religion is a general declaration for the liberation of mankind. It takes a realistic and practical approach that employs suitable means to confront any human situation. When it is impeded by obstacles of understanding, it speaks out, making its message absolutely clear. But when it faces the impediments of social systems and tyrannical authorities, it confronts them with a physical struggle, launching a campaign of *jihād* to destroy all tyranny and establish God's authority in its place.

This religion of Islam moves within a human practical situation. Its struggle against ignorance is not one between theories. As *jāhiliyyah* is represented in a social order and an authority, then this religion must have its own social order and authority in order to confront *jāhiliyyah* with equal and suitable means. Moreover, it must begin its struggle to ensure that religion belongs entirely to God, which means that no submission may be offered to anyone else.

Such is the positive and practical approach of this religion of Islam. It is nothing like the defeatists say, even though they may be sincere and well intentioned. They may even wish to be Muslims but the true image of this religion may be obscure in their minds.

For our part, we praise God for having guided us to this understanding. We would not have been able to have such clarity of understanding without God's guidance.

3

God's Will at Work

Know that one-fifth of whatever booty you may acquire in war is for God and the Messenger, and for the near of kin, the orphans, the needy and the traveller in need. [This you must observe] if you believe in God and what We revealed to Our servant on the day when the true was distinguished from the false, the day when the two hosts met in battle. God has power over all things. (41)

وَٱعْلَمُوٓا۟ أَنَّمَا غَنِمْتُم مِّن شَىْءٍ فَأَنَّ لِلَّهِ
خُمُسَهُۥ وَلِلرَّسُولِ وَلِذِى ٱلْقُرْبَىٰ
وَٱلْيَتَٰمَىٰ وَٱلْمَسَٰكِينِ وَٱبْنِ
ٱلسَّبِيلِ إِن كُنتُمْ ءَامَنتُم بِٱللَّهِ
وَمَآ أَنزَلْنَا عَلَىٰ عَبْدِنَا يَوْمَ ٱلْفُرْقَانِ
يَوْمَ ٱلْتَقَى ٱلْجَمْعَانِ ۗ وَٱللَّهُ عَلَىٰ كُلِّ
شَىْءٍ قَدِيرٌ ﴿٤١﴾

[Remember the day] when you were at the near end of the valley and they were at the farthest end, with the caravan down below you. If you had made prior arrangements to meet there, you would have differed on the exact timing and location. But it was all brought about so that God might accomplish something He willed to be done, and so that anyone who was destined to perish might perish in clear evidence of the truth and anyone destined to live might live in clear evidence of the truth. God certainly hears all and knows all. (42)

إِذْ أَنتُم بِٱلْعُدْوَةِ ٱلدُّنْيَا وَهُم
بِٱلْعُدْوَةِ ٱلْقُصْوَىٰ وَٱلرَّكْبُ
أَسْفَلَ مِنكُمْ ۚ وَلَوْ تَوَاعَدتُّمْ
لَٱخْتَلَفْتُمْ فِى ٱلْمِيعَٰدِ ۙ وَلَٰكِن
لِّيَقْضِىَ ٱللَّهُ أَمْرًا كَانَ مَفْعُولًا
لِّيَهْلِكَ مَنْ هَلَكَ عَنۢ بَيِّنَةٍ
وَيَحْيَىٰ مَنْ حَىَّ عَنۢ بَيِّنَةٍ ۗ وَإِنَّ
ٱللَّهَ لَسَمِيعٌ عَلِيمٌ ﴿٤٢﴾

إِذْ يُرِيكَهُمُ ٱللَّهُ فِى مَنَامِكَ قَلِيلًا
وَلَوْ أَرَىٰكَهُمْ كَثِيرًا لَّفَشِلْتُمْ
وَلَتَنَٰزَعْتُمْ فِى ٱلْأَمْرِ وَلَٰكِنَّ ٱللَّهَ
سَلَّمَ إِنَّهُۥ عَلِيمٌۢ بِذَاتِ ٱلصُّدُورِ ﴿٤٣﴾

God made them appear to you in your dream as few in number. Had He shown them to you as a large force, you would have lost heart and would surely have been in dispute about what to do. But this God has spared you. He has full knowledge of what is in people's hearts. (43)

وَإِذْ يُرِيكُمُوهُمْ إِذِ ٱلْتَقَيْتُمْ فِىٓ
أَعْيُنِكُمْ قَلِيلًا وَيُقَلِّلُكُمْ فِىٓ
أَعْيُنِهِمْ لِيَقْضِىَ ٱللَّهُ أَمْرًا كَانَ
مَفْعُولًا وَإِلَى ٱللَّهِ تُرْجَعُ ٱلْأُمُورُ ﴿٤٤﴾

When you actually met, He made them appear few in your eyes, just as He made you appear as a small band in their eyes, so that God might accomplish something He willed to be done. To God shall all things return. (44)

يَٰٓأَيُّهَا ٱلَّذِينَ ءَامَنُوٓا۟ إِذَا لَقِيتُمْ فِئَةً
فَٱثْبُتُوا۟ وَٱذْكُرُوا۟ ٱللَّهَ كَثِيرًا
لَّعَلَّكُمْ تُفْلِحُونَ ﴿٤٥﴾

Believers, when you meet an enemy force, be firm, and remember God often, so that you may be successful. (45)

وَأَطِيعُوا۟ ٱللَّهَ وَرَسُولَهُۥ وَلَا تَنَٰزَعُوا۟
فَتَفْشَلُوا۟ وَتَذْهَبَ رِيحُكُمْ وَٱصْبِرُوٓا۟
إِنَّ ٱللَّهَ مَعَ ٱلصَّٰبِرِينَ ﴿٤٦﴾

Obey God and His Messenger and do not dispute with one another, lest you lose heart and your moral strength. Be patient in adversity, for God is with those who are patient in adversity. (46)

وَلَا تَكُونُوا۟ كَٱلَّذِينَ خَرَجُوا۟ مِن
دِيَٰرِهِم بَطَرًا وَرِئَآءَ ٱلنَّاسِ
وَيَصُدُّونَ عَن سَبِيلِ ٱللَّهِ وَٱللَّهُ
بِمَا يَعْمَلُونَ مُحِيطٌ ﴿٤٧﴾

Do not be like those who left their homes full of self-conceit, seeking to be seen and praised by others. They debar others from the path of God; but God has knowledge of all that they do. (47)

Satan made their deeds seem fair to them, and said: 'No one can overcome you today, and I will stand firm by you.' But when the two hosts came within sight of each other, he turned on his heels and said: 'I am done with you, for I can see what you cannot. I fear God, for God is severe in retribution.' (48)

وَإِذْ زَيَّنَ لَهُمُ ٱلشَّيْطَـٰنُ أَعْمَـٰلَهُمْ
وَقَالَ لَا غَالِبَ لَكُمُ ٱلْيَوْمَ مِنَ
ٱلنَّاسِ وَإِنِّى جَارٌ لَّكُمْ ۖ فَلَمَّا
تَرَآءَتِ ٱلْفِئَتَانِ نَكَصَ عَلَىٰ عَقِبَيْهِ
وَقَالَ إِنِّى بَرِىٓءٌ مِّنكُمْ إِنِّىٓ أَرَىٰ
مَا لَا تَرَوْنَ إِنِّىٓ أَخَافُ ٱللَّهَ ۚ وَٱللَّهُ
شَدِيدُ ٱلْعِقَابِ ﴿٤٨﴾

The hypocrites and those in whose hearts there was disease said: 'Their faith has deluded these people.' But he who puts his trust in God knows that God is Almighty, Wise. (49)

إِذْ يَقُولُ ٱلْمُنَـٰفِقُونَ وَٱلَّذِينَ
فِى قُلُوبِهِم مَّرَضٌ غَرَّ هَـٰٓؤُلَآءِ دِينُهُمْ ۗ
وَمَن يَتَوَكَّلْ عَلَى ٱللَّهِ فَإِنَّ ٱللَّهَ
عَزِيزٌ حَكِيمٌ ﴿٤٩﴾

If you could but see how the angels gather up the souls of the unbelievers. They strike them on their faces and their backs and [say]: 'Taste the punishment of burning, (50)

وَلَوْ تَرَىٰٓ إِذْ يَتَوَفَّى ٱلَّذِينَ كَفَرُوا۟ ۙ
ٱلْمَلَـٰٓئِكَةُ يَضْرِبُونَ وُجُوهَهُمْ
وَأَدْبَـٰرَهُمْ وَذُوقُوا۟ عَذَابَ
ٱلْحَرِيقِ ﴿٥٠﴾

in return for what your own hands have committed. Never does God do any injustice to His servants.' (51)

ذَٰلِكَ بِمَا قَدَّمَتْ أَيْدِيكُمْ وَأَنَّ
ٱللَّهَ لَيْسَ بِظَلَّـٰمٍ لِّلْعَبِيدِ ﴿٥١﴾

Like Pharaoh's people and those who lived before them, they denied God's revelations; so God took them to task for their sins. God is Mighty, severe in retribution. (52)

كَدَأْبِ ءَالِ فِرْعَوْنَ وَٱلَّذِينَ مِن
قَبْلِهِمْ كَفَرُوا۟ بِـَٔايَٰتِ ٱللَّهِ فَأَخَذَهُمُ
ٱللَّهُ بِذُنُوبِهِمْ إِنَّ ٱللَّهَ قَوِىٌّ شَدِيدُ
ٱلْعِقَابِ ﴿٥٢﴾

This is because God would never alter the favours He bestows on a community unless they change what is in their hearts. God hears all and knows all. (53)

ذَٰلِكَ بِأَنَّ ٱللَّهَ لَمْ يَكُ مُغَيِّرًا نِّعْمَةً أَنْعَمَهَا
عَلَىٰ قَوْمٍ حَتَّىٰ يُغَيِّرُوا۟ مَا بِأَنفُسِهِمْ وَأَنَّ ٱللَّهَ
سَمِيعٌ عَلِيمٌ ﴿٥٣﴾

Like Pharaoh's people and those who lived before them, they disbelieved in their Lord's revelations; so We destroyed them for their sins, as We caused Pharaoh's people to drown. They were wrongdoers all. (54)

كَدَأْبِ ءَالِ فِرْعَوْنَ وَٱلَّذِينَ مِن
قَبْلِهِمْ كَذَّبُوا۟ بِـَٔايَٰتِ رَبِّهِمْ فَأَهْلَكْنَٰهُم
بِذُنُوبِهِمْ وَأَغْرَقْنَآ ءَالَ فِرْعَوْنَ
وَكُلٌّ كَانُوا۟ ظَٰلِمِينَ ﴿٥٤﴾

Overview

The transition from the end of the previous passage to the beginning of the present one is very smooth. The beginning here continues to outline rulings concerning fighting, which were started with the last couple of verses in the previous passage. Those ran as follows: "*Say to the unbelievers that if they desist, all that is past shall be forgiven them; but if they persist [in their erring ways], let them remember what happened to the like of them in former times. Fight them until there is no more oppression, and all submission is made to God alone. If they desist, God is certainly aware of all they do. But if they turn away, know that God is your Lord Supreme. How splendid is this Lord Supreme, and how splendid is this giver of support.*" (Verses 38– 40) The opening verse in this passage continues these rulings, outlining those that apply to spoils that are gained as a result of victory in battle.

The ultimate objective of any campaign of *jihād* was clearly stated in the statement instructing the believers to "*fight them until there is no more oppression, and all submission is made to God alone.*" (Verse 39) It is undertaken for the sake of God, and for well-defined goals that are related to the faith God has revealed and the code of living He has laid down. Ownership of the spoils of war has also been settled, with a statement that they belong to God and His Messenger. The fighters themselves are given no say in this, so that their effort is made purely for God's sake, to earn His pleasure. Nevertheless, the Qur'ānic approach provides practical regulations for practical situations. The fact remains that there are fighters and spoils of war. The fighters go on a campaign of *jihād* ready to sacrifice their lives and property, paying for their own arms and equipment, and also providing equipment for other fighters who cannot buy their own weapons. Those same fighters take the booty which is only the result of their own steadfastness and determination. Since God has already purged their hearts of any greedy thoughts concerning this booty, declaring that it belongs totally to God and His Messenger, it is now appropriate that they are given part of it. They feel that this new gift is being made to them by God and His Messenger to meet practical needs and satisfy real feelings, leaving no room for any dispute over its division.

Such is the nature of the code of living laid down by God who is well aware of human nature. It is finely balanced, holistic in its approach, satisfying real needs and feelings, and ensuring no ill feelings over such material gains.

When the Fighting is Over

"*Know that one-fifth of whatever booty you may acquire in war is for God and the Messenger, and for the near of kin, the orphans, the needy and the traveller in need. [This you must observe] if you believe in God and what We revealed to Our servant on the day when the true was distinguished from the false, the day when the two hosts met in battle. God has power over all things.*" (Verse 41) Much controversy is found in reports and among scholars on several points relating to the meaning of this verse. The main points of debate are as follows:

- Are the "spoils of war" mentioned in the opening verse of the *sūrah* the same as the "booty" mentioned here or are they two different things? The Qur'ānic text uses two different terms to refer to them.

- Since four-fifths are given to the fighters and divided among them, how is the remaining portion of one-fifth to be divided?
- Is the one-fifth portion that belongs to God to be divided in turn into five equal shares? If so, one of these belongs to God, but is this share the same as that which belongs to God's Messenger? Or is the Messenger's share a separate one?
- Does the Messenger's share (i.e. one-fifth of one-fifth of the whole booty) belong to him personally? Or is it transferred to every Muslim ruler after him?
- Is the share assigned to "the near of kin" exclusive to the Prophet's relatives of the clans of Hāshim and 'Abd al-Muṭṭalib, as was the case during the Prophet's time? Or does a Muslim ruler have any discretion over its distribution?
- Are these fixed and equal shares into which the original portion of one-fifth of the booty must be divided? Or do the Prophet and the Muslim rulers who succeed him have discretionary authority over its usage and spending?

There are further points of debate over other matters of detail. Following our usual approach in this commentary, we prefer not to discuss such controversial points, leaving them to be pursued in specialized studies. Moreover, the whole question of spoils of war is far removed from the practical realities of the Muslim world today. This is not something that is facing us at the present time. We do not have a Muslim state led by an Islamic leadership, fighting a campaign of *jihād* which may give it spoils of war that need to be divided according to Islamic regulations. Our situation today is similar to the period when Islam was addressing humanity for the first time. Human beings have reverted to the type of *jāhiliyyah*, or ignorance, that prevailed then, associating partners with God that give them their man-made laws. This religion has gone back to its starting point calling on human beings to adopt it anew. It wants them to declare that they believe that "there is no deity other than God and Muḥammad is God's Messenger." This means in practical terms that Godhead, sovereignty and all authority belong to God alone. In all these aspects we receive guidance from God's Messenger only. We acknowledge allegiance only to an Islamic leadership that strives to re-establish Islam in practical life, dissociating ourselves from all other types of society and leadership.

This is the real issue that confronts the Islamic faith today. At the outset there is no other issue to consider. There is no question of booty because no campaign of *jihād* is being launched. Indeed there is no single organizational or community issue, either at the internal or external level. The reason for this is very simple: there is no independent Islamic entity in need of specific rules to regulate its relations with other communities and societies.

Islam employs a very practical and realistic method. It does not preoccupy itself with issues that have no significance in reality. Hence, it does not concern itself with providing rules for such issues. Its outlook is too serious for that. Such an exercise may be pursued by those who devote their spare time to academic discussion that has no bearing on reality. Their time, however, would have been much more fruitfully utilized, had they dedicated it for the re-establishment of Islamic society according to the practical Islamic approach, starting with a call on people to believe in God's oneness and the message of the Prophet Muḥammad. For this leads to a situation where some people accept the faith. They, thus, establish a community that has its own leadership, allegiance and independent entity. God then settles the dispute between this community and other people on the basis of truth. Only at this stage would scholars need to deduce rules and regulations to address the various questions that may confront that community, internally and externally. This is when such scholarly exercise has real value, because it is relevant to practical and real questions and issues.

Recognizing this serious approach of Islam, we do not wish to engage in any discussion of the juristic details concerning the question of booty and spoils of war until the time is right for such discussion. That is when God wills to bring into being an Islamic society which launches a campaign of *jihād* that leads to the acquisition of spoils of war. When that occurs regulations will be needed to divide such spoils. In this commentary it is sufficient for our purposes to concentrate on the basic issue of faith in the historical progress of the Muslim community and the method of education to which it is exposed. This is a constant factor we find in God's book which is not subject to change at any time. Everything else is of secondary value.

The general rule outlined in the Qur'ānic verse states: "*Know that one-fifth of whatever booty you may acquire in war is for God and the Messenger, and for the near of kin, the orphans, the needy and the traveller in need.*" (Verse 41) This rule assigns four-fifths of anything gained in battle to the fighters themselves. The remaining one-fifth is left to God's Messenger (peace be upon him) and Muslim leaders implementing God's law and striving to further God's cause. They are required to dispense with it only "for God and the Messenger, and for the near of kin, the orphans, the needy and the traveller in need," so as to satisfy real needs when such booty has been gained.

If You Truly Believe

Following this, we have a permanent directive in the following statement: "*[This you must observe] if you believe in God and what We revealed to Our servant on the day when the true was distinguished from the false, the day when the two hosts met in battle. God has power over all things.*" (Verse 41)

True faith has certain essential indicators to prove it. God makes His recognition of true faith for the fighters in Badr conditional on their acceptance of His ruling on the question of the spoils of war. If they accept then they are truly believers in God and what He revealed to His Messenger. In fact such acceptance is a practical demonstration of faith.

The real meaning of faith is thus stated clearly in the Qur'ān, without equivocation. It does not admit anything of the wide variety of interpretations and controversial details introduced by the different schools and sects. Such schools opened the way for argument, academic controversy and logical debate, which led, in turn, to accusations and counter accusations. It then became possible to brand someone as an unbeliever and for the refutation of such an allegation to no longer rely on the clear and basic essentials of faith. Instead, they relied on prejudice and the need to score a point against opponents. Thus people began to accuse others of unbelief because of disagreement on points of detail, while others sought to refute such accusations by following very strict lines of thought and action. Both attitudes were products of historical circumstances. The divine faith is clear, well defined, free from ambiguity and extremism. The Prophet says: "To be a true believer does not come about through wishful thinking. True faith is that which is firmly rooted in one's heart and to which credence is given by practice." To be a true believer presupposes acceptance of God's law and its implementation in real life. Conversely, the rejection of God's law and the implementation of a law other than the one He has laid down, in matters large or small, constitutes unbelief.

God's law provides rulings that are clear and decisive. One example of these is provided in this verse: "*Know that one-fifth of whatever booty you may acquire in war is for God and the Messenger, and for the near of kin, the orphans, the needy and the traveller in need. [This you must observe] if you believe in God and what We revealed to Our servant on the day when the true was distinguished from the false, the day when the two hosts met in battle.*" (Verse 41) The same applies to all categorical statements that delineate the nature of true faith and its framework which we read in the divine book.

God has taken away the ownership of the spoils of war from those who actually collected them on the battlefield, and assigned that ownership to God and His Messenger, as stated clearly at the opening of the *sūrah*. His purpose was that those who fight for God's cause may have only pure motives. Thus, they would be able to remove from their minds all thoughts and temptations that relate to the life of this world. They would be able then to submit themselves totally to God, fighting the battle for God's cause, under His banner, in obedience to Him and to earn His pleasure. They accept His rule over their lives as they accept it over all their affairs, making no dissent or objection. This is the practical meaning of true faith, as clearly explained in the first verse of the *sūrah* which vested all authority over the spoils of war in God and the Messenger: "*They ask you about the spoils of war. Say: The spoils of war belong to God and the Messenger. So, have fear of God and set right your internal relations. Obey God and His Messenger, if you are true believers.*" (Verse 1)

When they accepted God's ruling, demonstrating that faith is deeply rooted in their hearts, God gave them back four-fifths of the spoils of war, and retained one-fifth in its original ownership, i.e. belonging to God and His Messenger. The Prophet was then to dispense with it for the welfare of those in the Muslim community who needed help, be they near of kin, orphans, needy or wayfarers. When the share of four-fifths was given back to them, the Muslims were well aware that they did not own it by right of fighting or victory. They went to war for God's sake, and achieved victory for His faith. They only deserved this share of four-fifths because God granted it to them, just as He determined the outcome of the battle and indeed all their affairs, and just as He granted them victory. They are reminded here anew that obeying this new order is a manifestation of faith. It is indeed both the condition and the outcome of being true believers: *"Know that one-fifth of whatever booty you may acquire in war is for God and the Messenger, and for the near of kin, the orphans, the needy and the traveller in need. [This you must observe] if you believe in God and what We revealed to Our servant on the day when the true was distinguished from the false, the day when the two hosts met in battle."* (Verse 41) We see clearly how Qur'ānic statements support one another in confirming an essential and decisive principle of Islam that relates to the true meaning of having faith.

Let us now reflect for a moment on God's description of His Messenger (peace be upon him) as "Our servant", at this particular point where the ownership of the spoils of war is stated as clearly belonging to God and the Messenger: "*if you believe in God and what We revealed to Our servant on the day when the true was distinguished from the false, the day when the two hosts met in battle.*" (Verse 41) It is indeed an inspiring description. Being a truly obedient servant of God is the essence of faith, and, at the same time, the highest position any human being can achieve when being honoured by God. Hence it is expressly mentioned at the point when God's Messenger is required to convey God's orders and assign the task of dispensing what God placed at his disposal.

This is indeed the case in real life: being a servant of God is not merely a position of honour; it is the highest position to which a human being can aspire. True submission to God alone protects people from being enslaved by their own desires or by other human beings. No human being can attain this highest position unless he refuses to submit to his own desires or to anyone other than God.

Those who are too proud to submit themselves to God alone are automatically enslaved by their own desires and caprice, which is the worst type of slavery. They lose their sense of free will with which God has favoured human beings. They sink to the level of animals and soon descend to the worst rank of animals. They take themselves down to a level that God describes as "*the lowest of the low*," (95: 5) after they have been created "*in the fairest form.*" (95: 4) They are willing to accept enslavement by others like them when they allow such people to conduct their lives according to narrow-minded theories and philosophies that are ignorant, deficient and arrogant.

Such people are also ready to submit to 'certainties' which they are told to be inevitable and to admit no discussion, such as the certainties of history, economic development and evolution! There is indeed a long list of such materialist certainties and inevitabilities which enslave man and keep his head in the sand.

A Criterion of Distinction

We need now to discuss the description of the Battle of Badr as the "*day when the true was distinguished from the false*," as it occurs in the first verse of the present passage.

The Battle of Badr, which started and finished according to God's own planning, direction and help, was indeed a criterion of distinction between truth and falsehood, as most commentators say. However, we are speaking here of a distinction that is much wider and far more profound. The truth, as meant here, is that original truth on the basis of which the whole structure of the heavens and the earth is established, as also the nature of all living things. It is the truth represented in the concept of God's oneness, and His being the only deity who has the overall sovereignty, and authority over the universe. It is He who plans all that takes place. Everything in the universe: the heavens, the earth, animate and inanimate objects submit to His authority that admits no partnership with anyone. His will is enforceable without question. Falsehood, on the other hand, is incidental, although at the time of Badr it spread over the whole earth, beclouding people's vision so that they could not distinguish the original truth. It also created tyrannical deities that ruled over people's lives and conducted their affairs. That was the nature of the distinction that took place at Badr, when the original truth was distinguished from the tyrannical falsehood so that they could no longer be confused.

The far-reaching and profound significance of the distinction between the truth and falsehood that took place at Badr was multi-dimensional. It separated the truth from falsehood within people's hearts and consciences. This provided, in effect, a complete distinction between absolute monotheism that assigns authority over human feelings, behaviour, morals, worship and submission to God alone, and polytheism in all its shapes and forms. This certainly includes mental submission to anyone other than God, be that a human being, a desire, a social value or a tradition.

Badr also separated truth from falsehood in daily life situations. It provided a clear separation between people's practical enslavement by other people, desires, values, laws and traditions on the one hand, and accepting, in all these matters, God's judgement, recognizing that He has no associate or partner, and that He is the only Lord and legislator. Thus human beings were able to raise their heads high, rejecting all tyranny and bending to no authority other than that of God, the only law-giver.

The Battle of Badr also separated two different stages in the history of the Islamic movement: the stage of grouping, perseverance and steadfastness, and the stage of strength, pre-emption and taking the initiative. The religion of Islam represents a new concept of life, a code of living, a social order and a system of state and government. All these are results of the liberation of humanity all over the world which Islam achieves through the establishment of God's sovereignty in human life and by rejecting all tyranny. As such, Islam must always acquire strength and take the initiative. It is not in the nature of Islam to remain in waiting for events and developments. It cannot remain a collection of beliefs that are represented in worship rituals and moral behaviour. It must take action to establish its new concept, practice its code of living and lay the foundation of its new social order and state. This requires the removal of all physical and material impediments that hinder the practical implementation of its constitution in the life of the Muslim community at first, and later in human life as a whole. Needless to say, God has given us all these for practical implementation.

Badr also separated two epochs in human history. Prior to the establishment of the Islamic system, humanity as a whole was a totally different entity. The new Islamic concept of life and the new Muslim community meant a rebirth of humanity, while the new set of values provided the foundation of a new social order and a new code of law. After Badr, these were no longer the sole property of the Muslims alone. They gradually became the property of all humanity, which came to be profoundly influenced by them, within the land of Islam and outside it. This applied to those who adopted a friendly attitude to Islam, and also to those who were hostile. The Crusaders who marched from the West to exterminate Islam in its own territory were strongly influenced by the traditions of the Muslim society they came to destroy. When they went home, they put an end to the feudal system that prevailed in Europe, after they had seen the lingering traditions of the Islamic system. Encouraged by the Jews and Crusaders living in the Muslim areas, the Tartars marched from the East to put an end to Islam. They, however, were eventually influenced by the Islamic faith. They not only adopted Islam, but went further to spread it across vast new areas and establish a new Islamic state that flourished close to the European hinterland from the fifteenth to the twentieth centuries. Ever since the Battle of Badr, human history is strongly influenced by that great distinction between the truth and falsehood, whether in the land of Islam or in the land of its opponents.

Badr also provided a clear distinction between two outlooks defining the causes of defeat and victory. The battle took place at a time when all apparent factors clearly indicated a victory for the unbelievers and predicted a defeat for the Muslims. The hypocrites and those sick at heart declared: "*Their faith has deluded these people.*" (Verse 49) Since it was the first major battle between the unbelieving majority and the Muslim minority, God willed that it should take place in this particular fashion in order to provide a clear distinction between causes of victory and defeat. Strong faith was thus able to overcome numerical strength and superior equipment so that people should know that victory belongs to the faith that has the elements of strength and is designed to bring out the best in human beings. Those who believe in the true faith must strive hard and join the battle against falsehood, without waiting until they have the same material strength as their enemy. They should be aware that they have another type of strength that can tip the balance in their favour. These are not idle words. This is an evident reality.

The Battle of Badr was also a distinction between the truth and falsehood in a different sense, which we derive from God's statement in the early part of the *sūrah*: "*God promised you that one of the two hosts would fall to you. It was your wish that the one which was not powerful to be yours, but it was God's will to establish the truth in accordance with His words and to wipe out the unbelievers. Thus He would certainly establish the truth firmly and show falsehood to be false, however hateful this might be to the evildoers.*" (Verses 7–8)

Those Muslims who marched with the Prophet from Madinah wanted only to capture the trade caravan led by Abū Sufyān. God, however, wanted something else for them. He wanted them to miss out on capturing the trade caravan and to meet in battle the army led by Abū Jahl. He wanted them to go through a hard battle when fighters are killed and prisoners are taken. He did not want them to have an easy mission which ended in the capture of handsome booty. Furthermore, He told them that He willed this in order to "*establish the truth firmly and show falsehood to be false.*" (Verse 8)

This is a clear reference to a fundamental issue. In human society, the truth cannot be established and falsehood cannot be clearly seen as false on the basis of any theoretical exposition of each, or even by an academic belief that the one is true and the other is false. The establishment of truth and the eradication of falsehood in the real world can only come about when the might of falsehood is smashed and the authority of truth is triumphant. This takes place when victory is achieved by the army of truth over the forces of falsehood. This religion is not a mere theory for debate. It is a practical code of living.

God's purpose was certainly achieved with the truth firmly established as true and falsehood clearly seen as false. He has indeed stated His purpose behind bringing His Messenger out of his hometown with the truth, allowing the caravan (the host of little might) to escape its chasers and bringing about the encounter with the mighty host, so that the battle could take place.

All this is a criterion of distinction characteristic of the method of operation of Islam. We are thus able to clearly see the nature of this method of operation and how it is perceived by Muslims. Today we feel the need and the importance of this criterion as we witness ambiguity creeping into people's perception of basic Islamic concepts. Indeed some of those who call others to embrace this religion are not free from such ambiguity.

The Battle of Badr was indeed a way to separate the true from the false in the sense of this whole range of concepts.

"*God has power over all things.*" (Verse 41) The Battle of Badr was an indisputable example of the working of God's power. It was an event that cannot be explained in any way other than its being brought about by God's power which can easily accomplish whatever He wants.

In Clear Evidence of the Truth

At this point the *sūrah* refers once more to the Battle of Badr, portraying its scenes and events in a splendid style, to bring it all alive before our eyes. It also points out the fact that it was God who conducted the battle, so that we almost see God's hand shaping events as they take place. Moreover, the *sūrah* tells us the purpose behind God's determination of the course of events.

> *[Remember the day] when you were at the near end of the valley and they were at the farthest end, with the caravan down below you. If you had made prior arrangements to meet there, you would have differed on the exact timing and location. But it was all brought about so that God might accomplish something He willed to be done, and so that anyone who was destined to perish might perish in clear evidence of the truth and anyone destined to live might live in clear evidence of the truth. God certainly hears all and knows all. God made them appear to you in your dream as few in number. Had He shown them to you as a large force, you would have lost heart and would surely have been in dispute about what to do. But this God has spared you. He has full knowledge of what is in people's hearts. When you actually met, He made them appear few in your eyes, just as He made you appear as a small band in their eyes, so that God might accomplish something He willed to be done. To God shall all things return.* (Verses 42–44)

The battle is about to start, with each of the two combatants taking position, and with a clear pointer to the subtle and elaborate planning behind it all. We can visualize how God's hand brings each party to its position, while the caravan manages to slip away. The very words unveil God's planning as the Prophet sees his dream, and as each party sees the other as small in number, which tempts each party with the prospect of victory. Only the Qur'ānic style can portray scenes so vividly, and bring them alive in such a concise method of expression.

Reference has already been made to the scenes portrayed in this part of the *sūrah*. When the Muslims left Madinah, they finally encamped at the end of the valley that was closer to Madinah, while the army of unbelievers took its position at the other end. There was a small hill separating the two sides. As for the caravan, Abū Sufyān managed to slip away with it to the coastal area, below the positions of both hosts.

Neither of the two armies was aware of the position of the other. It was God who brought them both to their positions by the hill, in order to accomplish a certain purpose of His own. Indeed, had they made prior arrangements to meet, they would not have taken their positions so close to each other and they would not have arrived there at the same time, as they actually did. God reminds the Muslim community of all this so that they always remember how God can accomplish any purpose He may have at any point in time. "*[Remember the day] when you were at the near end of the valley and they were at the farthest end, with the caravan down below you. If you had made prior arrangements to meet there, you would have differed on the exact timing and location. But it was all brought about so that God might accomplish something He willed to be done.*" (Verse 42) Behind such an unplanned meeting there was certainly a purpose which God made the Muslim community the means to achieve. Moreover, He arranged all the circumstances that helped its accomplishment.

What is this matter for the accomplishment of which God arranged all the necessary circumstances? It is the one which He describes in these terms: "*So that anyone who was destined to perish might perish in clear evidence of the truth and anyone destined to live might live in clear evidence of the truth.*" (Verse 42) The verb 'perish' may be used to express its direct meaning, or may be used to denote disbelief and rejection of the faith. The same applies to 'live' which could express life and may refer to faith itself. The latter meaning is nearer and clearer in this particular instance. In the same sense God says in the Qur'ān: "*Is he who was dead and whom We have raised to life, and for whom We set up a light to see his way among men, to be compared to one who is in deep darkness out of which he cannot emerge?*" (6: 122) Here denial of the true faith is described as death, while embracing the divine faith is portrayed as having life. This is indeed how Islam views the nature of faith and denying it. The basis for giving more weight to this meaning in this particular instance is the fact that the Battle of Badr was, as God describes it, a day which separated truth from falsehood. Hence, anyone who denies the faith after Badr does so in clear evidence of the truth. Likewise, anyone who believes does so on the basis of the clear evidence pointing to the truth provided by the battle itself.

With all the circumstances surrounding the Battle of Badr, the battle itself provided an irrefutable evidence of elaborate planning that dwarfs, by comparison, any plans human beings may devise, and points to a power that is totally different from that of human beings. It proved that this faith is supported by the Lord who takes care of its advocates when they demonstrate their sincerity and remain steadfast in their struggle for its cause. Had material strength been the decisive factor the unbelievers would not have been vanquished on the day of Badr, and the believers would not have scored such a great and decisive victory.

The unbelievers themselves said to their own ally who offered to support them with a battalion of his tribesmen: "If we are fighting men like us, we are more than a match to them. But if we are fighting God, as Muḥammad claims, then no human force can stand in opposition to God." Had mere knowledge been sufficient, they were certainly aware that they were taking a stand in opposition to God Himself, as they were told by Muḥammad, the man who personified honesty and spoke nothing but the truth. They were certain that no one was a match for God Almighty. If after all this they perished on account of their denial of the faith, they perished after having had very clear evidence of the truth.

A Purpose to Be Accomplished

Such are the thoughts that come immediately to mind when we try to understand God's statement: "*So that anyone who was destined to perish might perish in clear evidence of the truth and anyone destined to live might live in clear evidence of the truth.*" (Verse 42) However, the statement also imparts a different sense.

That the truth achieved victory in the battle between its advocates and the supporters of falsehood, after it had also triumphed in people's hearts, helps to put matters clearly in front of our eyes. No ambiguity or confusion is left after the victory at Badr has clarified all issues. Anyone who chooses to perish, i.e. rejects the true faith, no longer has any doubt concerning the truth after it had made its presence so clearly felt. Similarly, anyone who chooses life, i.e. embraces the faith, has no doubt that he is making his choice in favour of the truth which will always enjoy God's support against the tyrants who try to suppress it.

This takes us back to what we mentioned in our introduction when we spoke of the need to launch a *jihād* campaign to destroy the forces of evil and tyranny, and to enable the truth to triumph. Such *jihād* helps to make the truth clear to all, "*so that anyone who was destined to perish might perish in clear evidence of the truth and anyone destined to live might live in clear evidence of the truth.*" (Verse 42) Again, this understanding of the statement makes it easier for us to understand the significance of a later statement in this *sūrah*, in which the following directive is given: "*Make ready against them whatever force and war mounts you can muster, so that you may strike terror into the enemies of God who are also your own enemies.*" (Verse 60) Putting forces on the alert to frighten the enemy may help to make the truth clear in certain hearts and minds which only understand the language of force.

The comment that follows on this aspect of God's planning and execution of the battle and the purpose behind it all takes the following form: "*God certainly hears all and knows all.*" (Verse 42) Nothing that is said by the parties supporting truth or falsehood, and nothing that they may harbour in their hearts behind their words or actions escapes God as He puts His plan into action in full knowledge of all that is hidden or apparent. He does indeed hear all and know all.

This statement and the comment that follows occur in the middle of the account given in the *sūrah* of the events of the battle and its course. The next verse continues with this account: "*God made them appear to you in your dream as few in number. Had He shown them to you as a large force, you would have lost heart and would surely have been in dispute about what to do. But this God has spared you. He has full knowledge of what is in people's hearts.*" (Verse 43) Part of God's planning for the battle was that His Messenger should see the unbelievers in his dream as small in number, having no real strength. He told his companions of this and it gave them encouragement. Here God's Messenger is told the reason for this vision. Had God shown him a large force, it would have demoralized his Companions, who were no more than a small group of believers who joined him on an expedition, neither expecting a battle nor prepared for one. This would have weakened them and caused them to be in dispute over whether to fight or to avoid a confrontation. Such a dispute is the worst thing to happen to an army on the verge of meeting an enemy force: "*But this God has spared you. He has full knowledge of what is in people's hearts.*" (Verse 43)

It was an aspect of God's grace that He, knowing the weakness of the Muslim group in that particular situation, showed the unbelievers to His Messenger as small in number, whereas they were truly a much larger force. That dream had true significance. Their numerical strength was of little consequence, as their minds were devoid of broad vision, and their hearts deprived of faith. It was this true picture that God showed to His Messenger to reassure the small Muslim force. God was fully aware of their feelings and their inmost thoughts, as they were aware of their numerical weakness and lack of equipment. He was also aware of what would be the effect on them of their knowledge of their enemy's numerical superiority. Needless to say, they would have been reluctant to confront the enemy. It was, then, part of God's planning that they should think their enemy to have a smaller fighting force than it actually had.

When the two hosts actually met face to face, that which the Prophet saw in his true dream was repeated, but it was this time by actual eyesight and by both sides. This was again part of God's elaborate planning of which the believers are reminded in this review of the battle and its events: *"When you actually met, He made them appear few in your eyes, just as He made you appear as a small band in their eyes, so that God might accomplish something He willed to be done. To God shall all things return."* (Verse 44) This particular aspect of God's scheme encouraged both parties to go to war. The believers saw their enemies as a small force because they were looking at them from the viewpoint of real strength, while the unbelievers considered the believers to be of little consequence, because they judged them only by appearances. With the two facts shaping the way each party looked at the other, the purpose of God's planning was accomplished and His will was done. *"To God shall all things return."* (Verse 44) This is the appropriate comment on the accomplishment of what God willed. This is a matter that rests with God alone. He brings it into being by His will and shapes it with His power. It is never removed from His will or His divine wisdom. Indeed nothing takes place in the whole universe except what He has willed.

Since all things are conducted by God and victory is granted by Him, while neither numerical strength nor superior firepower can resolve a confrontation or determine the outcome of a battle, the believers should remain steadfast and persevere when they meet unbelievers in battle. What they should do, however, is to have the proper equipment for the battle and take the measures that keep on the right footing their relationship with God who has the final say over all matters. It is He who grants effective support and commands all power and authority. They must also avoid the causes of defeat which led the unbelievers to be vanquished despite their great numbers and superior equipment. They must rid themselves of conceit, arrogance and falsehood. They should guard against falling prey to Satan's deception, for it was he who led the unbelievers to their destruction. They must place their trust in God alone.

Eliminating Causes of Failure

> *Believers, when you meet an enemy force, be firm, and remember God often, so that you may be successful. Obey God and His Messenger and do not dispute with one another, lest you lose heart and your moral strength. Be patient in adversity, for God is with those who are patient in adversity. Do not be like those who left their homes full of self-conceit, seeking to be seen and praised by others. They debar others from the path of God; but God has knowledge of all that they do. Satan made their deeds seem fair to them, and said: 'No one can overcome you today, and I will stand firm by you.' But when the two hosts came within sight of each other, he turned on his heels and said: 'I am done with you, for I can see what you cannot. I fear God, for God is severe in retribution.' The hypocrites and those in whose hearts there was disease said: 'Their faith has deluded these people.' But he who puts his trust in God knows that God is Almighty, Wise.* (Verses 45–49)

In these verses we have a host of inspiring touches, rules, directives, scenes and attitudes; all relating to the battle. Ideas, feelings and inner thoughts are portrayed which normally need much greater space to describe, but they are all most vividly delineated here in the unique style of the Qur'ān. They start with an address to the believers, which is one of many in the *sūrah*, instructing them to stand firm when they meet their enemy. They should also try to acquire all that is needed to ensure victory. This includes a steadfast attitude, frequent remembrance of God to maintain their relationship with Him, obedience to God and His Messenger, avoidance of internal conflict and dispute, patience in adversity, perseverance in battle, and steering away from conceit, showing off and persecution of others.

Steadfastness is the first step to victory, and the party that is more steadfast is the one which has the upper hand. Although the believers cannot tell, their enemy may be suffering even more than what they themselves are suffering. Their enemy may even be enduring more pain, although that enemy could not hope to receive support from God as they hope to do. It may be that if the believers only remain steadfast for a moment longer, their enemy will collapse and be vanquished. Why should the believers ever feel shaken when they are certain that they will have either one of the best two alternatives: victory or martyrdom? Their enemy, on the other hand, aims at nothing further than the life of this world. This explains why unbelievers are so keen to achieve material superiority in this life which is the ultimate they hope for, since they have no hope in the life to come.

Frequent remembrance of God at the time when an encounter with the enemy is imminent is a constant directive to believers. It is a consistent teaching that becomes well engraved in the hearts of believers. Indeed the Qur'ān shows it as a feature of the community of believers in their long history.

The Qur'ān tells us about the sorcerers Pharaoh gathered for a contest with Moses. When they submitted to the faith after they had realized that it represented the truth, Pharaoh issued them with a highly frightening warning outlining the punishment which he would inflict on them, unless they abandoned their new faith. Their response was: "*You want to take vengeance on us only because we have believed in the signs of our Lord when they were shown to us. Our Lord, grant us abundance of patience in adversity, and let us die as people who have surrendered themselves to You.*" (7: 126) The Qur'ān also mentions the case of a small band of believers among the Children of Israel who were facing the might of Goliath and his army: "*When they came face to face with Goliath and his troops, they prayed, 'Our Lord, grant us patience, make firm our steps, and grant us victory over the unbelievers.'*" (2: 250)

In the Qur'ānic accounts of the attitudes of believing communities as they were fighting their battles we read the following statement: "*Many a Prophet has fought with many devout men alongside him. They never lost heart on account of what they had to suffer in God's cause, and neither did they weaken nor succumb. God loves those who are patient in adversity. All that they said was this: 'Our Lord! forgive us our sins and our excesses in our affairs. Make firm our steps, and give us victory over the unbelievers.'*"(3: 146–147)

This type of education was well taken by the early Muslim community. They adopted the same attitude whenever they had to meet an enemy in battle. Later, the Qur'ān speaks about those who suffered a reversal in the Battle of Uḥud. When they were required to go on a new campaign the following day, they showed that they could rise to the highest level of steadfastness: *"When other people warned them: 'A big force has gathered against you, so fear them,' that only strengthened their faith and they answered: 'God is enough for us; He is the best Guardian.'"* (3: 173)

Remembering God at the time of encountering an enemy is useful in a variety of ways. To start with, it provides a direct link with the Power that can never be overcome. It is a demonstration of placing all trust in God who is certain to support His servants. At the same time it brings to the forefront the nature of the battle, its causes and goals. It is a battle for God, to establish His authority on earth and to overthrow all tyrants who try to usurp this authority. In short it is a fight to make God's word supreme. It has no motive of imposing the authority of any person, group or nation, or making any personal or national gain. It also emphasizes the importance of the duty of remembering God even at the most difficult time.

Obedience to God and His Messenger ensures that the believers go into the battle submitting themselves totally to God. There will be no room for any cause of conflict or dispute: "*Do not dispute with one another, lest you lose heart and your moral strength.*" (Verse 46) People fall into dispute when they have different authorities which they look to for leadership and guidance, or when desire is the ultimate factor that shapes people's views and ideas. When people obey only God and His Messenger, the main cause of dispute between them disappears, no matter how much their views differ over the question under discussion. Having different views is never a cause of dispute and conflict. What causes conflict is desire, making everyone insist that his view is the one to follow, even when it appears to be wrong. Desire causes 'self' to be placed in opposition to 'right' and attaching more importance to self in the first place. For this reason, Muslims are given this directive to obey God and His Messenger at the time of battle. It is a question of discipline that is essential in battle. It is an obedience to the High Command which reflects itself in a genuine obedience to the leader in command of the Muslim forces. Thus it is different from the rigid and superficial discipline in the ranks of armies that do not fight for God's cause, and in which loyalty to commanders is not based on loyalty and submission to God. The gulf between the two is great indeed.

Steadfastness and patience in adversity are also essential in any fight, whether internal within oneself, or on the battlefield: *"Be patient in adversity, for God is with those who are patient in adversity."* (Verse 46) Being with God will certainly ensure success and victory for those who are steadfast.

The last directive is given as follows: "*Do not be like those who left their homes full of self-conceit, seeking to be seen and praised by others. They debar others from the path of God; but God has knowledge of all that they do.*" (Verse 47) The purpose of this directive is to protect the community of believers against going out to fight, with an attitude of conceit, keen to show off, boasting of their own strength and using the blessing of power God has granted them for a purpose other than that of which He approves. Believers go out to fight for God's cause, to establish His authority and Lordship over human life, and to ensure people's submission to Him alone. They seek to destroy the tyrants who usurp God's authority and claim sovereignty for themselves, having no basis for their claim in the form of a permission granted by God or His law. They fight to declare the liberation of mankind throughout the world from any bondage to any authority, since such bondage represents a humiliation of man. Believers fight in order to protect people's rights, freedom and integrity, not to humiliate other races and peoples through the abuse of the power God has granted them. They go out to fight seeking no personal gain whatsoever. Victory brings them nothing other than having obeyed God's command to go on *jihād*, to establish the code of living He has revealed, to make God's word supreme and to seek His grace and pleasure. Even the spoils of war that believers may gain are viewed as an aspect of grace bestowed by none other than God.

False Pretences, False Promises

The believers had just seen the Quraysh leave their homes full of self-conceit, eager to be praised by others. They also witnessed the consequences of such an arrogant demonstration. The Quraysh mustered all their pride, power and prestige to defy God and His Messenger. By the end of the day the Quraysh returned home with their pride tarnished, their prestige shattered and their might totally destroyed. Here God reminds the community of believers of a recent situation that gave them much to think about: "*Do not be like those who left their homes full of self-conceit, seeking to be seen and praised by others. They debar others from the path of God; but God has knowledge of all that they do."* (Verse 47)

All the arrogance, self-conceit, and praise-seeking were clear in what Abū Jahl, who commanded the Quraysh forces in the battle, said to Abū Sufyān's messenger. The latter was the leader of the trade caravan the Muslims sought to intercept in compensation for their property confiscated by the Quraysh. When he and his caravan managed to escape unharmed by his Muslim pursuers, he sent a message to Abū Jahl asking him to return with the Quraysh army, as there was no longer any reason for the Quraysh to fight the Muslims. Abū Jahl said: "No. By God we will not go back home until we have reached Badr. We will stay there for three days, slaughtering camels for food, feeding whoever comes to us, drinking wine and listening to music and singers. The Arabs will then hold us in awe for the rest of time." When Abū Sufyān's messenger told him of Abū Jahl's answer, he said: "Pity to my people. This is the action of 'Amr ibn Hishām (i.e. Abū Jahl). He does not wish to come back because he put himself at the helm and acted unjustly. Injustice brings shame and bad omen. If Muḥammad wins the fight, we will be humiliated." Abū Sufyān was a man of foresight: Muḥammad (peace be upon him) scored a great victory and the unbelievers were badly humiliated as a result of their arrogance, injustice and debarring of other people from God's path. The Battle of Badr was a very severe blow to them. "*God has knowledge of all that they do.*" Nothing escapes Him. Nor can their might stand up to His power. He overpowers them and knows all their actions.

The *sūrah* goes on to describe how Satan persuaded the unbelievers to go out for a fight that led to their defeat and humiliation: "*Satan made their deeds seem fair to them, and said: 'No one can overcome you today, and I will stand firm by you.' But when the two hosts came within sight of each other, he turned on his heels and said: 'I am done with you, for I can see what you cannot. I fear God, for God is severe in retribution.'"* (Verse 48)

We have several reports that refer to this verse and to what it relates. However, none of these is attributed to the Prophet himself, with the exception of one that is graded as poor in authenticity. This report attributes the following statement to the Prophet: "Iblīs is never seen to be more insignificant, humiliated or depressed as he normally is on the day of attendance at 'Arafāt, as he witnesses God's forgiveness, mercy and grace being bestowed on people; except for what he saw on the day of Badr." People asked the Prophet: 'What did he see on the day of Badr?' He answered: "He saw Gabriel marshalling the angels."

The other reports quote 'Abdullāh ibn 'Abbās, 'Urwah ibn al-Zubayr, Qatādah, al-Ḥasan and Muḥammad ibn Ka'b. Here are some examples of these, related by al-Ṭabarī: "Ibn 'Abbās reports: Iblīs came on the day of Badr with a company of satans raising a banner in the form of a man from the Mudlij clan, while Satan himself took the form of Surāqah ibn Mālik. He said to the unbelievers, 'No human host can overcome you today, and I will stand firm by you.' When the two armies were marshalled, the Prophet took a handful of dust and threw it at the unbelievers. They started to flee. Jubayr came to Iblīs only to find him holding a man from the unbelievers by the hand. Iblīs withdrew his hand quickly and retreated with his assistants. The man said: 'Surāqah, have you not pledged to stand firm by us?' He said: 'I see what you cannot see. I fear God, for God is severe in retribution.'"

'Urwah ibn al-Zubayr reports: "When the Quraysh made up their minds to go out in defence of the caravan, they remembered the conflict between them and the Bakr tribe. They were so worried that they began to have second thoughts. Iblīs appeared to them in the shape of Surāqah ibn Mālik of the Mudlij clan, who was a highly respected chief of the Kinānah tribe. He said to them: 'I shall stand firm by you and make sure that the Kinānah will not try to attack you from behind while you are away.' They continued with their preparations and moved fast."

Qatādah reports on the subject of the verse mentioning how Satan persuaded the unbelievers to take up arms against the Muslims: "We have been told that he (meaning Satan) saw Gabriel with the angels coming down to support the believers and he claimed that he had no power to counter that of the angels. He said as he saw them: "*I am done with you, for I can see what you cannot. I fear God.*" (Verse 48) He was certainly lying for he, a sworn enemy of God, had no fear of God in his heart. He realized that he had no power and could extend no protection to anyone. It is in his nature to let down those who believe in him and do his bidding. Once the truth comes face to face with falsehood, he turns away, unscrupulously letting them down and declaring that he has nothing to do with them."

Following our chosen approach in this commentary, we prefer not to discuss matters which relate to the world that lies beyond our human perception in any degree of detail, when we do not have a Qur'ānic statement or a highly authentic *ḥadīth* to explain them. Such matters require a statement of this type to formulate a conceptual belief. However, we do not adopt a negative attitude either. In this particular case, we have a Qur'ānic statement that tells us that Satan did make their deeds seem fair to the unbelievers and encouraged them to raise an army and march to fight the Muslims, promising them support and protection. Later when the two hosts were within sight of each other, "*he turned on his heels and said: 'I am done with you, for I can see what you cannot. I fear God, for God is severe in retribution.'*" (Verse 48) Thus he let them down, keeping no promise he had given them, and leaving them to suffer the outcome of their actions on their own. We have no idea how he made their actions seem fair to them, nor how he said to them that they could not be overcome by any human power on that particular day. Neither do we have any idea how Satan promised them support and assured them of his protection, nor how he turned on his heels and said what is reported in the Qur'ān of his statements.

We cannot say anything about 'how' all these matters took place and in what form they were done. Everything that concerns Satan belongs to the realm that lies beyond the reach of our human perception. We have no way of knowing exactly 'how' such matters occur, except in as much as the Qur'ānic statement relates. The statement we have here confirms the event but does not mention how it happened. We prefer not to go any further than that.

We do not support the line of thinking advocated by the school of Sheikh Muḥammad 'Abduh which tries to find an interpretation that denies any physical presence or effect for anything that belongs to the world beyond. In connection with this particular verse, Shaikh Rashīd Riḍā says:

> "*Satan made their deeds seem fair to them, and said: No one can overcome you today, and I will stand firm by you.*" The verse implies an order to the Prophet to tell the believers how Satan made the deeds of the unbelievers seem fair to them by his whispering to them and giving them the impression that no force could overcome them, whether it be the weak band of Muḥammad's followers or

any other tribe, because they could command a larger and more courageous force. He further impressed on them that he was going to give them firm support. Al-Bayḍāwī says in his commentary: 'Satan misguided them into believing that by following him in such actions as they might have thought to earn God's pleasure would be sufficient to protect them. They were so deceived that they prayed to God to give victory to the group which followed the better of the two religions.'

"When the two hosts came within sight of each other, he turned on his heels." When the two armies drew close to each other and each could have a clear idea of what situation the other was in, and before the actual battle started, he drew back and turned away. Commentators who say that 'coming within sight of each other' means drawing close to each other are rather mistaken. What is meant here is that at this juncture he stopped his whisperings to them and his attempts to delude them. The statement is figurative in the sense that Satan's whispering is depicted in terms of a movement similar to that of a person coming towards something he wants, and the stopping of these whispers as leaving that thing alone and turning away from it. The Qur'ānic account goes further to indicate that Satan abandons them and disassociates himself from them altogether: *"(He) said: 'I am done with you, for I can see what you cannot. I fear God, for God is severe in retribution.'"* This means that as he declared he had nothing to do with them, he feared that they were doomed, particularly since he saw that God had sent the angels to support the Muslims. The phrase ending this verse, *"God is severe in retribution,"* may be part of Satan's own statement and it may be a new statement commenting on the event itself...

The meaning of these statements, then, is that the disciples of the evil one were active among the unbelievers, working on their evil souls, whispering to them to delude them and to give them a false sense of power. At the same time the angels were working on the noble souls of the believers to give them support and to increase their confidence that God's promise of victory would certainly come true.[1]

---

1. M. Rashīd Riḍā, *Tafsīr al-Manār*. Dār al-Ma'rifah, Beirut, Vol. X, pp. 27–28

There is a clear tendency here to interpret the actions of the angels as merely making an impression on the souls of the believers. This commentator also states firmly that the angels did not take part in the fighting, despite the fact that God says to the angels: "*Strike, then, their necks and strike off their every fingertip.*" (Verse 12) He further describes Satan's actions as working on the unbelievers' souls. Such interpretation is typical of the line this school follows. It is similar to the interpretation given by Shaikh Muḥammad ʿAbduh when he comments on *Sūrah* 105 which describes how God destroyed the Abyssinians who came with a large army to destroy the Kaʿbah and at the head of the army marched an elephant. The *sūrah* states: "*Have you not seen how your Lord dealt with the people of the elephant? Did He not cause their treacherous plan to be futile, and send against them flights of birds, which pelted them with stones of sand and clay? Thus He made them like devoured dry leaves.*" (105: 1–5) In his commentary Shaikh Muḥammad ʿAbduh says that those 'stones of sand and clay' could be only the smallpox virus. Such an approach carries matters too far. It unnecessarily seeks to interpret matters that belong to the world beyond in terms of what is familiar to us in our world, when there is nothing to prevent these statements from meaning exactly what they say. All that is needed is not to try to go further than the clear meaning of every such statement. This is our chosen approach.[2]

Deception Compounded by Short-Sightedness

While Satan was working hard, trying to delude the unbelievers and encouraging them to go out in force to fight the believers then abandoning them at their time of need, the hypocrites and those who were sick at heart thought the worst of what fate the Muslims would be facing. They looked at the small band of believers facing up to a much superior force. Thinking only in material terms, they felt that the believers brought upon themselves a woeful doom, deluded by their faith, thinking that faith would bring them victory or at least give them protection: "*The hypocrites and those in whose hearts there was disease said: 'Their faith has deluded these people.'*" (Verse 49) Some

2. The author comments on this *sūrah* in detail and discusses Shaikh ʿAbduh's view in Vol. 30 of the Arabic edition, published in English as Vol. 30 of *In the Shade of the Qur'ān* by MWH London Publishers, 1979, pp. 293–309. – Editor's note.

scholars say about this group that they were Makkans who looked favourably upon Islam but who stopped short of accepting it. They went out with the Quraysh army, uncertain of their own attitude. When they realized how superior the forces of the unbelievers were they said this about the Muslims.

The hypocrites and those who are sick at heart are unable to understand the true causes of defeat or victory. They only look at appearances and have no means of understanding the true nature of anything that is not physically apparent. They cannot appreciate the power of faith and what effect trusting God and relying on Him bring about. They cannot see how believers cannot be overawed by forces that do not rely on a firm belief in God. Hence it is understandable that they should think the believers to be deluded by their faith, bringing themselves to ruin as they faced a far superior force.

Any situation may have the same physical appearance in the eyes of believers and those whose hearts are devoid of faith. What is different, however, is how they look at any situation and how they evaluate it. Unbelievers do not see anything beyond the physical appearance, while those who have faith see the reality that lies beyond it. They are able to see all the forces that have an influence on it and balance between them accurately. The fact that believers understand and from which they derive reassurance is that to which the conclusion of this verse alludes: "*But he who puts his trust in God knows that God is Almighty, Wise.*" (Verse 49) But this fact is withheld from those hearts that have no faith. Yet it is the one that tilts the balance and determines the outcome of the conflict between the two groups every time and everywhere.

On the day of Badr the hypocrites and those who were sick at heart said about the Muslim group, '*their faith has deluded these people.*' This is the same thing that such people say whenever they see the advocates of Islam confronting the mightier forces of tyranny, when their main equipment is basically this religion, their unshakeable faith in its truth, their burning desire to defend what God has made sacred and their reliance on God and trust in Him.

The hypocrites and those who are sick at heart stand idle, watching the advocates of Islam as they firmly stand up to the forces of falsehood, deriding their attitude that makes little of the dangers to which they expose themselves when they take on such mightier forces. At the same time, they are full of admiration for such people who are willing to take such great risks for their cause. They cannot understand why anyone should be willing to be exposed to such great dangers. They view everything in life, including faith and religion, as little more than a business deal. If they feel they can profit by it then they will take it up without question, but if it involves risk taking, then they do not want to have anything to do with it. They are unable to see matters from the point of view of a believer, and they cannot evaluate matters using the perspective of faith. From a believer's point of view, the deal is a highly profitable one in all circumstances. It leads to one of the two best eventualities: victory which brings about the implementation of faith in practical life or martyrdom which ensures admittance into heaven. Besides, the balance of power is viewed differently by the believer. God Himself is involved, but the hypocrites and those who are sick at heart do not take God's power into account.

The advocates of Islam, wherever they may be and in whichever period in history they live, are called upon to use the standard of faith when they evaluate matters. They must look at everything in the light of God's guidance. They must not be overawed by the mighty forces of evil, thinking that they have little power of their own. How could they think themselves to be weak when they have God on their side? They must always pay heed to the instructions God gives to the believers: *"He who puts his trust in God knows that God is Almighty, Wise."* (Verse 49)

Divine Justice for All

At this juncture the *sūrah* portrays a scene of God's direct intervention in the battle. We see the angels acting on God's instructions and by His permission, reproaching the unbelievers and meting out punishment to them. They gather their souls in a very harsh manner and dole out to them the sort of treatment that befits their arrogance and conceit. Even in the most difficult of times they remind them of their evil deeds and tell them of their inevitable destiny. There is no injustice in what they are about to suffer. It is only what they deserve. When this scene is painted, the *sūrah* follows it by a statement making clear that punishing the unbelievers for their misdeeds is a constant law that God has set into operation: *"Like Pharaoh's people and those who lived before them."* (Verses 52 and 54) *"This is because God would never alter the favours He bestows on a community unless they change what is in their hearts."* (Verse 53)

It is according to this law that He took Pharaoh and his people to task, and according to it He takes to task any person or community guilty of the same type of action: "*If you could but see how the angels gather up the souls of the unbelievers. They strike them on their faces and their backs and [say]: 'Taste the punishment of burning, in return for what your own hands have committed. Never does God do any injustice to His servants.' Like Pharaoh's people and those who lived before them, they denied God's revelations; so God took them to task for their sins. God is mighty, severe in retribution. This is because God would never alter the favours He bestows on a community unless they change what is in their hearts. God hears all and knows all. Like Pharaoh's people and those who lived before them, they disbelieved in their Lord's revelations; so We destroyed them for their sins, as We caused Pharaoh's people to drown. They were wrongdoers all.*" (Verses 50–54)

The first two of these verses may be intended to refer to what the unbelievers were made to suffer at the Battle of Badr when the angels took part in the fighting carrying out God's orders. He had issued to them an express order: "*Strike, then, their necks and strike off their every fingertip. This is because they have defied God and His Messenger. Whoever defies God and His Messenger [will find out that] God is severe in retribution.*" (Verses 12–13) When we commented on this statement (p. 95), we mentioned that we do not know how the angels strike the necks of human beings or how they strike off their fingertips. However, our ignorance of how this is done should not tempt us to try to give this statement any meaning other than its apparent one, which makes it clear that there was an order from God to the angels to strike. We know that the angels "*do not disobey God in whatever He commands them, but always do whatever they are bidden to do.*" (66: 6) In this case these two verses serve as a reminder of what the angels did on the day of Badr and an explanation of what they actually did to the unbelievers.

These two verses, however, may also be taken as a reference to a continuing situation that applies whenever the angels gather the souls of unbelievers. In this case the opening phrase, '*if you could but see*', may be understood as an address to anyone with eyes to see. This type of address is used frequently to direct attention to certain matters that need to be contemplated.

Whichever possibility we take, the Qur'ānic statement portrays a fearful picture of the unbelievers as the angels gather their souls, adding humiliation to their misery and combining physical suffering with death: *"If you could but see how the angels gather up the souls of the unbelievers. They strike them on their faces and their backs."* (Verse 50) The mode of expression then changes from that of reporting to an address: *"Taste the punishment of burning."* This serves to bring the scene alive as though it is happening now in front of our eyes. We almost see the fire of hell and how it burns fiercely. The unbelievers are severely reproached as they are pushed into it: *"[this is] in return for what your own hands have committed."* (Verse 51) It is all a fitting recompense. You deserve it all on account of what you have done: *"Never does God do any injustice to His servants."* (Verse 51)

This statement and the scene of the punishment of burning it portrays raise the question: is it a warning the angels give to the unbelievers pointing out to them what they are going to suffer and showing it as if it is taking place now? Or do they actually suffer the punishment of burning as soon as their souls are gathered by the angels? Both situations are possible. There is no reason to preclude either. We do not wish to add anything further because this is again something that belongs to the world that lies beyond human perception. It is known only to God. As for us, we only need to believe that it will definitely take place. Indeed there is nothing to stop it happening. But when will that be? The answer is known only to God whose knowledge is absolute, encompassing the universe and all that it contains.

The *sūrah* then states a fundamental fact that is relevant to this scene. The infliction of suffering and humiliation on the unbelievers is a permanent law that does not change. It was set into operation a long time ago and it continues to operate without fail: *"Like Pharaoh's people and those who lived before them, they denied God's revelations; so God took them to task for their sins. God is mighty, severe in retribution."* (Verse 52) God does not determine the fate of human beings haphazardly or on the basis of sudden whims. Their fate follows a law that is meant to apply at all times. What happened to those unbelievers at Badr is likely to happen to them at all times. The same type of thing happened to Pharaoh's people and to other communities before them, because *"they denied God's revelations; so God took them to task for their sins."* (Verse 52) They could not protect themselves against His punishment: *"God is mighty, severe in retribution."* (Verse 52)

What Changes God's Blessings?

God had bestowed His grace on them, giving them plenty of provisions, granting them power, and allowing their generations to follow one another. All this God grants to human beings to test them so that they may choose whether to be grateful to Him for His blessings or not. But they chose to be ungrateful, denying God and using His blessings to tyrannize. They felt that the power they were given was theirs by right and they denied God's revelations. Hence they deserved their severe punishment in accordance with the law God had set in operation. Therefore, God altered the blessings with which He had favoured them, and destroyed them altogether: *"This is because God would never alter the favours He bestows on a community unless they change what is in their hearts. God hears all and knows all. Like Pharaoh's people and those who lived before them, they disbelieved in their Lord's revelations; so We destroyed them for their sins, as We caused Pharaoh's people to drown. They were wrongdoers all."* (Verses 53–54)

God destroyed them only after they had denied His revelations. He did not punish them with destruction prior to that, although they were unbelievers, because He is Compassionate, Merciful: *"We would never inflict punishment on anyone until We have sent a Messenger."* (17: 15) Pharaoh's people and those who had gone before them adopting the same attitude of denying God's revelations and suffering the punishment of destruction are described here as "wrongdoers". This is a very frequent usage in the Qur'ān, depicting the rejection of the faith or the association of partners with God as "wrongdoing".

We need to reflect a little on the statement that this verse makes: *"This is because God would never alter the favours He bestows on a community unless they change what is in their hearts."* (Verse 53) It confirms the essential aspect of fairness in God's treatment of human beings. He does not deprive them of any favour He has granted them unless they change their intentions, attitudes, behaviour and general situation. By doing so, they deserve that God should alter what He has given them by way of testing them and withdrawing the favours and blessings He has bestowed on them. They have shown no gratitude for such blessings and favours. On the other hand, God bestows a great honour on man when He makes His will applicable to man on the basis of man's own actions. A change in the fate of human beings depends on a practical change in their own intentions, behaviour, practices and general situation. All this they choose for themselves. Moreover, human beings are given a great responsibility, commensurate to the great honour God has granted them. They can ensure that the grace and favours God grants them remain permanently with them and that they are given an increase of this by knowing, appreciating and showing gratitude. On the other hand, they can ensure that all these are removed from them if they behave with arrogance, deny God's favours, entertain evil intentions and adopt deviant practices.

This great fact is central to the Islamic concept of man, how God's will applies to him as well as his relationship with the universe and what takes place in it. Here we see the position of honour granted by God to man and we appreciate the latitude man has been given in determining his own destiny and shaping the events that take place around him. He is indeed an actor who makes his contribution by God's permission. Indeed the working of God's will takes place through his deeds and actions. Thus man is freed from the humiliating state of passivity imposed on him by materialistic philosophies which regard him as a passive creature who has no influence on the major trends that continue their inevitable movement with total disregard to him and his actions. These include economy, history and evolution. According to these philosophies, man has no option other than to submit to these trends with all humility.

The same fact makes it absolutely clear that there is an inevitable relationship in human life between action and reward. It also gives us a clear idea of God's absolute, unfailing justice that transforms this relationship into a law set into operation by God's will. It ensures that not a single one of God's servants will suffer the slightest injustice:

> *Never does God do any injustice to His servants.* (Verse 51)
>
> *This is because God would never alter the favours He bestows on a community unless they change what is in their hearts.* (Verse 53)
>
> *We destroyed them for their sins, as We caused Pharaoh's people to drown. They were wrongdoers all.* (Verse 54)

All praise be to God, the Lord of all the worlds.

4

Delineation of Loyalties

Indeed, the worst of all creatures in God's sight are the ones who have denied the truth, and therefore will not believe; (55)

إِنَّ شَرَّ ٱلدَّوَآبِّ عِندَ ٱللَّهِ ٱلَّذِينَ كَفَرُواْ
فَهُمۡ لَا يُؤۡمِنُونَ ﴿٥٥﴾

those with whom you have concluded a treaty, and then they break their treaty at every occasion, entertaining no sense of fearing God. (56)

ٱلَّذِينَ عَٰهَدتَّ مِنۡهُمۡ ثُمَّ يَنقُضُونَ
عَهۡدَهُمۡ فِي كُلِّ مَرَّةٖ وَهُمۡ
لَا يَتَّقُونَ ﴿٥٦﴾

Should you meet them in battle, make of them a fearsome example for those who follow them, so that they may reflect and take it to heart. (57)

فَإِمَّا تَثۡقَفَنَّهُمۡ فِي ٱلۡحَرۡبِ فَشَرِّدۡ بِهِم
مَّنۡ خَلۡفَهُمۡ لَعَلَّهُمۡ يَذَّكَّرُونَ ﴿٥٧﴾

And if you fear treachery from any folk, cast [your treaty with them] back to them in a fair manner. God does not love the treacherous. (58)

وَإِمَّا تَخَافَنَّ مِن قَوۡمٍ خِيَانَةٗ فَٱنۢبِذۡ
إِلَيۡهِمۡ عَلَىٰ سَوَآءٍۚ إِنَّ ٱللَّهَ لَا يُحِبُّ
ٱلۡخَآئِنِينَ ﴿٥٨﴾

Let not those who disbelieve reckon that they shall escape. They can never be beyond [God's] grasp. (59)

وَلَا يَحۡسَبَنَّ ٱلَّذِينَ كَفَرُواْ سَبَقُوٓاْۚ
إِنَّهُمۡ لَا يُعۡجِزُونَ ﴿٥٩﴾

Make ready against them whatever force and war mounts you can muster, so that you may strike terror into the enemies of God who are also your own enemies, and others besides them of whom you may be unaware, but of whom God is well aware. Whatever you may spend in God's cause shall be repaid to you in full, and you shall not be wronged. (60)

وَأَعِدُّوا۟ لَهُم مَّا ٱسْتَطَعْتُم مِّن قُوَّةٍ
وَمِن رِّبَاطِ ٱلْخَيْلِ تُرْهِبُونَ بِهِۦ
عَدُوَّ ٱللَّهِ وَعَدُوَّكُمْ وَءَاخَرِينَ مِن
دُونِهِمْ لَا تَعْلَمُونَهُمُ ٱللَّهُ يَعْلَمُهُمْ ۚ
وَمَا تُنفِقُوا۟ مِن شَىْءٍ فِى سَبِيلِ ٱللَّهِ
يُوَفَّ إِلَيْكُمْ وَأَنتُمْ لَا تُظْلَمُونَ ﴿٦٠﴾

If they incline to peace, then incline you to it as well, and place your trust in God. He alone hears all and knows all. (61)

وَإِن جَنَحُوا۟ لِلسَّلْمِ فَٱجْنَحْ لَهَا وَتَوَكَّلْ
عَلَى ٱللَّهِ ۚ إِنَّهُۥ هُوَ ٱلسَّمِيعُ ٱلْعَلِيمُ ﴿٦١﴾

Should they seek to deceive you, God is all-sufficient for you. He it is who has strengthened you with His help and rallied the believers round you, (62)

وَإِن يُرِيدُوٓا۟ أَن يَخْدَعُوكَ فَإِنَّ
حَسْبَكَ ٱللَّهُ ۚ هُوَ ٱلَّذِىٓ أَيَّدَكَ بِنَصْرِهِۦ
وَبِٱلْمُؤْمِنِينَ ﴿٦٢﴾

uniting their hearts. If you were to spend all that is on earth you could not have so united their hearts, but God has united them. He is Mighty and Wise. (63)

وَأَلَّفَ بَيْنَ قُلُوبِهِمْ ۚ لَوْ أَنفَقْتَ مَا فِى
ٱلْأَرْضِ جَمِيعًا مَّآ أَلَّفْتَ بَيْنَ
قُلُوبِهِمْ وَلَٰكِنَّ ٱللَّهَ أَلَّفَ بَيْنَهُمْ ۚ
إِنَّهُۥ عَزِيزٌ حَكِيمٌ ﴿٦٣﴾

Prophet, God is enough for you and those of the believers who follow you. (64)

يَٰٓأَيُّهَا ٱلنَّبِىُّ حَسْبُكَ ٱللَّهُ وَمَنِ ٱتَّبَعَكَ
مِنَ ٱلْمُؤْمِنِينَ ﴿٦٤﴾

Prophet, urge the believers to fight. If there are twenty steadfast men among you, they will overcome two hundred, and if there are a hundred of you, they will defeat a thousand of those who disbelieve, for those are devoid of understanding. (65)

يَـٰٓأَيُّهَا ٱلنَّبِيُّ حَرِّضِ ٱلْمُؤْمِنِينَ عَلَى ٱلْقِتَالِ إِن يَكُن مِّنكُمْ عِشْرُونَ صَـٰبِرُونَ يَغْلِبُوا۟ مِا۟ئَتَيْنِ وَإِن يَكُن مِّنكُم مِّا۟ئَةٌ يَغْلِبُوٓا۟ أَلْفًا مِّنَ ٱلَّذِينَ كَفَرُوٓا۟ بِأَنَّهُمْ قَوْمٌ لَّا يَفْقَهُونَ ٦٥

Now God has lightened your burden, for He knows that you are weak. So, if there are a hundred steadfast men among you, they will overcome two hundred, and if there are a thousand of you they will, by God's will, defeat two thousand. God is with those who are steadfast. (66)

ٱلْـَٔـٰنَ خَفَّفَ ٱللَّهُ عَنكُمْ وَعَلِمَ أَنَّ فِيكُمْ ضَعْفًا فَإِن يَكُن مِّنكُم مِّا۟ئَةٌ صَابِرَةٌ يَغْلِبُوا۟ مِا۟ئَتَيْنِ وَإِن يَكُن مِّنكُمْ أَلْفٌ يَغْلِبُوٓا۟ أَلْفَيْنِ بِإِذْنِ ٱللَّهِ وَٱللَّهُ مَعَ ٱلصَّـٰبِرِينَ ٦٦

It does not behove a Prophet to have captives unless he has battled strenuously in the land. You may desire the fleeting gains of this world, but God desires for you the good of the life to come. God is Almighty, Wise. (67)

مَا كَانَ لِنَبِيٍّ أَن يَكُونَ لَهُۥٓ أَسْرَىٰ حَتَّىٰ يُثْخِنَ فِى ٱلْأَرْضِ تُرِيدُونَ عَرَضَ ٱلدُّنْيَا وَٱللَّهُ يُرِيدُ ٱلْـَٔاخِرَةَ وَٱللَّهُ عَزِيزٌ حَكِيمٌ ٦٧

Had it not been for a decree from God that had already gone forth, you would have been severely punished for what you have taken. (68)

لَّوْلَا كِتَـٰبٌ مِّنَ ٱللَّهِ سَبَقَ لَمَسَّكُمْ فِيمَآ أَخَذْتُمْ عَذَابٌ عَظِيمٌ ٦٨

Enjoy, then, what you have gained, as lawful and good, and remain God-fearing; indeed God is much Forgiving, most Merciful. (69)

فَكُلُوا۟ مِمَّا غَنِمْتُمْ حَلَـٰلًا طَيِّبًا وَٱتَّقُوا۟ ٱللَّهَ إِنَّ ٱللَّهَ غَفُورٌ رَّحِيمٌ ٦٩

Prophet, say to the captives who are in your hands: If God finds goodness in your hearts, He will give you something better than all that has been taken from you, and He will forgive you your sins. God is much Forgiving, Merciful. (70)

يَـٰٓأَيُّهَا ٱلنَّبِىُّ قُل لِّمَن فِىٓ أَيۡدِيكُم مِّنَ ٱلۡأَسۡرَىٰٓ إِن يَعۡلَمِ ٱللَّهُ فِى قُلُوبِكُمۡ خَيۡرًا يُؤۡتِكُمۡ خَيۡرًا مِّمَّآ أُخِذَ مِنكُمۡ وَيَغۡفِرۡ لَكُمۡۗ وَٱللَّهُ غَفُورٌ رَّحِيمٌ ٧٠

Should they seek to play false with you, they were previously false to God Himself, but He gave [you] mastery over them. God is All-knowing, Wise. (71)

وَإِن يُرِيدُواْ خِيَانَتَكَ فَقَدۡ خَانُواْ ٱللَّهَ مِن قَبۡلُ فَأَمۡكَنَ مِنۡهُمۡۗ وَٱللَّهُ عَلِيمٌ حَكِيمٌ ٧١

Those who believe and have migrated and striven hard, with their possessions and their lives, for God's cause, as well as those who give them shelter and support – these are friends and protectors of one another. As for those who believe but have not migrated [to join you], you owe no duty of protection to them until they have migrated. Yet, should they appeal to you for support, on grounds of faith, it is your duty to support them, except against a people with whom you have a treaty. God sees all that you do. (72)

إِنَّ ٱلَّذِينَ ءَامَنُواْ وَهَاجَرُواْ وَجَـٰهَدُواْ بِأَمۡوَٰلِهِمۡ وَأَنفُسِهِمۡ فِى سَبِيلِ ٱللَّهِ وَٱلَّذِينَ ءَاوَواْ وَّنَصَرُوٓاْ أُوْلَـٰٓئِكَ بَعۡضُهُمۡ أَوۡلِيَآءُ بَعۡضٍۚ وَٱلَّذِينَ ءَامَنُواْ وَلَمۡ يُهَاجِرُواْ مَا لَكُم مِّن وَلَـٰيَتِهِم مِّن شَىۡءٍ حَتَّىٰ يُهَاجِرُواْۚ وَإِنِ ٱسۡتَنصَرُوكُمۡ فِى ٱلدِّينِ فَعَلَيۡكُمُ ٱلنَّصۡرُ إِلَّا عَلَىٰ قَوۡمٍ بَيۡنَكُمۡ وَبَيۡنَهُم مِّيثَـٰقٌۗ وَٱللَّهُ بِمَا تَعۡمَلُونَ بَصِيرٌ ٧٢

The unbelievers are allies of one another. Unless you do likewise, there will be oppression on earth and much corruption. (73)

وَٱلَّذِينَ كَفَرُواْ بَعۡضُهُمۡ أَوۡلِيَآءُ بَعۡضٍۚ إِلَّا تَفۡعَلُوهُ تَكُن فِتۡنَةٌ فِى ٱلۡأَرۡضِ وَفَسَادٌ كَبِيرٌ ٧٣

Those who believe and have migrated and striven hard for God's cause, as well as those who give them shelter and support are indeed the true believers. Forgiveness of sins, and most generous provisions await them. (74)

وَٱلَّذِينَ ءَامَنُوا۟ وَهَاجَرُوا۟ وَجَٰهَدُوا۟
فِى سَبِيلِ ٱللَّهِ وَٱلَّذِينَ ءَاوَوا۟ وَّنَصَرُوٓا۟
أُو۟لَٰٓئِكَ هُمُ ٱلْمُؤْمِنُونَ حَقًّا ۚ لَّهُم
مَّغْفِرَةٌ وَرِزْقٌ كَرِيمٌ ﴿٧٤﴾

And those who subsequently come to believe, and migrate and strive hard with you [for God's cause] shall also belong to you. Those who are bound by ties of blood have the first claim on one another in accordance with God's decree. God has full knowledge of everything. (75)

وَٱلَّذِينَ ءَامَنُوا۟ مِنۢ بَعْدُ وَهَاجَرُوا۟
وَجَٰهَدُوا۟ مَعَكُمْ فَأُو۟لَٰٓئِكَ مِنكُمْ ۚ
وَأُو۟لُوا۟ ٱلْأَرْحَامِ بَعْضُهُمْ أَوْلَىٰ بِبَعْضٍ
فِى كِتَٰبِ ٱللَّهِ ۗ إِنَّ ٱللَّهَ بِكُلِّ شَىْءٍ
عَلِيمٌۢ ﴿٧٥﴾

Overview

This final passage of the *sūrah* includes a number of rules for dealing with other camps and communities in times of peace and war. It also speaks of the internal organization of the Muslim community and the regulation of its relations with other communities. It speaks of the Islamic view of pledges and covenants in all situations, as well as the ties of blood, race, homeland and faith. This gives us a host of rules and regulations in all these matters. Some of these are final and apply in all situations, while others are provisional, dealing with the situation that prevailed at the time. These were to be amended later, when *Sūrah* 9, Repentance, was revealed towards the end of the Madinan period. These rules and regulations include:

- Those who enter into a treaty with the Muslims and then break their treaty are the worst creatures. The Muslims should, therefore, teach them a lesson that strikes fear in their hearts and in the hearts of those who follow them, contemplating a similar breach of their own treaty or thinking of launching a treacherous attack on the Muslim community.

- Those groups who have concluded a treaty with the Muslims, but the Muslim leadership has reason to believe that they may be involved in treacherous action, may be put on notice of termination of their treaty. When this is done, the Islamic leadership is free to fight them, teach them a lesson and make of them an example for those who take a similar attitude.
- The Muslim community, which represents the camp following God's guidance, must always be prepared, maintain a position of strength, be as well equipped as possible, so that it is always held in awe by other communities. This will ensure better security for the land of Islam, as hostile forces will think twice before launching an attack on it. It will also make such forces submit to the requirement of allowing the advocates of the faith to fulfil their task of making God's message known to people and calling on them to accept it. They will also refrain from trying to prevent anyone in their land from accepting the faith if he wishes to do so. Sovereignty will thus be acknowledged to belong to God alone, and no one other than Him may lay claim to it.
- If any party of unbelievers is inclined to have an agreement of peaceful co-existence with the Muslim community, the Muslim leadership will accept this and conclude such an agreement. If they entertain thoughts of treachery, and there is no visible evidence of such thoughts, the Muslims will entrust the whole matter to God who will take care of any would-be traitors.
- *Jihād* is a duty of Muslims, even when they are heavily outnumbered. With God's help, they can achieve victory. Each one of them is equal to ten of the enemy. In the worst situations when the Muslims are at their weakest, everyone of them is equal to two of the enemy force. The duty of *jihād* does not wait until parity with the enemy is achieved. All that the Muslims should do is to mobilize their best forces, place their full trust in God, remain patient in adversity and steadfast in battle. Moreover, they must leave the rest to God. After all, they have a power that other camps do not have.

- The first goal of the Muslim community is to destroy the power of tyranny by all available means. If the taking of captives in battle and releasing them for ransom does not help achieve that, then such measures are to be discounted. It is a permanent rule that God's Messengers and their followers should not take captives until they have demonstrated their power, destroyed the might of their enemy and established their own authority. When that has been accomplished, there may be no harm in taking captives and receiving ransom for their release.
- Spoils of war are permissible for the Muslims to take. The same is the case with ransom in return for the release of any captives they might have taken after they have strenuously battled and demonstrated their power.
- When captives are taken by the Muslims, these captives should be given a good idea of Islam. They should also be encouraged to accept it. They should be told that God promises them what is superior to what is taken from them, whether in spoils of war or in ransom. They should also be warned against any attempt of treachery.
- The central bond that brings people together in Muslim society is that of faith. Loyalty and allegiance in that society are based on faith and organization at the same time. Those who have accepted the faith and migrated to its land and those who welcomed them into their land, giving them full support, are one single group with mutual ties of faith and duties of protection. By contrast, those who accepted the faith without moving to the land of Islam have no commitment of mutual protection with the Muslim camp. This means that there is no duty binding the Muslim state to give them support. The Muslim community will give them active support only when they are attacked because of their faith by a group who have no covenant with the Muslims.
- The fact that the central bond in Muslim society is faith does not preclude that relatives have an added bond of loyalty when the two main requirements of faith and organization are fulfilled. Blood relationship does not initiate any tie of loyalty when the bond of faith is not in existence.

This is a brief outline of the rules and regulations included in this final passage of the *sūrah*, outlining the most important elements of the Islamic system dealing with internal and external affairs.

When Treaties Are Breached

Verses 55–63 at the beginning of this passage deal primarily with a real situation that the Muslim community had to come to grips with at the time when the first Muslim state was established in Madinah. These verses provided the Islamic leadership with guidance and rules to apply in dealing with that situation. They represent a basic element in the international relations between the Muslim community and other groups. They remained in force, with minor amendments that were subsequently incorporated.

These verses make it clear that it is perfectly appropriate to conclude agreements of peaceful co-existence with other communities and groups, as long as such agreements are certain to be taken seriously, respected and honoured. If the other camp manipulates these agreements and uses them as a shield to cover up its treacherous designs, taking steps to launch an assault against the Muslims, then the Muslim leadership is fully entitled to terminate these agreements, making the other side fully aware of that termination. Once this is done, the Muslim leadership is free to choose the time when to attack, making sure that any such attack is powerful enough to strike fear in the heart of all who contemplate a hostile attitude towards the Muslim society, whether openly or in secret. On the other hand, those who are interested in a genuine peace with the Muslim camp, have no intention of opposing the Islamic message or stopping its advocacy, and demonstrate their inclination to peace, may enjoy such a relationship of real peace.

All this was clearly meant to deal with real situations that affected relations between the Muslim state and neighbouring camps. When the Muslim state enjoys security, having no physical impediments to its task of conveying God's message to people everywhere, it has no reason to refuse peaceful co-existence. At the same time, it does not allow for peace agreements to be used as a cover-up for intended treachery.

The practical situation in Madinah that these verses addressed resulted from the circumstances of the early period of the Prophet's settlement in that city. These are outlined by Imām Ibn al-Qayyim in his priceless book *Zād al-Ma'ād.* Although this summary is quoted in the Prologue to this volume, it is useful to repeat it here.

This is a chapter setting an outline of the Prophet's attitude to the unbelievers and the hypocrites, right from the time when he first received his message until he departed from this life:

The first revelation bestowed on him was "*Read in the name of your Lord who created.*" (96: 1) This was the point at which he became a Prophet. It was an order to him to read, alone. No order was given at this point that he should deliver any message. Later on, God revealed to him: "*You that are wrapped up in your cloak! Arise and warn.*" (74: 1–2) Thus He made him a Prophet when He said to him, 'Read', and then made him a Messenger when He told him, 'Arise and warn.' He then ordered him to warn his immediate clan. He followed this by warning his own people, then the other Arab tribes close to Makkah, then all the Arabs, and finally all mankind.

The Prophet thus spent more than a dozen years after his initial prophethood advocating his message, without fighting. He was ordered throughout this period not to take up arms; rather, he should remain patient and forbearing. Then he received permission to migrate, and another permission to fight. God then ordered him to fight those who wage war against him, and not to fight those who stand aside, refraining from such a fight. Later, the Prophet was ordered to fight the unbelievers until all submission is made only to God.

At this point, the unbelievers were divided into three categories with regard to their relationship with the Prophet (peace be upon him). In the first category were those with whom he concluded a peace treaty. The second category included those who were at war with the Prophet, while the third were those who had submitted to his authority and were under his protection.

The Prophet was ordered to fulfil his obligations under any peace treaty as long as the other party fulfilled their obligations. Should he fear that they may resort to treachery, he should give them notice of the termination of their treaty. He must not fight them until he had informed them of such termination. He was also ordered to fight any party which violated their peace treaty with him.

When *Sūrah* 9, Repentance, was revealed, it outlined the rulings applicable to each of the three categories. Thus, the Prophet was ordered to fight those of the people of earlier revelations who waged war against him until they had been subdued and agreed to pay submission tax, or *jizyah*, or accept Islam. He was further ordered to strive hard against the unbelievers and the hypocrites. Thus, he struggled against the unbelievers with sword and spear, and against the hypocrites with logic and argument. He was also ordered in *Sūrah* 9 to declare a general disavowal, terminating all treaties with unbelievers.

However, the people who held peace treaties with the Prophet were divided into three groups. The first were those who had been unfaithful to their treaties and were in clear violation of them: these he was ordered to fight. He actually fought them and was victorious. The second group included those with a treaty lasting for a specific time. If these had honoured their obligations under the treaty and did not aid others against the Prophet and the Muslim community, the Prophet was ordered to honour their treaty for as long as it lasted. The third group included those who had no treaty with the Prophet but had not fought with him and also those who had an open treaty specifying no time. He was ordered to give all these groups four months' notice, after which he could fight them.

Thus, the Prophet fought and killed those who were treacherous, violating their treaty, and put on four-months' notice those without a treaty or with an open-ended one. He was also to honour his obligations to those who honoured theirs under their treaties. All those in this category adopted Islam before the end of their respective terms. He imposed *jizyah* or submission tax on those under his authority.[1]

When we closely examine this scholarly summary in the light of the events of the period and the dates of the revelation of the different

1. Ibn al-Qayyim, *Zād al-Ma'ād,* Mu'assasat al-Risālah, Beirut, 1994, Vol. 3, pp. 158–161.

Qur'ānic verses and *sūrah*s outlining these rules and regulations we definitely conclude that the verses we are looking at in this *sūrah* represent a middle stage between the situation in the early days of the Islamic reign in Madinah and that which prevailed after the revelation of *Sūrah* 9, Repentance. All relevant statements must be studied in this light. Although the verses we have here include some very basic rules, they do not put these in their final form. These are finally stated in *Sūrah* 9. The events which took place later in the Prophet's lifetime represent a practical example of how these rules are to be implemented.

The Worst of All Creatures

> *Indeed, the worst of all creatures in God's sight are the ones who have denied the truth, and therefore will not believe; those with whom you have concluded a treaty, and then they break their treaty at every occasion, entertaining no sense of fearing God.* (Verses 55–56)

The Arabic term used in this verse for "creatures" signifies walking, which makes the description sound like, "the worst of those that walk on earth." This term applies to all walking creatures, particularly animals, but includes human beings. However, it has clear additional connotations when it refers to humans. It makes those to whom it refers appear like animals. Thus those humans become the worst of all animals that walk on earth. These are the hardened unbelievers who will not accept the faith. They are the ones who break their treaties all the time and do not entertain any sense of fearing God.

Several reports speak of which groups were meant in this statement. Different reports mention the three Jewish tribes of Qaynuqā', al-Naḍīr and Qurayẓah, while other reports suggest that they were the Bedouin Arabs in the areas around Madinah. Historical events and the statement itself admit all these possibilities, as all of these groups did break their treaties with the Prophet, one after the other. The pagan Arabs were guilty of this on several occasions. What is important is that we should know that these verses speak of actual events that took place before the Battle of Badr and after it, till the time when these verses were revealed. However, the rule that they outline, which also explains the nature of those who break their treaties, applies to all such situations. Those who have become hardened in disbelief *"will not believe."* Their very nature has gone awry and they have become the worst of creatures. They break every agreement they make. Thus they shed yet another human characteristic, namely, faithfulness. They run loose, like animals, except that animals are restricted by their nature while these know no restriction. In God's sight, they are the worst of all creatures.

Those people who cannot be trusted to honour an agreement they make must not be allowed to feel secure, just like they deprived others of enjoying a sense of security. Their punishment is that they should live in fear and that they should become an example to those who follow their suit. God's Messenger and his followers in succeeding generations are commanded to mete out punishment to them on every occasion: "*Should you meet them in battle, make of them a fearsome example for those who follow them, so that they may reflect and take it to heart.*" (Verse 57)

This verse paints an image of a ferocious attack that is bound to strike fear into the hearts of the enemies. The image is so powerful that hearing it is enough to make people flee. We need not ask about those who are at the receiving end of such punishment. God commands His Messenger to level such a powerful strike against those who are in the habit of violating their treaties and who have broken all human restraints. Such a strike has the dual purpose of protecting the Muslim community and destroying the power of those who try to undermine its position. This should deter all people from trying to stop the Islamic march.

Striking Terror into the Enemy

Those who believe in Islam should have a clear understanding of the nature of its method of operation. It is essential that Islam should have real power as well as a reputation of power. Thus, as it starts its mission to liberate mankind all over the world from tyranny, it strikes fear into the hearts of all tyrants who do their utmost to check its tide. Those who think that this religion will confine itself to preaching and to the explanation of its message when the forces of evil try to put every type of impediment in its way have little understanding of its true nature.

This is the first ruling which deals with the case of actual violation of treaties that have been concluded with the Muslim community. The violators are to be dealt a heavy blow so that they, as well as those who sympathize with them, are intimidated and are actually overawed by the Muslims.

The second ruling deals with a different situation: that of fearing and expecting treachery. There should be clear signs that a particular group or community are actually contemplating such violation of a treaty. In this case the Prophet is directed to take the following approach: "*And if you fear treachery from any folk, cast [your treaty with them] back to them in a fair manner. God does not love the treacherous.*" (Verse 58)

Islam here sets out a code of practice. When a treaty is concluded, the Muslim community will undoubtedly honour it. If they fear that the other party is about to violate it, then the Muslims declare the termination of the treaty, without any attempt to cheat or deceive the other party. What is meant here is an open and clear termination of a treaty so that each party realizes that peaceful relations are over. Islam attaches a very high value to honesty and integrity in order to ensure peace and security. Launching a treacherous attack on people who rely on covenants that remain in force is alien to the nature of Islam. Islam does not terrorize those who have not taken precautions even when it fears treachery from them. However, when a treaty has been publicly terminated, then trying to outwit the enemy is perfectly acceptable because each side should be on its guard. If an enemy falls for a trick, they pay the price of naïvety. No method of outwitting the enemy can then be described as treachery.

Islam wants humanity to rise above worldly temptations and to be sublime. Hence, it does not allow treachery for the sake of achieving a cheap victory at a time when it strives for the noblest of causes and aims. People who have honourable aims cannot utilize dishonourable means. Islam finds treachery repugnant and looks at traitors who violate their treaties with contempt. Therefore, it does not accept that Muslims violate their covenants for the achievement of any objective, noble as it may be. The human soul is a complete whole. When it allows itself to resort to disgraceful means it cannot maintain its noble aims. He is not a Muslim who claims that the ends justify the means. Such a principle is alien to Islamic thinking and cannot fit with Islamic sensitivities. Within the human self there can be no gulf to separate the ends from the means. Reaching a clean shore does not tempt a Muslim to walk through a muddy pool, because the shore will not remain clean after dirty feet have walked there. Hence, *"God does not love the treacherous."* (Verse 58)

We should remember that these regulations were revealed at a time when the whole of humanity could not have aspired to such a high level. The law of the jungle, which meant that the powerful could use their power without restraint, was the one that prevailed. The same law of the jungle continued to dominate in all *jāhiliyyah* communities until the eighteenth century. Europe had no concept of international codes and laws except for what it learnt through its dealings with the Muslim world. Yet in practical reality Europe has not attained any level approaching this high peak, not even after it adopted, only in theory, something it calls 'international law'. Those who admire so-called 'advanced law making' should try to understand the realities as they compare Islamic law to all contemporary legal codes.

In return for such clear honesty God promises victory to the Muslims and He tells them that the unbelievers have no real power: "*Let not those who disbelieve reckon that they shall escape. They can never be beyond [God's] grasp.*" (Verse 59) Their treachery will not enable them to take the lead and outstrip the Muslims, because God will not abandon the Muslims or allow the traitors to triumph. The unbelievers are too weak to escape from God when He moves against them. Nor can they escape from the Muslims when God is supporting them. Hence those who resort only to clean and lawful means, seeking God's pleasure, need not worry when they see others who employ foul means surging ahead. They achieve victory through God's help, because they strive to implement His law and make His word supreme. Their efforts aim to liberate humanity from the worship of creatures, so that it may worship only the Creator.

Islam, however, sets out to make real preparations that are within the capability of the Muslims so that victory becomes achievable. It does not raise the sights of the Muslim community towards that sublime horizon without making sure that it has firm ground on which it can stand. Islam also takes every practical step which has been proven through experience to be of immense value in the achievement of victory. Islam also makes sure that the Muslim community is well prepared for its practical tasks that serve its sublime objectives: "*Make ready against them whatever force and war mounts you can muster, so that you may strike terror into the enemies of God who are also your own enemies, and others besides them of whom you may be unaware, but of whom God is well aware. Whatever you may spend in God's cause shall be repaid to you in full, and you shall not be wronged.*" (Verse 60)

To make all practical preparations is a duty that goes hand in hand with the duty of *jihād*. The verse gives a clear order to prepare all forces and power within the means of the Muslim community. It makes special mention of cavalry because that was then the main equipment in war. Had the Qur'ān ordered them to prepare equipment that was unknown to them, they would have found these a complete mystery. Far be it from God to address anyone with mysteries. What is most important to remember here is that the directive is of a very broad nature. Hence, in our translation of the verse we use the expression 'war mount' to denote every necessary type of feasible equipment: "*Make ready against them whatever force and war mounts you can muster.*" (Verse 60)

Getting All Forces Ready

Islam certainly needs physical might which is kept ready to use for the fulfilment of its mission of liberating mankind throughout the world. The first purpose that this power serves is to establish peace and security for those who choose to accept the Islamic faith so that they do not suffer any persecution as a result of their choice. Secondly, it deters the enemies of Islam from contemplating aggression against the land of Islam. Thirdly, such enemies should be so intimidated that they do not ever entertain any thought of trying to check the tide of Islam as it goes about the fulfilment of its mission of liberation. Lastly, this power is to be used to break any force that claims the attributes of God and enforces its laws and legislation on human beings and refuses to accept that all sovereignty belongs to God alone.

Islam is not merely a system of divinity that is established once it has been consciously accepted as a faith and practised as a set of worship rituals. Islam is a practical code of living which stands face to face against other codes and systems that are supported by physical force. Hence, Islam has no option but to break those forces and remove the authorities that implement those codes which stand in opposition to its code of living devised and revealed by God Himself.

No Muslim should ever mince words when he declares this basic truth. There is nothing to be ashamed of in the nature of the Islamic approach. Islam does not have a man-made system, and does not seek to establish the authority of a leader, a state, a class, or a race. It does not try to enslave serfs so that they cultivate the plantations of the aristocracy, like the Romans used to do. Nor does it try to exploit markets and raw materials, as Western capitalism has been doing. It is not the aim of Islam to impose a human system devised by a short-sighted, narrow-minded and ignorant human being, as Communism was keen to do. Islam has a system devised by God whose knowledge and wisdom are absolute. It aims to establish God's absolute sovereignty in order that all mankind be free from subjugation to any worldly authority.

This is the fundamental truth which needs to be driven home to those defeatists who put Islam on the defensive, trying to seek excuses for *jihād* in Islamic history.

It is pertinent to know the limits of the Muslim community's duty to prepare its forces. The Qur'ānic verse states: *"Make ready against them whatever force and war mounts you can muster."* This goes as far as the maximum ability of the Muslims, so that they do not overlook any element of power which they are able to get ready. The verse also makes clear the prime purpose for which such forces are mobilized: "*So that you may strike terror into the enemies of God who are also your own enemies, and others besides them of whom you may be unaware, but of whom God is well aware.*"

The objective, then, is to strike terror into the hearts of God's enemies who are also the enemies of the advocates of Islam throughout the world, be they open with their hostility and known to the Muslim community, or others who may be discreet with their real feelings, not openly stating their hostile attitude to Islam. God is certainly aware of their true feelings and sympathies. Such people are intimidated by the might of Islam even though they may not suffer its consequences directly. The Muslims are required to gather all the strength they can have so that they remain feared by other people. This is essential so that God's word remains supreme and all submission is to God alone.

Acquiring such forces and having them ready can only be done if the resources are there. Since the Islamic system lays much stress on collective responsibility and mutual support, the duty of *jihād* goes hand in hand with the duty of spending money for God's cause:

"*Whatever you may spend in God's cause shall be repaid to you in full, and you shall not be wronged.*" (Verse 60) Both *jihād* and spending money for God's cause are thus purged of all worldly and personal aims and purposes as well as all national and community feelings and aspirations. They must always be pure, undertaken 'for God's cause,' to establish His authority and to earn His pleasure.

Thus, right at the outset, Islam rules out any war undertaken for the glory of individuals and states. It rejects all campaigns that seek to exploit resources and open markets, or to subjugate and humiliate other communities. Islam has nothing to do with any war that tries to establish the superiority of one class, race, nation, or state over another. The only type of campaign which Islam approves of is one undertaken for God's cause. Needless to say, God does not wish to grant supremacy to any one race, nation, class, or individual. He only wants His own sovereignty and authority to be recognized by all people. God is in no need of anyone or any community. The recognition of His sovereignty and submission to Him alone bring honour, freedom, goodness and blessings to all mankind.

When Peace is a Real Prospect

The third ruling given in this passage deals with the case of those who wish to live in peace with the Muslim community and give clear indications by word and action that they are genuine in their desire to have a friendly and peaceful relationship with the Muslims. With respect to these, the Prophet is instructed: *"If they incline to peace, then incline you to it as well, and place your trust in God. He alone hears all and knows all."* (Verse 61) The use of the term 'incline' here is very apt as it gives connotations of a gentle attitude that prefers peace and friendly relations. The instruction to be inclined to peace is coupled with that of placing our trust in God who hears and knows everything and is certainly aware of all that is harboured behind words and appearances. Placing our trust in God is sufficient for ensuring protection and security.

It is important to recall here Imām Ibn al-Qayyim's summary which we quoted earlier, outlining the various categories of unbelievers and their attitudes to the Prophet Muḥammad and his attitude to each of them, from the time when he first settled in Madinah to the Battle of Badr when this new ruling was revealed. Referring to this summary, we realize that this particular ruling applied to those unbelievers who did not fight against the Prophet, preferring to have peaceful relations with the Muslim community. God instructs His Messenger here to leave this group alone, and to extend friendly and peaceful relations to them. This remained in effect until the revelation of *Sūrah* 9, several years later. That *sūrah* gives a four-months' notice to all groups which had no treaty with the Prophet or had a treaty with no specific time limit to define their attitudes. Their decisions would then determine what their relations with the Muslim state would be like in the future. Hence the ruling we have here is not final. Its provisions do not apply to all people. We have to consider it within the framework of its relevant circumstances and the attitude taken by the Prophet later in his life, as he received new revelations on the subject.

The ruling, however, had a kind of general application at the time. The Prophet implemented it until the revelation of *Sūrah* 9, Repentance. One aspect of its implementation was the conclusion of the peace treaty of al-Ḥudaybiyah in the sixth year after the Prophet's settlement in Madinah.

Some scholars tend to consider this ruling final and permanent. They explain the inclination to peace as the acceptance of *jizyah*,[2] or submission tax. This interpretation, however, does not fit with the historical events of the period. The provisions that regulate levying *jizyah* are included in the next *sūrah*, revealed sometime after the eighth year of the Islamic calendar, while the present verse was revealed in the second year, after the Battle of Badr, when the rules of *jizyah* had not yet been outlined. When we review events and the dates of various revelations and consider the practical nature of the Islamic approach, we come to the conclusion that it is perhaps more accurate to say that this particular ruling was not meant to be final at the time. It was amended later when the final rulings were revealed in *Sūrah* 9, which classified all people according to their attitude to Islam into three groups: those who are hostile and fighting Islam, those who are Muslims implementing God's law, and those who accept the Islamic rule, paying *jizyah* and honouring their agreements with Muslims. These are the final rules that represent the final outcome of Islamic *jihād*. Any other

2. *Jizyah* is a submission tax paid by non-Muslims in areas which accept the rule of the Muslim state in return for protection by the Muslims from any outside aggression. – Editor's note.

situation should be changed into one of these three in order to fall in line with the final pattern. These three situations are outlined by the following *ḥadīth* related by Muslim and Imām Aḥmad on the authority of Yazīd ibn al-Khaṭīb:

> When the Prophet despatched an expedition or an army, he would enjoin its commander to remain God-fearing and to take good care of the Muslims under his command. He would then say to them: "Set out on your campaign in the name of God and to serve His cause. Fight those who deny God. When you meet your enemies call on them to accept one of three options. Accept from them whichever option they prefer and leave them alone. Call on them to accept Islam. If they respond favourably, then accept that from them and call on them to move from their land to that of the *Muhājirīn* [i.e. the Prophet's Companions who migrated with him to Madinah]. Inform them that if they do so, they will have the same obligations and privileges that apply to the *Muhājirīn*. If they choose to remain in their own land, then make it clear to them that they will be in the same position as the desert Arabs who are Muslims. All rules that apply to believers are also applicable to them but they will have no share of any spoils gained in war or without a fight unless they join forces with the Muslims in their *jihād* campaigns. If they refuse, then make it clear to them that they have to pay *jizyah*. If they are willing to do so, then accept that from them and leave them alone. If they refuse then pray for God's help and fight them."

This *ḥadīth* is problematic in one aspect, namely because it mentions the *Muhājirīn* and *jizyah* at the same time. It is confirmed that the *jizyah* was not imposed until the eighth year. It was not levied from the Arabs who were unbelievers because they accepted Islam before its provisions were revealed. It was applied to the Magians who were similarly unbelievers. Had those provisions been revealed at a time when there were unbelievers in the Arabian Peninsula, it would have been levied from them, as Imām Ibn al-Qayyim points out. This is also the view of Abū Ḥanīfah and one of two views attributed to Imām Aḥmad.

Be that as it may, what we conclude is that there is no final rulings of universal application in this verse: *"If they incline to peace, then incline you to it as well, and place your trust in God. He alone hears all and knows all."* (Verse 61) At the time when this *sūrah* was revealed, God instructed His Messenger to remain at peace with those groups who refrained from fighting him and the Muslims, whether they entered into a formal treaty with the Muslims or not. The Prophet continued to accept a peaceful relationship with unbelievers and people of earlier revelations until *Sūrah* 9 was revealed, when he could only accept one of two alternatives: either they embraced Islam or paid *jizyah* which indicated a state of peace. Otherwise, the only alternative was war, whenever this was feasible for the Muslims to undertake, so that all people submit to God alone.

Where to Place All Trust

I have dwelt rather extensively on the provisional nature of the rule outlined in this verse, which requires the Prophet and the Muslims to reciprocate any inclination to peace by the unbelievers. My aim is to clarify a certain aspect of confusion that arises from the spiritual and intellectual defeatism reflected in the work of many of those who write about Islamic *jihād*. Such people feel the pressure of modern values that prevail in international relations. Lacking a clear understanding of the true nature of Islam as they are, they find it too much for the divine faith to adopt a single and permanent approach towards all humanity, giving all people a choice between three alternatives: acceptance of Islam, payment of *jizyah* or being at war with Islam. They realize that all forces of *jāhiliyyah* are mobilized against Islam and its followers, while those who profess to be Muslims, without fully understanding or seriously appreciating the true nature of Islam, are too weak to stand up to the combined forces of other creeds and religions. They also feel that those at the forefront of Islamic advocacy are too small in number and have little power to reckon with. Hence, such writers try to impose a different interpretation on Qur'ānic statements and *aḥadīth* so that they can be seen to be in line with the situation in our present world with all its pressures on contemporary Muslims. They find the single approach of Islam and the three choices it offers too hard to swallow.

Such writers often interpret statements that have a provisional nature or qualified application as final, permanent and having general and universal application. When they tackle the final statements they interpret these in the light of those provisional ones to which they have applied a final import. Thus, they come up with the idea that Islamic *jihād* is merely a defensive operation to protect Muslim people and their land when they are attacked, and that Islam will always accept any offer of peace. To them, peace is merely a state of non-belligerence which, in practical terms, means that the other camp will not attack the land of Islam. According to their understanding, Islam should shrink inside its borders at all times. It has no right to call on others to accept its message or to submit to God's law, unless such a call takes the form of a speech, statement or bulletin. When it comes to material forces, Islam has no right to attack the ruling forces in *jāhiliyyah* societies unless it first comes under attack, in which case Islam is right to defend itself.

Had those spiritually and intellectually defeatist people wanted to find in the rules and laws of their faith elements which can deal with a situation like the present one, without imposing any arbitrary interpretation on any statement, they would have been able to understand how Islam faced a situation that is not dissimilar to what we face today. They would then have been able to say that in similar situations Islam adopted such and such policy, but that does not constitute the final or the permanent Islamic attitude. It was merely a set of temporary measures that were necessary in a special situation or in an emergency. Within the same context, it is useful to look at examples of rulings and practices of a transitional nature, undertaken to meet emergencies.

- In the early days after his settlement in Madinah, the Prophet concluded a peace and defence treaty with the Jews and the unbelievers in and around Madinah. The treaty made it clear that the supreme authority in Madinah belonged to the Prophet, and committed the other groups to defend the city against the Quraysh. The signatories agreed that they would not extend any support to any aggressor who attacked Madinah. None would make any pact with the unbelievers who were hostile to the Muslims without the prior agreement of the Prophet. At the same time, God instructed the Prophet to extend peaceful and friendly treatment to any group who were inclined towards peace, even though they did not sign a treaty with him. He was to maintain that peaceful situation as long as they were committed to peace. All this changed later, as already explained.

- When the events known as the Expedition of the Moat took place, with the Arab unbelievers mobilizing large forces and surrounding Madinah, the Qurayẓah Jews violated their treaty with the Muslim state. The Prophet was worried that the Muslims might be in very serious trouble as a result of a planned pincer attack. To ease the situation the Prophet offered to make a deal with the chiefs of the second largest force, namely the Ghaṭafān tribe, which would have them withdrawing all their forces in return for having one-third of Madinah's harvest. That agreement would have left the Quraysh alone in the position of attack and the Muslims would most probably have been able to gain a quick victory against them. This was only an offer and no agreement was signed.
- Before having the agreement signed and witnessed, the Prophet consulted the two leaders of the *Anṣār*, Saʿd ibn Muʿādh and Saʿd ibn ʿUbādah. They asked him: "Is this something you would like us to do? In this case, we will accept it for your sake. Or is it something God has ordered and we have to accept it? Or is it something you are doing for our sake?" The Prophet answered: "I am doing it for you, having seen all the Arabs joining forces against you." He added that all he wanted was to break up the unity of their enemies for the present.

Saʿd ibn Muʿādh said:

> Messenger of God, when we were, like these people, idolaters, unaware of any religion other than the worship of idols, they did not hope to get a single fruit from Madinah except as a present from us or if we sold it to them. Now that God has honoured us with Islam and guided us to it and has given us the honour and strength of having you in our midst, would we willingly give them our goods? We have no need for this agreement. We will give them nothing but the sword until God makes His judgement between us.

The Prophet was pleased with this reply and said: "You do what you wish." Turning to the Ghaṭafān chiefs, he said: "You may go now, for we have nothing to offer you except the sword." What the Prophet thought of doing on this occasion was merely a temporary measure in an emergency situation. It was by no means indicative of a final rule.

- The Prophet also concluded the peace agreement at al-Ḥudaybiyah with the Quraysh when they were still associating partners with God. The terms of the agreement were far from satisfactory to many Muslims. The agreement stipulated that neither party would go to war against the other for ten years. People would live in peace and security. The Prophet and his companions would go back without entering Makkah, to return in a year's time when they would be allowed in the city for three days only, having no armament other than swords in their shields. If an unbeliever should seek to join the Muslims, they would turn him back, but if a Muslim sought to join the unbelievers, they would not have to send him back. Acting on God's instruction, the Prophet accepted those seemingly unfair conditions for a definite purpose known to Him. In similar circumstances the leaders of the Muslim community could take action on a similar basis.

The practical nature of the Islamic faith makes it necessary to face up to any situation with adequate means. Islam takes a practical and flexible approach which is at the same time clear and firmly based. If we seek in Islamic teachings a basis for positive action to deal with any practical situation, we will not need to twist Qur'ānic or *aḥadīth* statements, or give them arbitrary interpretations. What is needed is to fear God and to refrain from any attempt to make His faith subservient to evil and ignorant realities. We must also guard against adopting a defeatist attitude which puts Islam on the defensive when it is a faith that is meant to govern and regulate people's lives. It satisfies, from a position of strength, all the needs of practical life. Praise be to God for having guided us to His faith.

Uniting Believers' Hearts

When God instructed His Messenger, the Prophet Muḥammad (peace be upon him), to accept the state of non-belligerency from any community which offered him it and to incline to peace whenever they so inclined, He also directed him to rely on Him and place his trust in Him. He further reassured him that He knows precisely what all people hide as guarded secrets: "*If they incline to peace, then incline you to it as well, and place your trust in God. He alone hears all and knows all.*" (Verse 61)

Furthermore, God assured him that they would not be able to deceive him, should they try to do so. If their peace offer was merely a cover-up for their real intentions of treachery, he could always rely on God who is sure to protect him. It was He who granted him victory in the Battle of Badr, when He strengthened him with His own help and with the believers. It was He who established their brotherhood based on faith and united their hearts which could not have been united by any other means: "*Should they seek to deceive you, God is all-sufficient for you. He it is who has strengthened you with His help and rallied the believers round you, uniting their hearts. If you were to spend all that is on earth you could not have so united their hearts, but God has united them. He is Mighty and Wise.*" (Verses 62–63)

The Prophet is here reassured that he would not need anything other than God's help, for that is more than sufficient for protection from any treachery. It was He who gave strength and support to His Messenger in the first place, when he rallied the believers round him. They were true to their pledges. They came to be a united force, after they had had divergent loyalties. They were often in open hostility against one another and fought their tribal wars with determined ferocity. The reference here may be to the two tribes of Madinah, the Aws and the Khazraj, who constituted the *Anṣār*. In pre-Islamic days, their enmity and protracted disputes were so fierce that there could not be any sort of peace between them, let alone a bond of brotherhood which Islam forged. However, this verse may also be intended as a reference to the *Muhājirīn*, who migrated with the Prophet from Makkah to Madinah. They also had the same sort of internal disputes and enmity as the *Anṣār*. Or it may be that the verse means them all together. Indeed the whole of Arabia was alike in its internal hostilities.

It was a great miracle which could never have been accomplished by anyone other than God, through the faith He revealed. Hearts that had always been hostile, and natures that had been rebellious, were solidly united. Their hostility was replaced by love and unity of a standard that serves as a symbol for life in heaven: *"We shall have removed from their hearts any lurking feelings of malice, [and they shall rest] as brothers, face to face, on raised couches."* (15: 47)

This faith is remarkable indeed. When it touches people's hearts, it pours into them a mixture of love, familiarity and compassion that is certain to soften them and establish between them a firm and deeply-rooted bond. Words, looks, touches and heartbeats all become lyrics and odes expressing mutual love, compassion, loyalty, support and forbearance. What is the secret of such a profound transformation? The secret is known only to God. However, its effects are clear to the believers themselves.

The faith of Islam makes its appeal to mankind on the basis of pure love that has its roots in faith in God and is nourished by dedication to His cause. When human beings make a favourable response to that appeal, the miracle that can only be worked out by God takes place in reality.

The Prophet (peace be upon him) said: "Some of God's servants who are neither prophets nor martyrs shall have on the Day of Judgement a position so close to God that prophets and martyrs would love to have." His Companions said: "Messenger of God, will you please tell us who these people are." He said: "These are people who love one another for God's sake only. They have no relation of kinship or business interests with one another. By God, their faces are radiant with light, and they have light. They shall experience no fear or sadness when other people are overtaken by fear and sadness." [Related by Abū Dāwūd.]

The Prophet also said: "When a Muslim meets his Muslim brother and they shake hands, their sins shall fall off just like leaves fall off a dry tree on a windy day. Their sins shall be forgiven them, even though they appear to be as huge as sea foam." [Related by al-Ṭabarānī.]

God's Messenger made several statements on this point. His actions confirm that such love, and unity constitutes an essential factor in his message. The community that he built on the basis of love provides the best proof that such love was not merely flowery words or idealistic actions by a few individuals. It was a firmly established reality that came into being by God's will. It is only He who can bring about such a real unity of hearts.

Matching Superior Forces

The *sūrah* moves on to reassure the Prophet and the Muslim community yet again that God is on their side. This is more than enough for them to ensure their victory. The Prophet is also instructed to encourage the believers to fight for God's cause. They are equal to a force that outnumbers them by ten to one. Even at their weakest, the believers are more than a match for twice their number.

> *Prophet, God is enough for you and those of the believers who follow you. Prophet, urge the believers to fight. If there are twenty steadfast men among you, they will overcome two hundred, and if there are a hundred of you, they will defeat a thousand of those who disbelieve, for those are devoid of understanding. Now God has lightened your burden, for He knows that you are weak. So, if there are a hundred steadfast men among you, they will overcome two hundred, and if there are a thousand of you they will, by God's will, defeat two thousand. God is with those who are steadfast.* (Verses 64–66)

We pause here a little to contemplate the difference between God's invincible, overwhelming power and the small force which tries to suppress the advocates of the divine message. The difference is too huge to allow any meaningful comparison. Hence, the outcome of the battle is a foregone conclusion. This is what is implied in the statement: *"Prophet, God is enough for you and those of the believers who follow you."* (Verse 64)

This is followed by an order to the Prophet to urge the believers to fight for God's cause, now that every soul is ready for the engagement, every heart is full with expectation and all are confident, reassured: *"Prophet, urge the believers to fight."* (Verse 65) Rouse them to arms, for they are a match for their enemies, even though they may be much inferior in number: *"If there are twenty steadfast men among you, they will overcome two hundred, and if there are a hundred of you, they will defeat a thousand of those who disbelieve."* (Verse 65) The reason for such a great difference in real power comes as a surprise, but it is true, incisive: *"For those are devoid of understanding."* (Verse 65)

What is the link between understanding and victory? There may be very little on the surface, but the link is very real and strong. The believers are distinguished by the fact that they know their way which they have chosen after deep thought. They understand the course they follow in this life and they are well aware of the purpose of their existence and their goals. They have a perfect understanding of the nature of Godhead and the nature of servitude to God. They know that God must be the only master in the universe, and that none of His servants can associate any partners with Him. They realize that they, the Muslim community, are the group that follow divine guidance, whose task is to liberate humanity, by God's will, from servitude to creatures so that they worship God alone. They are the ones to be entrusted with power on earth, not to exercise superiority over others, but to ensure that the word of God reigns supreme. Their mission is to struggle for God's cause, build a proper human civilization, and establish the rule of justice among all people.

All this understanding pours enlightenment, confidence, strength and reassurance into the believers' hearts. They are thus motivated to go into their campaigns of *jihād* with certainty of the outcome. This alone multiplies their strength. Their enemies, on the other hand, are "devoid of understanding". Their hearts are sealed, and their eyes are blinded. Their forces are without power, although they may appear to be superior. That is because their link to the source of real power has been severed.

This relative power of one to ten is the original balance of power between the believers who are full of understanding and the unbelievers who are devoid of it. Even when the Muslims who remain steadfast are at their weakest, this ratio is two to one: *"Now God has lightened your burden, for He knows that you are weak. So, if there are a hundred steadfast men among you, they will overcome two hundred, and if there are a thousand of you they will, by God's will, defeat two thousand. God is with those who are steadfast."* (Verse 66)

Some scholars and Qur'ānic commentators have taken these verses to imply a commandment to the believers that, when they are strong, no one may run away from ten of the unbelievers, or from two in the case of weakness. There are considerable differences on points of detail, which we prefer not to go into. It is our considered opinion that these verses make a statement of fact in estimating the believers' strength when they confront their enemies. This is an estimate made according to God's own measure, which is the true measure. These verses are also meant to inform the believers of this fact so that they have more confidence and reassurance. God certainly knows best, but in our considered view, these statements do not stipulate rules to be implemented.

Rulings on Captives of War

The *sūrah* moves on to outline certain rulings that are relevant to taking prisoners of war and what to do with them. This comes in the context of the Prophet's action with regard to the captives taken in the Battle of Badr. The captives themselves are invited to accept the faith, which provides them with a prospect giving them more than fair compensation for the loss they suffered:

> *It does not behove a Prophet to have captives unless he has battled strenuously in the land. You may desire the fleeting gains of this world, but God desires for you the good of the life to come. God is almighty, wise. Had it not been for a decree from God that had already gone forth, you would have been severely punished for what you have taken. Enjoy, then, what you have gained, as lawful and good, and remain God-fearing; indeed God is much forgiving, most merciful. Prophet, say to the captives who are in your hands: 'If God finds goodness in your hearts, He will give you something better than all that has been taken from you, and He will forgive you your sins. God is much forgiving, merciful.' Should they seek to play false with you, they were previously false to God Himself, but He gave [you] mastery over them. God is All-knowing, Wise.* (Verses 67–71)

Ibn Isḥāq relates within the context of his account of the events of the Battle of Badr: "The Prophet was in the shed erected for him, with Sa'd ibn Mu'ādh and a number of the *Anṣār* close on hand guarding the Prophet against any possible surprise attack by the unbelievers. When the Muslim fighters started to take prisoners, the Prophet noticed that Sa'd did not look very pleased. He asked him: 'You do not seem very happy, Sa'd with what our Companions are doing?' Sa'd answered: 'That is true, Messenger of God. This is the first major defeat God has inflicted on the unbelievers. I would have preferred to do away with their men, rather than keep them alive.'"

Imām Aḥmad relates on the authority of ʿUmar ibn al-Khaṭṭāb: "On the day of the battle, God inflicted a heavy defeat on the unbelievers, with 70 of them killed and 70 taken prisoner. The Prophet consulted some of his companions about what to do with the prisoners. Abū Bakr said: 'Messenger of God, these are our cousins and tribesmen. I suggest that you take ransom from them, which we could use to improve our position *vis-à-vis* the unbelievers. Besides, they will still have a chance to follow God's guidance and thus come to support us.' The Prophet then asked ʿUmar ibn al-Khaṭṭāb for his view, and ʿUmar said: 'I do not share Abū Bakr's view. I suggest that you give me my relative to kill, and you give ʿAqīl ibn Abī Ṭālib to his brother ʿAlī to kill, and you give Ḥamzah his brother to kill. We thus demonstrate in front of God that we have no sympathy whatsoever with the unbelievers. After all, these are their elite.' The Prophet felt more inclined to Abū Bakr's view and accepted ransom from them."

ʿUmar continues his account of this event: "On the next day, I went to the Prophet to find him and Abū Bakr with tears in their eyes. I said: 'What makes you and your Companion cry? If I find it in me to cry, I will, and if not, I will pretend to join you in your crying.' The Prophet said that they were crying 'because of what our Companions advised of taking ransom. I have been shown the punishment you would have suffered closer to you than this tree, (pointing to a nearby tree.)' Soon afterwards, these verses were revealed: "*It does not behove a Prophet to have captives unless he has battled strenuously in the land. You may desire the fleeting gains of this world, but God desires for you the good of the life to come. God is Almighty, Wise. Had it not been for a decree from God that had already gone forth, you would have been severely punished for what you have taken. Enjoy, then, what you have gained, as lawful and good, and remain God-fearing; indeed God is much Forgiving, most Merciful.*" (Verses 67–69) This last verse makes it clear that the spoils of war are lawful to take." [This *ḥadīth* is also related by Muslim, Abū Dāwūd, and al-Tirmidhī with different chains of transmission]

Imām Aḥmad relates on Anas's authority: "The Prophet consulted his companions concerning the captives taken in the Battle of Badr, saying to them: 'God has given you power over them.' ʿUmar stood up and said: 'Messenger of God, kill them.' The Prophet turned away from him, and then said: 'God has given you power over them, and only yesterday they were your brethren.' 'Umar repeated his suggestion, but the Prophet turned away from him and repeated his question. Abū Bakr stood up and said: 'Messenger of God, it may be wise to pardon them and accept ransom from them.' The Prophet's face cheered up. Then God revealed the verse saying: '*Had it not been for a decree from God that had already gone forth, you would have been severely punished for what you have taken.*'" (Verse 68)

God's Preferred Option

Yet another *ḥadīth* reported by 'Abdullāh ibn Mas'ūd explains this incident. "On the day of Badr the Prophet asked his Companions what they thought he should do about prisoners of war. Abū Bakr said: 'Messenger of God, they are your own people and your tribesmen. Spare them and offer them the chance to repent of their past attitude.' 'Umar said: 'Messenger of God, they have accused you of lying and they have chased you out of your city. Put them to death.' 'Abdullāh ibn Rawāḥah said: 'Messenger of God, you are now in a valley where there is a lot of wood. Light a big fire and throw them into it.' The Prophet remained silent making no rejoinder, then he went into his home. Some people thought he would take Abū Bakr's view, and others thought 'Umar's view would be upheld, while still others felt that the Prophet might adopt the view of 'Abdullāh ibn Rawāḥah. The Prophet then came out and said: 'God makes some people's hearts so soft that they become softer than milk, and He makes other people's hearts harden until they become harder than bricks. Abū Bakr, your attitude is similar to that of Abraham (peace be upon him) as he said, '*he that follows me belongs to me. As for him who disobeys me, well, You are surely most Forgiving, Merciful.*' (14: 36) And you are also like Jesus (peace be upon him) as he said: '*If You punish them, they are Your servants; and if You forgive them, You are indeed Almighty, Wise.*' (5: 118) As for you 'Umar, you are like Moses (peace be upon him) as he said: '*Our Lord, wipe out their wealth and firm up their hearts so they would not believe until they see painful torment.*' (10: 88) And you are also like Noah (peace be upon him) as he said: '*My Lord, do not leave on earth a single unbeliever.*' (71: 26) You are in poverty, so no one may be set free without a ransom, or else, he should be beheaded."

'Abdullāh ibn Mas'ūd reports: "I said: 'Messenger of God, except Suhayl ibn Bayḍā'. For he is considering becoming a Muslim.' The Prophet was silent for a while. Never until that day did I fear that rocks could fall on my head from the sky. I remained so worried until the Prophet said: 'With the exception of Suhayl ibn Bayḍā'.' Shortly afterwards God revealed the verses: "*It does not behove a Prophet to have captives unless he has battled strenuously in the land. You may desire the fleeting gains of this world, but God desires for you the good of the life to come. God is Almighty, Wise. Had it not been for a decree from God that had already gone forth, you would have been severely punished for what you have taken. Enjoy, then, what you have gained, as lawful and good, and remain God-fearing; indeed God is much Forgiving, most Merciful.*" (Verses 67–69)

The killing mentioned in these verses aims to give strength to the Muslims and weaken their enemies, until the Muslims reached a stage when they could set prisoners free either as a favour or for a ransom. Hence the reproach of the Muslims. The Battle of Badr was the first major battle between the Muslims and the unbelievers. The Muslims were still small in number, compared with the unbelievers. Hence, any reduction of the number of fighters among the unbelievers would have a weakening effect on them, and would hurt their pride, deterring them from launching another campaign against the Muslims. This would have achieved a much higher objective than they could achieve by taking ransom, poor as they were.

There was another concept to establish in people's hearts, which was beautifully stated by 'Umar: "We demonstrate in front of God that there is no sympathy whatsoever in our hearts with the unbelievers."

We feel – and God knows best – that these are the two main reasons why God did not like the Muslims to take prisoners at Badr and then set them free for ransom. It was in the light of these circumstances that God said: "*It does not behove a Prophet to have captives unless he has battled strenuously in the land.*" (Verse 67) Hence the Qur'ānic reproach of the Muslims who accepted ransom in return for setting the prisoners free: "*You may desire the fleeting gains of this world.*" (Verse 67) Because of this preference for the fleeting good of the present life you have taken them prisoners instead of killing them, and you accepted ransom in return for their freedom. "*But God desires for you the good of the life to come.*" (Verse 67) Needless to say, the Muslims should prefer the option God prefers, because it is always the one to bring them good. To seek the hereafter means to abandon the pursuit of the fleeting comforts of this world.

"God is Almighty, Wise." (Verse 67) He has enabled you to achieve victory for a specific, wise purpose which He accomplishes through inflicting such a heavy defeat on the unbelievers. *"Thus He would certainly establish the truth firmly and show falsehood to be false, however hateful this might be to the evildoers."* (Verse 8) *"Had it not been for a decree from God that had already gone forth, you would have been severely punished for what you have taken."* (Verse 68)

God had previously decreed that He would forgive the believers who took part in the Battle of Badr whatever they might subsequently do. That preceding decree spared them the punishment which would have attended their acceptance of the ransom. God then showered on them more of His grace, by making the spoils of war lawful for them to take, while it was forbidden to the followers of earlier prophets. He reminds them of their need to remain God-fearing as He also reminds them of His grace and forgiveness. Thus their feelings towards their Lord remain well balanced. They are not tempted by God's mercy to the extent that they lose sight of their need to remain always God-fearing: *"Enjoy, then, what you have gained, as lawful and good, and remain God-fearing; indeed God is much-Forgiving, most Merciful."* (Verse 69)

Seeking to Deceive God

Now the *sūrah* addresses those captives, giving them hope and promising a future which is far better than the life they used to lead. They are also promised what is superior to the property they lost, in addition to forgiveness and mercy: *"Prophet, say to the captives who are in your hands: If God finds goodness in your hearts, He will give you something better than all that has been taken from you, and He will forgive you your sins. God is much-Forgiving, Merciful."* (Verse 70) But all this depends on them opening their hearts to the light of faith. God will then find goodness in them. That goodness is the very fact of believing in God. It is goodness at its purest. Indeed all goodness stems from it.

From the Islamic point of view, keeping prisoners of war in the hands of believers is only a means of opening up the essence of goodness that may be deep in their hearts. Thus their nature becomes recipient to the call to accept the divine faith and follow guidance. No vengeance is to be exacted on those prisoners of war. Such was the practice of the Byzantines and other conquerors. But Islam follows a totally different approach.

Al-Zuhrī relates that the Quraysh sent people to pay the ransom of their prisoners. Each clan paid whatever was accepted from them in ransom. Al-ʿAbbās (the Prophet's uncle who was among the captives) said: "Messenger of God, I have been a Muslim." The Prophet said: "God knows better whether you were truly a Muslim. If it is true, He will certainly reward you. To all appearances, you were against us. Therefore, you have to pay ransom for yourself, your two nephews, Nawfal and ʿAqīl, and also for your ally ʿUtbah ibn ʿAmr." He said: "I do not have enough for all this, Messenger of God." The Prophet said: "What about the money you and your wife, Umm al-Faḍl, have hidden underground. You said to her: If I am killed on this trip of mine, this money is to be shared between my three sons, al-Faḍl, ʿAbdullāh and Qutham." He said: "I do know for certain that you are God's Messenger. This is something of which no one has any knowledge except myself and my wife. Will you please, then, count as advance payment the 20 ounces of gold your companions have taken from me?" The Prophet said: "No. That is something God has given to us." Al-ʿAbbās then paid the ransom money for himself, his two nephews and his ally. God then revealed the verse which says: "*Prophet, say to the captives who are in your hands: If God finds goodness in your hearts, He will give you something better than all that has been taken from you, and He will forgive you your sins. God is much-Forgiving, Merciful.*" (Verse 70) Al-ʿAbbās later said: "God has replaced my loss, giving me for those 20 ounces twenty slaves who carry on with my business. I am still hoping for God's forgiveness as well."

At the same time that the captives are given this prospect of hope, they are warned against any attempt to play false with God's Messenger (peace be upon him). They have already experienced the outcome of playing false to God: "*Should they seek to play false with you, they were previously false to God Himself, but He gave [you] mastery over them. God is All-knowing, Wise.*" (Verse 71) Their treachery to God took the form of associating partners with Him after He had formed their nature to always recognize Him as the only Lord, but they were never true to their pledges. If they seek to play false with God's Messenger when they are captives in his hands, they should remember the result of their first treachery which led them to be taken prisoner and gave mastery over them to God's Messenger and his followers. God is certainly aware of the thoughts they harbour and He is wise as He inflicts punishment on them: *"God is All-knowing, Wise."* (Verse 71)

In his commentary on the Qur'ān, al-Qurṭubī quotes Ibn al- ʿArabī's comments:

> When those unbelievers were taken prisoners, some of them started talking about adopting Islam, without showing any real intention to do so, nor did they make any unequivocal acknowledgement of its being the true faith. It looked as if they might have wanted to win favour with the Muslims without moving themselves away from the unbelievers. Our scholars have made it clear that when an unbeliever does that and only pays lip service to Islam without taking steps to be a true believer, he remains an unbeliever. If the same is done by a believer, he is not a believer at all, unless it all be only thoughts that occur to him and he is unable to get rid of them. God has pardoned people such fleeting thoughts. God tells His Messenger the truth as He says to him: *"Should they seek to play false with you,"* which means that if they are only trying to deceive you with what they say about Islam and their willingness to accept it, then this is only their habit. *"They were previously false to God Himself,"* when they disbelieved and tried to kill you and then waged war against you. However, should what they are saying be honest and there is true goodness in their hearts, God will certainly be aware of that and will accept it from them. He will then reward them with something which is far superior to what was taken from them and with His forgiveness of their past treachery.[3]

Definition of Relations

The *sūrah*'s final passage outlines the internal and external relations of the Muslim community. Rulings concerning these relations are also outlined. This gives us a clear idea of the nature of the Muslim community itself and the basis on which it is founded. The essential ties which bring that community together are not those of blood,

3. M. al-Qurṭubī, Al-Jāmiʿ li-Aḥkām al-Qur'ān, Vol. VIII, p. 55

land, race, history, language or economy. Ties of family, country, nation or financial interests are of no importance. The only ties which are given weight and importance are those of faith, organized movement and its leadership. Hence, those who believe, migrate to the land of Islam, abandon all their earlier links with their own land, homes and nation, sacrifice their lives and possessions and strive for God's cause, as well as those who give them shelter and support and join them in their faith under the same leadership and in the same movement – all those are friends and protectors of one another. On the other hand, those who believe but have not yet migrated may not aspire to such status that provides for mutual protection. This is because they have not yet pledged their full loyalty to the Islamic leadership and have not yet abandoned all ties with the unbelievers, except the bond of faith. Within the Muslim community itself, blood relations have priority in inheritance and other matters. The unbelievers, on the other hand, are also patrons and allies of one another.

These are the main lines delineating loyalties and relationships as shown in these very clear verses: "*Those who believe and have migrated and striven hard, with their possessions and their lives, for God's cause, as well as those who give them shelter and support – these are friends and protectors of one another. As for those who believe but have not migrated [to join you], you owe no duty of protection to them until they have migrated. Yet, should they appeal to you for support, on grounds of faith, it is your duty to support them, except against a people with whom you have a treaty. God sees all that you do. The unbelievers are allies of one another. Unless you do likewise, there will be oppression on earth and much corruption. Those who believe and have migrated and striven hard for God's cause, as well as those who give them shelter and support are indeed the true believers. Forgiveness of sins, and most generous provisions await them. And those who subsequently come to believe, and migrate and strive hard with you [for God's cause] shall also belong to you. Those who are bound by ties of blood have the first claim on one another in accordance with God's decree. God has full knowledge of everything.*" (Verses 72–75)

Loyalty in a Muslim Community

In the early days of Islam, until the major Battle of Badr, the social bond that tied Muslims together involved inheritance and obligatory mutual support, sharing in the payment of any blood money for accidental killing. These ties replaced those of blood and family. When the state was established and acquired additional strength after God enabled it to score its most remarkable victory at Badr, the obligation of giving loyalty and support was maintained. As for inheritance and help in the payment of blood money, these were now confined, by God's order, to blood relatives within the Muslim community itself.

The migration mentioned here as a condition of such mutual commitment, in its special and general aspects, refers to the physical departure, by those who can, from the land of the unbelievers to the land of Islam. Those who were able to migrate but chose not to do so, because they did not want to abandon their ties, whether financial or family, with the unbelievers had no claim for protection by the Muslim community. This provision applied to some Bedouins and some individuals in Makkah who were not prevented from migrating. The Muslim community had an obligation to come to the support of those believers, particularly when they appealed for help on account of being harassed or persecuted on grounds of faith. The only exception was if they wanted such help against a people with whom the Muslim community had a treaty, as such treaties had a stronger claim to be honoured by the Muslims.

These statements and the rulings and provisions they outline give us a clear idea of the nature of the Muslim community, its essential factors and basic values. Nevertheless, a word about the emergence of this community and its foundation, method of action and commitments will clarify that better.

The message of Islam conveyed by God's Messenger, the Prophet Muḥammad (peace be upon him), is the last link in the long history of the call advocating submission to God alone undertaken by the noble prophets. Throughout history, this message has remained the same: that human beings should recognize their true Lord and Sustainer, God the only deity, and that they should submit to Him alone. All claims to lordship by human beings are null and void. Except for a few individuals here and there in history, mankind as a whole has never denied the existence of God or His sovereignty over the universe. It has rather erred in its understanding of His real attributes, or associated partners with Him, either in belief and worship or in assigning sovereignty. Both of these are forms of polytheism which take people out of the faith altogether. Each one of God's Messengers taught humanity the religion God wants people to follow. After a long while, people would start to deviate and steer away from it, back into *jāhiliyyah*, ignorance and polytheism, i.e. associating partners with God, either in belief and worship or in attributing sovereignty to them or both.

Throughout history the call to believe in God has had the same nature. Its purpose is self-surrender to God, which means to bring human beings into submission to the Supreme Lord alone, to free them from servitude to human beings so that they may devote themselves to the one true God. Thus, they would be freed from the clutches of human lordship and man-made laws, value systems and traditions. They would be able to acknowledge the sovereignty and authority of the one true God and follow His law in all spheres of life. This is the central issue of the message of Islam as preached by the Prophet Muḥammad and all the noble prophets and messengers sent before him (peace be upon them all). It wants people to acknowledge God's sovereignty, which is readily acknowledged by all the universe. Human life must be regulated by the same authority that regulates the entire universe. Thus, human beings will not have their own code of living and will not submit to an authority other than those governing the whole universe, including those aspects of human life over which human beings have no say.

As is well known, human beings are subject to the laws of nature God has set into operation in matters that affect their birth, growing up, health, illness, death and also those that determine the consequences of their own choices in the areas where they can exercise their free-will. They cannot change God's laws governing the universe or these aspects of their own life. It is only wise then for them to submit to God in those aspects of their life in which they have a free choice. When they do so they make God's law govern both aspects of their life, the one which follows God's natural laws and the one subject to their own will. They thus bring harmony into their life.

Jāhiliyyah, which may be defined as a state of ignorance based on giving sovereignty to human beings, is bound to bring about a clash between the natural and the free-will aspects of human life. To counter *jāhiliyyah* in human life all prophets, including Muḥammad, God's final Messenger, advocated submission to God alone. It must be said that ignorance is not represented by an abstract theory. In certain periods of history, ignorance had no theoretical representation whatsoever. However, it always takes the form of a living movement in a society which has its own leadership, its own concepts and values, and its own traditions, habits and feelings. It is an organized society and there is close co-operation and loyalty between its individuals. It is always ready to defend its existence consciously or unconsciously. It crushes all elements which seem to be dangerous to its personality.

Since *jāhiliyyah* takes the form of an active movement in this fashion, rather than of a theory, then any attempt to abolish *jāhiliyyah* and bring people back to God through representing Islam merely as a theory is both useless and ineffective. *Jāhiliyyah* controls the practical world, and for its support there is a living and active organization. In this situation, mere theoretical efforts cannot be a match for it. When the purpose is to abolish the existing system and to replace it with a new one that is different in character, principles, as well as in all general and particular aspects, it stands to reason that this new system should come into the battlefield as an organized movement and a viable community. It must also have the advantage of a more powerful strategy, social organization and firmer ties between its individuals. Only then can it hope to replace the existing system.

The Practical Manifestation of Islamic Theory

The theoretical foundation of Islam, in every period of history, has been the declaration by which a human being bears witness that 'there is no deity other than God.' This means that God is the sustainer, the ruler and the real sovereign. This must take the form of a firm belief that is deeply rooted in one's heart and manifested in both addressing all worship to God alone and putting His laws into practice. This declaration cannot be deemed to have been truly made with such complete acceptance of its meaning. It is only when a person accepts its significance fully that he is deemed to be a true Muslim.

From the theoretical point of view, the establishment of this rule means that people must refer to God in conducting any aspect of their lives. They cannot decide on any affair without first referring to God's injunctions that may be relevant to it and implement them. There is only one source to know God's guidance; that is, His Messenger. Thus, in the second part of the declaration by which a person becomes a Muslim we declare that we 'bear witness that Muḥammad is God's Messenger.'

This theoretical basis of the Islamic doctrine provides a complete code of living for the entirety of human life. A Muslim approaches every aspect of his individual or social life, whether within or outside the Islamic community, from the perspective of this code of living which also regulates the internal and external relations of the Muslim community.

As has already been explained, Islam cannot confine itself to a mere theory which people accept as a belief practised merely as worship rituals while remaining within the structure of the existing *jāhiliyyah* society. If true believers, numerous as they may be, do that, their presence within the *jāhiliyyah* society cannot lead to a real and practical existence of Islam. Those 'theoretical' Muslims who are part of the structure of the *jāhiliyyah* society will inevitably have to respond to its requirements. Whether they like it or not, they will try, consciously or subconsciously, to fulfil its basic needs and defend its existence, and they will try to counter whatever forces or factors are threatening that existence. Any living entity will always complete these tasks using all its organs without even consulting them. In practical terms, those individuals, who are theoretically Muslims, will continue to practically support and strengthen the *jāhiliyyah* society which they should, in theory, be trying to dismantle. They will remain living cells within its structure, supporting its continuing existence with all their talent, experience and capability. Their efforts should in fact be directed to using all their power, talent and experience for the establishment of an Islamic society.

For this reason, it is necessary that the theoretical foundation of Islam, i.e. the belief, should take in practice the form of an organized and active group right at the outset. It is also necessary that this group should separate itself from *jāhiliyyah* society and remain independent of, and distinct from it. After all, Islam aims to dismantle *jāhiliyyah* society altogether. At the centre of this new group there should be a new leadership. Such leadership first came in the person of the Prophet himself. In later generations, it has been delegated to those who strive for bringing people back to believing in God as the only deity in the universe and who accept His sovereignty, authority and laws. Every person who bears witness that there is no deity other than God and that Muḥammad is God's Messenger should cut off relations of loyalty to *jāhiliyyah* society, which he has forsaken, and its ignorant leadership, whether it takes the guise of priests, magicians or astrologers, or in the form of political, social or economic leadership, as was the case with the Quraysh at the time of the Prophet. Full and complete loyalty must be given to the new Islamic movement and the new Muslim leadership.

This decisive step must be taken at the very moment when a person makes this verbal declaration bearing witness that 'there is no deity other than God and Muḥammad is God's Messenger.' A Muslim society cannot come into existence without this. It does not become a reality when it is no more than a belief held by individual Muslims, numerous as they may be. They must form themselves into an active, harmonious and cooperative group with a separate and distinct existence. Like the limbs of a human body, all individuals in this group work together to strengthen its foundation, and to enable it to expand and defend itself against any external attack which threatens its existence. In all this, they must work under a leadership that is independent of that of *jāhiliyyah* society. The role of this leadership is to regulate, harmonize and direct their efforts to the strengthening of their Islamic character and to resist and abolish the hostile, *jāhiliyyah* set-up.

It was in this way that Islam was established the first time. It was founded on a creed which, though concise, encompassed all life. This creed immediately brought into action a viable and dynamic group of people who became independent and separate from the *jāhiliyyah* society that rose to challenge it. It never came as an abstract theory devoid of practical existence. Similarly, it can be brought about in the future only in the same manner. There is no other way for the survival of Islam, in any area or period of time, unless it wants to remain under the yoke of *jāhiliyyah*. Efforts to bring about a revival of Islam must always be equipped with a thorough understanding of its character which tries to be represented in a movement and in an organic system.

When we understand these basic elements in the nature of Islam and its method of action we can fully understand the import of the provisions that we read in the final passage of this *sūrah*. These organize relations within the Muslim community between those who migrated from Makkah and those who provided them with shelter and support in Madinah, and the relations of these together with those who did not migrate. All these relations are based on the understanding of the active and organized emergence of Islamic society.

Equipped with this understanding, we can now look at the relevant passage and the provisions it outlines.

Demarcation of Loyalties in Islamic Society

Those who believe and have migrated and striven hard, with their possessions and their lives, for God's cause, as well as those who give them shelter and support – these are friends and protectors of one another. As for those who believe but have not migrated [to join you], you owe no duty of protection to them until they have migrated. Yet, should they appeal to you for support, on grounds of faith, it is your duty to support them, except against a people with whom you have a treaty. God sees all that you do. The unbelievers are allies of one another. Unless you do likewise, there will be oppression on earth and much corruption. (Verses 72–73)

Everyone in Makkah who declared his or her belief that 'there is no deity other than God and that Muḥammad is God's Messenger' also disclaimed all loyalty to their family, clan, tribe or to the leadership of the *jāhiliyyah* society represented by the Quraysh. At the same time, they pledged every loyalty to Muḥammad, God's Messenger, and to the nucleus of the new society emerging under his leadership. On the other hand, the *jāhiliyyah* society tried to defend itself against the danger represented by the new group which broke away from it even before they clashed in the battlefield. It certainly tried to crush the new group in its early days.

At the same time, the Prophet established a bond of brotherhood between the members of the new group. In other words, he transformed those individuals who broke away from the *jāhiliyyah* society into a new community where a new bond of mutual loyalty was established. In the new community, the bond of faith replaced that of blood and family in other societies. Everyone in that community pledged their total loyalty to the new leadership and the new entity, thus replacing all past bonds and loyalties.

When a number of people in Madinah accepted Islam and pledged their total loyalty to the Islamic leadership, they made it clear that they would obey that leadership in all situations. They also pledged to strive to protect God's Messenger against his enemies, in the same way as they protected their own women, children and property. When all this was set in place, God allowed the Muslims of Makkah to migrate to Madinah. Thus, the new Muslim state was established in Madinah under the leadership of God's Messenger. The Prophet again established a bond of brotherhood between the *Muhājirīn*, i.e. the migrants, and the *Anṣār*, i.e. the supporters. Again this brotherhood replaced the bonds of blood and family with all that they entailed, including inheritance, payment of blood-money and other compensations for which the family and the clan were liable. "*Those who believe and have migrated and striven hard, with their possessions and their lives, for God's cause, as well as those who give them shelter and support – these are friends and protectors of one another.*" (Verse 72) They are mutual protectors in as much as they provide one another with support, and they are friends in as much as they inherit one another and provide help in the payment of blood-money for accidental death, and other compensations, as well as fulfilling the commitments and honouring the pledges that result from blood relations.

Other individuals then accepted Islam as a faith without practically joining the Muslim community, because they did not migrate to the land of Islam where God's law was implemented and the Muslim leadership was in full control. Those individuals were not part of the Muslim community which was able to fulfil its whole existence in its own land.

These individuals were in Makkah or were Bedouins living in the areas surrounding Madinah. This means that they adopted the faith but did not join the Islamic society, nor did they pledge their full loyalty to its leadership. These were not regarded as part of the Muslim community. With these, God did not require that the Muslim community have full loyalty, in all its aspects, because they were not, in practical terms, part of Islamic society. Hence, the rule regarding these individuals stated: "*As for those who believe but have not migrated [to join you], you owe no duty of protection to them until they have migrated. Yet, should they appeal to you for support, on grounds of faith, it is your duty to support them, except against a people with whom you have a treaty.*" (Verse 72)

This rule is perfectly understandable because it fits with the nature of Islam and its practical method of action. Those individuals were not part of the Muslim society and, therefore, they could not have a relationship of allegiance with it. Nevertheless, there is the bond of faith which, alone, does not provide for duties towards such individuals which the Islamic society is bound to fulfil. However, in the case where these individuals suffer aggression or an attempt to turn them away from their faith a provision in their favour is clearly stated. Should they in such a situation appeal to Muslims in the land of Islam for support, the Islamic society must support them. The only proviso is that giving such support should not violate any provision of a treaty the Muslim society might have with another party, even though that party might be the aggressor. What we have to understand here is that the first priority is given to what serves the interests of the Muslim community and its method of action with whatever contracts or transactions that this might produce. These have to be honoured even in the case where aggression is made against believers who have not joined the Islamic society which represents the practical existence of the Islamic faith.

This shows the great importance Islam attaches to its own active organization. The comment on this rule added at the end of the verse says: "*God sees all that you do.*" (Verse 72) Whatever human beings may do, God is aware of all their actions. He knows the preliminaries, incentives, motivations, the deeds as well as their effects and consequences.

Thus, Islamic society is an active and organic grouping where individuals are united by their loyalty, allegiance and mutual support of one another. The same characteristics apply to ignorant or *jāhiliyyah* societies: "*The unbelievers are allies of one another.*" (Verse 73) By nature, a *jāhiliyyah* society does not act as mere individuals. It behaves like a living entity whose organs move by nature to defend its existence and independence. Hence, the people in that society are, to all intents and purposes, friends and protectors of one another. Therefore, Islam must confront them as a society which demonstrates the same characteristics to a stronger and firmer degree.

Should the Muslims refrain from confronting them as a community whose individuals are united by mutual ties of loyalty and friendship, these Muslims would be subject to persecution by the *jāhiliyyah* society. They would not be able to resist that society since it moves against them as an integrated whole. Thus, *jāhiliyyah* would gain the upper hand against Islam, sovereignty would be given to human beings and people would be forced to submit themselves to other people. All this leads to much persecution and the worst type of corruption. "*Unless you do likewise, there will be oppression on earth and much corruption.*" (Verse 73)

This is a very serious warning. Muslims who do not establish their existence on the solid foundation of an active organization bound by a single loyalty and working under a single leadership shall have to answer to God for all the oppression and the corruption that results from their actions, in addition to what they suffer in their own lives as a result.

True Believers

Once more, the *sūrah* states the true nature of faith: "*Those who believe and have migrated and striven hard for God's cause, as well as those who give them shelter and support are indeed the true believers. Forgiveness of sins, and most generous provisions await them.*" (Verse 74) This is the true picture reflecting true faith. This verse tells us exactly how Islam gains its real existence. Islam does not become a reality with a declaration of its theoretical basis, or its adoption as a conceptual belief, or even with offering its worship rituals. The religion of Islam is a code of living which needs an active organization to implement it and put it into practice. When it remains in the form of beliefs only, its existence remains abstract. It does not become a true and practical existence without such an active organization dedicated to its implementation.

Those who belong to such an active organization are the true believers who are promised forgiveness and generous provisions. The provisions are mentioned here in relation to their striving, sacrificing their wealth, supporting their brethren and giving them shelter, with all the costs they bear in meeting these responsibilities. But in addition to such generous provisions, they are given forgiveness of sins, which counts as the best type of God's bounty.

Grouped with the first Muslim community of the *Muhājirīn* and the *Anṣār* are all those who later migrate and strive for God's cause, but the first community had its degree of excellence, as stated in other Qur'ānic verses. The addition is stated here to make it clear that these also belong to the Muslim community, and give it their allegiance. "*And those who subsequently come to believe, and migrate and strive hard with you [for God's cause] shall also belong to you.*" (Verse 75)

The requirement of migration continued to apply until Makkah had fallen to Islam. At that time, the whole of Arabia acknowledged the Islamic leadership and its entire population formed the Islamic community. The Prophet made it clear then that the requirement of migration was no longer operative, but people were required to work for Islam and strive hard in serving its cause. That was in the first round of Islamic triumph which ushered in a period of Islamic rule that continued for nearly twelve centuries. Throughout that period, Islamic law was implemented and the Muslim leadership acknowledged God's sovereignty and fulfilled its obligations under Islamic law. Today, when the whole world has reverted to *jāhiliyyah*, God's law is no longer implemented, sovereignty is usurped by tyrants everywhere and one group of people submit themselves to another, a new round begins. In this round, all provisional laws that applied in the first round may be applicable. Thus, a land may be established where Islam is implemented and to where Muslims should migrate. At a later stage, the rule of Islam will, by God's will, stretch over a wide area when migration will no longer be required. The duty of individual Muslims at this stage is again to work and strive hard for the Islamic cause, just as was the case in the first round.

The first period of building the Islamic existence had its own provisional laws and special duties. Loyalty on the basis of faith replaced blood and family relations in all shapes and forms, as well as rights and duties, including inheritance and mutual support in the payment of penalties and compensation for accidental killing. When the structure of Islamic society became well established after the resounding victory at Badr, the provisional laws applicable to that special period of construction were amended. The amendments re-established inheritance and mutual support in financial liabilities on the basis of family relationships, but only within the Muslim community in the land of Islam: "*Those who are bound by ties of blood have the first claim on one another in accordance with God's decree.*" (Verse 75)

To give priority in such matters to family and relatives, within the general framework of the Muslim community, after the practical existence of Islam has been firmly established meets a certain need of human nature. There is no harm in satisfying people's natural feelings as long as there is no conflict between such satisfaction and the fulfilment of Islamic duties. Islam does not negate or obliterate natural feelings, but it controls them so that they work in line with the more important requirements of its own existence as a faith. Thus, the satisfaction of people's natural needs and feelings is provided within the general framework of Islam and its requirements. This means that some special periods may have special provisions which are not included among the final provisions of Islamic law which are applicable in a well-established and secure Islamic community. This is how we must understand the requirements of the initial building stage as well as the general nature of Islam and its laws.

"*God has full knowledge of everything.*" (Verse 75) This is the appropriate comment on all these laws and regulations and how they interact and are coordinated. They have their basis in God's knowledge which is flawless, perfect and absolute.

The Nature of Islamic Society

As it builds the Muslim community on the basis of its unique approach, establishing its active organization which is bound together by the bond of faith, Islam aims to highlight and enhance the human qualities of man, giving them prominence in all aspects of life. We cannot fail to notice the clear consistency of the Islamic approach, with all its rules, regulations and laws.

There are certain aspects which man has in common with other animate objects, and some which he shares even with inanimate objects. These have caused those who advocate what may be termed as 'scientific ignorance' to claim on occasions that man is just another animal and on others that he belongs to the world of matter, like inanimate objects. Yet besides these features which man has in common with animals and matter, he has his own qualities and characteristics that distinguish him from both and make him absolutely unique. Ultimately, and under the pressure of undeniable facts, those who belong to 'scientific ignorance' have acknowledged man's uniqueness.

With its special approach defined by God Almighty, Islam highlights, enhances and strengthens the qualities that contribute to man's unique status. This is indeed the reason for making the bond of faith the basis of unity in the Muslim community and the mainstay of its organization.

Faith appeals to the highest human qualities and characteristics. Islam does not establish the Muslim community on any bond of descent, language, land, race, colour, interests or common destiny. These are ties which men have in common with animals.

These ties bring together flocks of animals and they can be seen in operation in stables, grazing land and in animal language. Faith, on the other hand, provides man with a full and complete explanation of his origin, existence and destiny, as well as those of the universe in which he lives. It makes him a creature far superior to matter. Faith is something which relates to man's spirit and understanding, the two qualities that make him unique and raise his humanity to its highest level to which no other creature can aspire.

The bond of faith and ideology is a free one which human beings choose by their own free-will, after proper consideration and study. The other ties are not only more fitting for animals, but are also imposed on man and he has no say in them. No human being can change his family descent or the race to which he belongs. Nor does he have any choice of the colour of his skin. All these matters are settled before he is even born. The same applies to the land or the country of his birth, and the language he speaks as a result of being raised within his particular community. Man has certain material interests and a common destiny with others, but these are also very difficult to change, because they apply to him as well as to his community. There is little room for man's free-will in all these matters. For this reason, Islam does not adopt any of these as the basic bond uniting its community. Faith, ideology and its practical approach of implementation are all matters of free choice. At any moment, a human being can declare his choice of these and determine the community to which he wishes to belong. No restriction is imposed on this choice as a result of man's colour, language, race, descent, the land of his birth or his material interests which may change from one community to another. This sums up the great honour assigned to man in Islamic philosophy.

A Community of Mankind

This Islamic approach making faith the basic social tie in Islamic society has produced remarkable results. Instead of stressing those traits which are common to both man and animal, the Islamic approach promotes and nurtures man's human qualities so that they become the dominant factors. The concrete remarkable result of this attitude was that the Islamic society became an open and all-inclusive community in which people of various races, nations, languages and colours were members. No obstacle prevented them from forming a coherent and open society. The rivers of higher talents and various abilities of all races of mankind flowed together into this vast ocean and worked in perfect harmony. Such a coherent mix gave rise to a high level of civilization in a very short period of time. It harnessed the capabilities, ideas and wisdom of all those peoples to produce a great civilization, in spite of the fact that in those times, travel was difficult and the means of communication were slow.

In this unique Islamic society Arabs, Persians, Syrians, Egyptians, Moroccans, Turks, Chinese, Indians, Romans, Greeks, Indonesians, Africans and people of other nations and races were gathered together. Their various characteristics were united, and with mutual cooperation, harmony and unity they took part in the construction of the Islamic community and the Islamic culture. This marvellous civilization was not an 'Arab' civilization but an Islamic one. At no time did it acquire a nationalistic guise, but was instead always based on faith.

All these peoples came together on an equal footing in a relationship of love, with their minds set on a single goal. They used their best abilities, developed the qualities of their races to the fullest, and brought the essence of their personal, national and historical experiences for the development of this united community, to which they all belonged as equal members and in which their common bond was through their relationship with their Lord. In this community their 'humanity' developed without any hindrance. Such characteristics were never witnessed in any other community in the entire history of mankind.

The best known society in ancient history was that of the Roman Empire. Peoples of various races, languages and characteristics lived in that society. But nothing of this was based on 'human relationship', nor did it aspire to any sublime ideal such as faith. Their society was ordered on a class system which provided for a class of 'nobles' and one of 'slaves'. Moreover, the Roman race, in general, had the leadership, and the other races were considered its subjects. Hence, this society could not rise to that high level of Islamic society, nor could it produce results and blessings of the type produced by Islamic society.

In recent history there have appeared other societies grouping together different peoples. We may cite the example of the British Empire. It bore a strong resemblance to the Roman society to which it was an heir. It was based on national greed, in which the British nation had the leadership because it was able to exploit the territories which it colonized. The same is true of other European empires. The Spanish and Portuguese Empires in their time, and the French Empire were equally oppressive. They all shared the same contemptible and ugly outlook.

Communism, on the other hand, wanted to establish a new type of society, demolishing the walls of race, colour, nation and land. But its society was not established on the basis of a universal human relationship, but on a class system. Thus, Communist society only reverses the emphasis of the old Roman society: nobles had the distinction in Rome, while in Communist society the proletariat dominate. The underlying emotions in this society are envy and hatred. Such a selfish and vengeful society cannot generate in its individuals anything except base emotions. Its very basis aims to excite, develop and strengthen animalistic characteristics. In its view, the most fundamental needs of human beings are those which they share with animals. These are food, shelter and sex. To Communism, the whole of human history is nothing but a struggle for food.

Islam, then, is the only divine way of life which brings out the noblest human characteristics, developing and using them for the construction of human society. In this respect, Islam has always remained unique. Those who opt for any other system, whether based on nationalism, colour and race, or on class struggle, or similar corrupt theories, are truly enemies of mankind. They are the ones who do not want man to develop those noble characteristics which have been given to him by his Creator. Nor do they wish to see a human society benefit from the harmonious blending of all those capabilities, experiences and characteristics which have been developed among the various races of mankind. Such people swim against the current and try to reverse the tide of human development. They wish human society to be based on the same factors which group animals together: a stable and a grazing land. They are not happy with that sublime level to which God has raised man and which provides a fitting basis for uniting human society.

It is most odd that a society based on the harnessing of the best human qualities is labelled as fanatic and reactionary, while the one that promotes animal characteristics is hailed as progressive and civilized. All values and considerations are turned upside down only to avoid making faith the basis of human society, when belief is the highest human characteristic.

But God will most certainly accomplish His purpose. This type of reversal into *jāhiliyyah*, or ignorance, and its animal values will not survive for ever in human life. God's will is certain to prevail. Humanity will try one day to establish its society on the basis by which God has honoured man and which provided the foundation of the first Islamic society that attained a highly distinctive position in human history. The image of that society will continue to loom large on the horizon and mankind will aspire to attain the same high level which it had experienced at a particular stage in history.

Index

Anṣār, 44, 45, 49, 53, 56, 73, 82, 85, 86, 192, 194, 198, 212, 214
Apostates, 40
'Aqabah, 44
'Aqīl ibn Abī Ṭālib, 199
Arab(s), 7, 16, 10, 48, 104, 104, 106, 121, 125, 160, 17, 179, 218
Arab, 192; civilization, 218; character, 16; feuds , 16; household, 16; memory, 16; mind, 16; society, 16, 17; tribal chivalry, 17; tribes, 17, 179; unbelievers, 17
Arabia, 12, 17, 37, 38, 43, 52, 194, 214
Arabian, 18; idols, 125; imperialism, 37; Peninsula, 12, 89, 189
Arabic, 107, 112, 181
Asia, 26
Al-'Āṣ ibn Hishām ibn al-Mughīrah, 41, 55
Al-'Āṣ ibn Munabbih, 41
Al-Aswad, 49
Aslam, 46
Astrologers, 210
'Ātikah bint 'Abd al-Muṭṭalib, 41
'Awf ibn al-Ḥārith, 49, 51
Aws, 39, 194

B

Badr, 2, 4, 39, 42, 45, 48, 53, 56, 57, 70, 73, 86, 90, 91, 93, 97, 98, 101, 102, 103, 144, 148, 153, 160, 165, 168, 200, 206
Bark al-Ghimād, 44
Al-Basūs, 16
Battle of Badr, 2, 3, 18, 37, 38, 43, 57, 62, 72, 88, 89, 96, 97, 100, 123, 126, 130, 130, 131, 147, 149, 150, 152, 160, 161, 167, 181, 187, 188, 198, 198, 199, 201, 205
Battle of Qādisiyyah, 20
Battle of Uḥud, 2, 92, 158
Battle of Yamāmah, 52
Al-Bayḍāwī, 163
Bedouins, 97, 212
Bedouin Arabs, 181
Belief(s), 80, 91, 109, 114, 125, 113, 115, 125, 148, 214
Believer(s), 57, 58, 59, 60, 63, 64, 65, 66, 67, 68, 69, 70, 71, 72, 74, 75, 76, 77, 78, 79, 81, 82, 83, 84, 85, 86, 87, 90, 91, 92, 92, 94, 94, 97, 98, 96, 166, 101, 102, 104, 106, 107, 107, 108, 110, 113, 114, 115, 133, 134, 138, 141, 144, 145, 145, 146, 153, 155, 156, 157, 158, 159, 164, 173, 175, 194, 196, 197, 202, 214,
Al-Bidāyah wa'l-Nihāyah, 39
Bilāl, 53
Blood money, 121, 206, 212
Booty, 58, 62, 73, 74, 84, 137, 141, 142, 143, 150
Britain, 35
British Empire, 218
British nation, 219
Buddhists, 26
Al-Bukhārī, 91, 97
Byzantine, 12, 20
Byzantines, 203

C

Caesar, 29, 37
Call of Islam, 36
Capitalist system, 35
Captive, 62, 87
Captives of War, 198
Charity, 80
Children of Israel, 157
Chinese, 218
Christ, 11, 19
Christian Europe, 9
Christian radio stations, 127
Christianity, 10
Christians, 10, 19
Church (es), 9, 14, 15
Co-existence, 178
Communism, 186, 219
Communist society, 219
Companion(s), 44, 45, 46, 47, 48, 52, 54, 56, 56, 57, 62, 76, 77, 78, 82, 81, 83, 123, 189, 203, 200, 102, 121, 154, 199, 203

you do, 174, 211, 213; shall all things return to, 138, 155; Submission to God, 109, 114, 134, 146; the Merciful, 65; Trust in God, 158; With God there is a great reward, 113; Word of God, 30; Worship of God, 38
God's; absolute sovereignty, 22, 186; authority, 15, 21, 9, 109, 134, 135; blessings, 45, 108, 169; bounty, 70, 115; cause, 5, 12, 14, 19, 20, 29, 36, 51, 61, 70, 73, 74, 101, 109, 144, 145, 157, 158, 159, 172, 174, 175, 185, 186, 187, 196, 197, 205, 211, 214; choice, 84; command, 159; creation, 94; creatures, 19; decree, 175; enemies, 55, 63, 186; existence, 104; favour, 170; forgiveness, 129, 160, 203; grace, 3, 45, 63, 73, 74, 116, 119, 129, 154; grasp, 184; greatness, 76; guidance, 110, 120, 136, 166, 176; help, 63, 90, 135, 176, 184, 189, 194; injunctions, 208; instruction(s), 166, 193; judgment, 148; knowledge, 114, 216; law of justice and fair play, 30; law(s), 9, 23, 100, 111, 133, 145, 188, 191, 207, 212, 215; leadership, 60; light, 19, 115; Lordship, 23, 120, 134; mercy, 130, 202; message, 17, 18, 71, 73, 98, 112, 122, 176, 178; messenger(s), 9, 11, 52, 62, 107, 108, 109, 110, 111, 114, 119, 120, 121, 122, 124, 128, 129, 142, 144, 146, 154, 182, 195, 203, 205, 207, 208, 211, 212; might, 87; name, 14, 15; natural law, 36; oneness, 32, 78, 81, 87, 95, 125, 143, 147; order(s), 10, 146, 167, 206; path, 18, 118, 130, 133, 138, 156, 159, 160 ; planning, 63, 96, 102, 103, 151, 154, 155; pleasure, 110, 163, 184; power, 101, 109, 150, 166; prior knowledge, 16; promise, 112, 127; punishment, 120, 133, 98; purpose, 150; revelation, 106, 120, 126, 140, 167, 168, 169; reward, 111; rule, 9; ruling, 58, 70, 74; scheme, 155; servants, 170, 195; sight, 18, 76, 107; soldier(s), 90, 92; sovereignty, 23, 38, 106, 148, 21, 215; support, 59, 92, 153; truth, 110; unlimited power, 59; way, 30; will, 59, 61, 64, 66, 71, 78, 79, 80, 83, 87, 88, 90, 91, 92, 96, 99, 121, 137, 170, 173, 196, 215; word, 34, 113, 158, 159; wrath, 68, 96, 97, 99, 101, 102
Godhead, 9, 23, 24, 31, 38, 105, 109, 111, 113, 120, 134, 142, 19, 197
Goliath, 157
Gratitude, 111, 112
Greeks, 218
Guidance, 108, 109, 110, 127, 142, 158, 203

H

Ḥadīth, 30, 36, 82, 97, 100, 101, 162, 189, 193, 200
Ḥakīm ibn Ḥizām, 41, 48
Ḥamzah ibn ʿAbd al-Muṭṭalib, 18, 43, 50, 53
Ḥanafi, 97, 99, 100
Ḥanẓalah ibn Abī Sufyān, 40
Ḥārith ibn ʿĀmir, 41
Al-Ḥārith ibn Kildah, 42
Al-Ḥārith ibn Mālik, 82
Ḥārithah ibn Surāqah, 51
Al-Ḥasan, 98, 161
Hāshim, 17, 51, 121, 142
Hāshimite, 17, 43, 51
Heaven(s), 82, 83, 113, 147, 195
Hell, 82, 101, 102, 118, 130, 131, 132
Hereafter, 202
Hijaz, 40
Al-Ḥubāb ibn al-Mundhir, 46, 93
Al-Ḥudaybiyah, 188, 193
Ḥudhayfah ibn Muḥsin, 20
Ḥunayn, 98
Ḥuwayṭib ibn ʿAbd al-ʿUzzā, 41
Hypocrite(s), 5, 6, 9, 17, 52, 71, 76, 139, 149, 156, 164, 165

I

Iblīs, 160, 161
Ibn ʿAbbās, 3, 72, 76, 99, 100, 101
Ibn al-ʿArabī, 100, 101, 205